ADAM
AND THE
FAMILY
OF
MAN

Jean de Fraine, S. J.

translated by Daniel Raible, C.PP.S.

ADAM AND THE

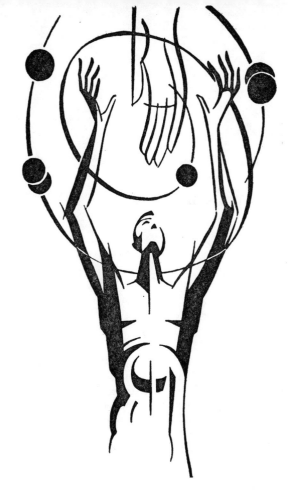

FAMILY OF MAN

alba house
A DIVISION OF ST. PAUL PUBLICATIONS
STATEN ISLAND, NEW YORK

Nihil Obstat:

Donald A. Panella, M.A., S.T.L., S.S.L.

Censor Deputatus

Imprimatur:

✠ Francis Cardinal Spellman

Archbishop of New York

May 6, 1965

The Nihil Obstat and Imprimatur are official declarations that a book or pamphlet is free of doctrinal or moral error. No implication is contained therein that those who have granted the Nihil Obstat and Imprimatur agree with the contents, opinions or statements expressed.

Library of Congress Catalog Card Number 65 - 15729

Designed, printed and bound in the U.S.A. by the Pauline Fathers and Brothers as part of their publishing apostolate. They were founded to spread Christ's message by means of the press, radio, motion pictures and television. A brochure on the Paulines can be obtained by sending a card to: Society of St. Paul, Vocation Office, 2187 Victory Boulevard, Staten Island, New York 10314.

Contents

Abbreviations

All Scripture texts are from the Confraternity Version except where that is not yet available. In the latter case the texts are from the Douay Version.

Following are the abbreviations used in this translation for the books of the Bible:

Genesis — Gn.
Exodus — Ex.
Leviticus — Lv.
Numbers — Nm.
Deuteronomy — Dt.
Josue — Jos.
Judges — Jg.
Ruth — Ru.
1 Kings (1 Samuel) — 1 K.
2 Kings (2 Samuel) — 2 K.
3 Kings (1 Kings) — 3 K.
4 Kings (2 Kings) — 4 K.
1 Paralipomenon (1 Chronicles) — 1 Par.
2 Paralipomenon (2 Chronicles) — 2 Par.
Esdras (Ezra) — Esd.
Nehemias (2 Esdras) — Neh.
Tobias (Tobit) — Tob.
Judith — Jud.
Esther — Est.
Job — Jb.

Psalms — Ps.
Proverbs — Prv.
Coheleth (Ecclesiastes) — Co.
Canticle of Canticles (Song of Solomon) — Ct.
Wisdom — Wis.
Sirach (Ben Sira or Ecclesiasticus) — Sir.
Isaia — Is.
Jeremia — Jer.
Lamentations — Lam.
Baruch — Bar.
Ezechiel — Ez.
Daniel — Dn.
Osee (Hosea) — Os.
Joel — Jl.
Amos — Amos
Abdia (Obadiah) — Ab.
Jona — Jon.
Michea (Micah) — Mi.
Nahum — Na.
Habacuc — Hb.

Sophonia (Zephaniah) — So.
Aggai (Haggai) — Ag.
Zacharia (Zechariah) — Za.
Malachia — Mal.
1 Machabees — 1 Mac.
2 Machabees — 2 Mac.
St. Matthew — Mt.
St. Mark — Mk.
St. Luke — Lk.
St. John — Jn.
Acts of the Apostles — Acts
Romans — Rom.
1 Corinthians — 1 Cor.
2 Corinthians — 2 Cor.
Galatians — Gal.
Ephesians — Eph.
Philippians — Phil.

Colossians — Col.
1 Thessalonians — 1 Th.
2 Thessalonians — 2 Th.
1 Timothy — 1 Tim.
2 Timothy — 2 Tim.
Titus — Tit.
Philemon — Phm.
Hebrews — Heb.
St. James — Jas.
1 St. Peter — 1 Pt.
2 St. Peter — 2 Pt.
1 St. John — 1 Jn.
2 St. John — 2 Jn.
3 St. John — 3 Jn.
St. Jude — Jude
Apocalypse (Revelation) — Ap.

Preface

It is not without a certain amount of trepidation that we pass these pages on to the public. Their subject matter—the biblical notion of "corporate personality" with "Adam and his descendants" as a striking epitome—might be considered dangerous, or at least risky, by certain persons because it will run counter to their accustomed modes of thought. In order to understand the content of the concept under study, it will be necessary to divest oneself of the ordinary philosophical categories and create a new Semitic or biblical mentality.

In this connection, we must all recall the memorable words of St. Pius X: "Spiritually we are all Semites." We must make a constant effort to accomodate ourselves to the Divine Word which is expressed in idioms more simple and more vital than our customary Western forms of speech. Instead of wishing to explain the Sacred Scriptures according to our Greek or "rationalistic" mode of thought, we must keep in mind that they are to be explained in accordance with their own proper ideas and modes of expression. Unless we do so, we will incur the reproach which St. Augustine levelled against some exegetes of his day: *Non pro sententia divinarum Scripturarum, sed pro sua dimicantes, ita ut eam velint Scripturarum esse quae sua est, cum potius eam quae Scripturarum est, suam esse velint.*" (Aug., de Gen. ad litt. in ML 34. 260) Far from defending our own point of view and imposing our own interpretation on the Word of God, we must humbly accept the divine gift such as it has been given to us.

We wish to thank most heartily the editors of *Museum Lessianum* for welcoming our work and extending to it their fraternal confidence in the persevering labor of exegetes which the encyclical *Divino Afflante Spiritu* urges.

1

The Concept of "Corporate Personality"

A. PRELIMINARY IDEAS

The problem of the relationship between the individual and the collectivity is taken for granted in human speculation. Man has always been interested in determining the correlation between his individuality and his membership in the social group. Far from finding a contradiction between the two, he has always realized that there is rather an undeniable affinity between the two.

In human affairs, especially, it is most important to determine exactly where the significance of the individual begins and ends and where the collectivity takes over. One must never lose sight of the fact that the interests of the individual (this is not said of certain specified individuals) and those of society are not absolutely the same. Any theory which *a priori* claims that the individual must be swallowed up in society, or *vice versa,* that the individual must be freed of all social constraint does not take cognizance of the true relationship between the two.[1]

The interests of the individual, if considered in their fullness, coincide to a certain extent with those of society. When contrasting them, one is not speaking of two completely separate entities, but rather of two aspects of one complex entity. In so far as an individual develops in any given society, he must sink his roots into the society; on the other hand, all true values are ultimately personal, that is to say they develop in a person, the one and only object of all laws and institutions. Just as each member of the

1 R. M. McIver, *Community. A Sociological Study,* London, 1924, 92.

human race reaches maturity and full flowering in a suitable environment, so each person must abandon himself, so to speak, to society: in order to find himself, he must lose himself.[2]

If it is true that society exists only in its members, it is likewise true that it exists most perfectly in its most disinguished members.

It is these latter more than the others who fulfill that condition of membership which points to a less atomistic and less mechanical concept of society.[3] Instead of considering themselves as mere objects juxtaposed to one another and sufficient unto themselves, the individuals (especially the more conspicuous ones) feel themselves members of a psychic whole, which surpasses them on the one hand, and on the other hand acts through them and finds its being in them. It is in this light that the individual, especially the more gifted one, finds the basis of his acting for others: "In every true society the individual members can fulfill the duties of other members and take their place by vicarious representation."[4]

These ideas we have just sketched apply in a special way to the religious society of biblical times. More than any other mentality, whether ancient or modern, "the Israelite genius tends to incorporate the destiny of the people (chosen) in a representative person."[5] There exists a biblical personalism which proclaims the integrity of the individual person in relation to the group, while at the same time admitting that the individual person can, under proper circumstances, represent the entire group. This is in opposition to an exaggerated individualism which sees in the individual the supreme unit of the social structure, the only solid basis and the only driving force of the group created by him,[6]

2 F. W. Jerusalem, *Soziologie des Rechts I. Gesetzmässigkeit und Kollektivität*, Jena, 1925, 401, speaking of the great personalities of the Middle Ages says: "the decisive fact is that they were always only representatives of collectivities, even though the latter might be concentrated in them themselves."

3 O. Spann, *Kategorienlehre*, Jena, 1939[2], 177n.

4 O. Spann, *Religionsphilosophie auf geschichtlicher Grundlage*, Vienna, 1947, 95.

5 A. M. Dubarle, in *Mélanges Lebreton* — RSR 39 (1951 / 52), I, 59.

6 Cf. G. Mehlis, *Lehrbuch der Geschichtsphilosophie*, Berlin, 1915, 301: "To regard personality as simply or absolutely valuable."

and an exaggerated collectivism which looks upon society as the driving power and basic norm of the individuals governed by it.[7]

In this present study we are not concerned with unusual groups, (such as the blind or a group in the state of panic), but only with social groups properly speaking. By that we mean all groups of social beings who are united with one another by a relatively firm bond[8] and who experience a feeling of togetherness among themselves so as to speak of themselves as "we."[9] When this common sharing extends to the fundamental conditions of human life (such as in the case of a village, a tribe, or a nation) we speak of it as a "community."[10] Within each natural community there is a place for the rights of the individual person.[11] In so far as he is a person, the "human being is socially speaking more than an individual being."[12] Personality as such combines both the collective and the individual, since "it includes all the ways of behavior which identify persons with one another (sociality) and all the ways which distinguish persons from one another (individuality."[13]

Basically the very idea of personality always includes a nuance of collectivity. This is particularly true of the biblical understanding

7 Th. Litt, *Individuum und Gemeinschaft*, 1924², 16, notes that in the collectivity, individuals are "merely parts, 'members' of the collective entirety, and they consist only in the latter and by means of the latter; whatever they are and have, whatever they are and have, whatever they experience or endure, that is granted to them exclusively by the entirety."

8 This is the definition of a "group" given by R. McIver, *Society. A Textbook of Sociology*, New York, 1937, 13.

9 C. Colley, *Social Organization*, New York, 1914, 23.

10 R. McIver, *Society*, 8. In German *Gemeinschaft* (a natural society) is opposed to *Gesellschaft* (a free society); cf. A. Rademacher, *Die Kirche als Gemeinschaft und Gesellschaft*, Augsburg, 1931, 17.

11 N. Berdiaeff, *Die menschliche Persönlichkeit und die überpersönlichen Werte*, Vienna, 1937, 13.

12 L. C. Morgan, *Individual and Person*, in AJS 34 (1928/29) 623-631, p. 629; A. Rademacher, *Die Kirche*, l.c., 17.

13 E. S. Bogardus, *Fundamentals of Social Psychology*, 1931², 103.

of the individual and the community.[14] On the other hand the books of the Old Testament picture Israel as having a somewhat collective sociological structure: "A certain organic solidarity uniting the group and a very great dependence of the individual on the community characterize the primitive organization of the Chosen People."[15] Throughout her history Israel preserved a particularly strong consciousness of her scoial and religious solidarity. She never looked upon herself as merely a formless mass of individuals, and always remained "a living whole with an organic body of rights, responsibilities and duties."[16]

On the other hand we must not exaggerate—as is done so often—the importance of the collectivity over the individual. Happily, at the present time no one accepts any longer the opinion of Rudolf Smend: "As the God of Israel," says this author, "Yahweh was particularly the God of the community; he kept himself aloof from the lesser groups of the people and especially from the individual member."[17] The English scholar W. Robertson Smith seconds the opinion: "Religion did not exist for the saving of individual souls but for the preservation and welfare of the society, and in all that was necessary to this end, and every man had to take his part, or break with the domestic and political community to which he belonged."[18]

The protests against these radical views have been growing louder and louder. In an important article on "The Nation and State in the Old Testament," W. Rudolph discredits "the baneful

14   J. De Fraine, *Individu et Société dans la religion de l'Ancien Testament*, in *Bb.* 33 (1952) 324-355 and 445-475.

15   A. Causse, *Du groupe ethnique à la communauté religieuse. Le problème sociologique de la religion d'Israel*, Paris, 1937, 20. — Cf. also L. Rost, *Die Vorstufen von Kirche und Synagoge im AT* (*BWANT IV*, 21) Stuttgart, 1938, 3.

16   J. Hempel, *Das Gottesvolk im Alten und Neuen Testament*, in *Auslanddeutschtum und evangelische Kirche*, Jahrbuch, Munich, 1933, 5-19, p. 9.

17   R. Smend, *Lehrbuch der alttestamentlichen Religionsgeschichte*, Fribourg, in B. and Leipzig, 1899², 102.

18   W. Robertson Smith, *Lectures on the Religion of the Semites*, London, 1927³, 29. For other examples, cf. J. De Fraine, *Individu et Société*, l.c., 325-6, 353, 455.

exaggeration" which "denies the existence of an intense individual piety in ancient Israel," and he adds: "Recourse to God in times of personal trials and for personal desires is not only mentioned in the Old Testament but is in itself readily understandable. However, it is true that the individual could not aspire to union with God in and of himself; he had always to come to God as an Israelite, as a member of the Chosen People."[19]

We have shown elsewhere[20] in what way the individual, as a member of the covenanted people, is called upon to play a not insignificant role. Both the ancient laws and the preaching of the prophets are directed primarily to the individual. Frequently in the historical episodes one finds references to personal culpability, which would not make sense if the individual were not morally responsible. Oaths, names signifying a personal relation with God (e.g. Elias—Yahweh is my God), prayer, personal worship—all these give evidence of a profound conviction of the value of the individual as a religious subject. On the other hand, it is undeniable the the individual Israelite felt himself firmly tied to the natural groups to which he belonged (family, village, nation).[21] This is evident from such practices as that of collective punishment, collective rewards, and the election of the people by covenant.

The point at issue is to see how the religious individual finds fulfillment and integrity, rather than hindrance to his development, in the midst of the group wherein he lived. Membership in larger groups such as the city, the clan, the nation, seems unthinkable without a conscious adherence to and collaboration with the group. The ethico-religious nature of the Chosen People makes it impossible to conceive of the religious life as anything but a free, therefore personal, carrying out of the divine covenant. There is no need to refer to *Jeremia,* to *Ezechiel,* to *Job,* or to psalm 72[22] (as is often done) to find the origin of personal religion.

19 W. Rudolph, *Volk und Staat im AT*, in: *Volk, Staat, Kirche, Ein Lehrgang der theologischen Fakultät Giessen*, Giessen 1933, 21-33, p. 21.
20 *Bb* 33 (1952) 329-55.
21 *Ibid.,* 445-450.
22 E. Meyer, *Geschichte des Altertums* V, Stuttgart, 1933[2], 216.

Throughout the history of Israel (such is the evidence of the Old Testament) the individual has always realized that he could come to God only as a member of the Chosen People. But at the same time "the Old Testament gives abundant evidence that divine Providence extends not only to the Chosen People but also to each member of that group."[23]

As is evident, one always comes back to the basic dialectic between the individual and the collectivity. Rather than look upon these two elements of Old Testament religion as contradictory, one must remember that the ancient Israelite did not at all consider them "as diametrically opposed."[24] Even in the most remote times (as far as we can tell from the sources available), there always existed a personal relationship between the individual and God and a benevolent attitude on God's part toward the individual. But at the same time, the people in its totality has always been, even in early times, the basic point of contact between God and man.[25]

The present essay wishes to demonstrate that the originality, on this point, of Old Testament piety (and this refers to certain elements of piety of the New Testament) is based on the fact that the union between the individual and the religious society bears certain very special characteristics of realism and reversibility. In virtue of a kind of identity, or at least an extreme physical cohesion, between a given individual and the group, the former is the representative *par excellence* of the group. Collective life centers in him; in so far as he represents the group, he can speak in its name, even while using the personal pronoun "I."[26]

23 G. Dalman, *Die Worte Jesu I*, Leipzig, 1930², 115.

24 J. Hempel, *Das Ethos des AT* (ZAW Beiheft 67), Berlin, 1938, 33. — Cf. D. Bonnhoeffer, *Sanctorum communio*, Berlin, 1930, 57: "Man, in that he is individual, is a genus."

25 F. Baumgärtel, *Die Eigenart der alttestamentlichen Frömmigkeit*, Schwerin in Mechlenburg, 1923, 25.

26 H. H. Rowley, *The Faith of Israel*, London, 1956, 118. Recently E. Best, *One Body in Christ*, London, 1955, 56 and 189, has suggested the term *"inclusive personality"* which emphasizes the "inclusion" of the group in a single person.

This quality of the individual which makes him the living and concrete expression of the community is well expressed in the concise formula of the British scholar Henry Wheeler Robinson (1872-1945): "corporate personality." This concept, which we will delineate very carefully, is not an *abstraction* of the twentieth century European scholar but is deeply rooted in the authentic biblical text and idioms.

We do not intend in any way in this essay to arbitrarily set up an *a priori idea* and then try to support it with scripture texts. Rather, as has been said so excellently: "the exegete must seek to discover a coherent view of things, a *synthesis;* he must not spend his time in defending a thesis. He wants to get behind the words and phrases to the living thought. This effort to sympathetically understand the thought of an ancient inspired author causes him to set in bold relief the unusual aspects of his work." [27]

Without defending a thesis or seeking an incontrovertible proof, we will strive to *show* the critical value of the notion of "corporate personality" by pointing out how it throws added light on a number of scriptural passages when they are read in its light. The only "proof" will be that of a phenomenological description. This will display all the various facets of the idea and command assent of the mind by the force of its inner reasonableness. Possibly in some cases the reader may not see the force of the explanation, but the proof, if there is one, lies in the universality with which the idea of "corporate personality" seems to fit so many texts. We are interested in a serious explanation which takes into account the many nuances of the text rather than a rigid principle which sweeps away all other explanations.

Before applying the idea to various texts, it will be well to give a working definition, even if it be a bit vague. This working hypothesis will enable us to determine whether or not the texts contain this idea, and if so, to what extent. It goes without saying that the elaboration of the idea is based on an examination of several striking texts, and that the idea will blossom out in fuller nuances as one progresses in applying it to various texts.

---

27   H. Cazelles, *Les poèmes du Serviteur,* in RSR 43 (1955), 2-51, p. 2.

B. *THE MAIN ASPECTS OF THE CONCEPT OF "CORPORATE PERSONALITY"*

The term "corporate personality" does not appear anywhere in the Bible. Nonetheless this term of contemporary exegesis merely unifies in a short formula the teaching of the Old Testament regarding the union between the individual and the community.

Here, according to the views of H. Wheeler Robinson, (views which we shall explain and criticize when necessary) is the meaning of the expression "corporate personality." [28]

28 Cf. H. Wheeler Robinson, *The Hebrew Conception of Corporate Personality*, in ZAW Bhft 66 (1936), 49-61; O. Eissfeldt, *Der zweite Internationale Alttestamentlertag* (4-10 Sept. in Göttingen), in *TB* 14 (1935) 234-49, col. 244-45. On several occasions beginning in 1911, H. Wheeler Robinson has treated the idea of "corporate personality:" cf. *The Christian Doctrine of Man*, Edinburgh, 1913[2] (1911); *The Religious Ideas of the Old Testament*, London, 1949[8] (1913); A. S. Peake, *The People and the Book*, Oxford, 1925, 353-82; D. C. Simpson, *The Psalmists*, Oxford, 1926, 67-87: "The Social Life of the Psalmists;" H. Wheeler Robinson, *The Old Testament. Its Making and Meaning*, London, 1937; *Redemption and Revelation*, London, 1944[3]; *Inspiration and Revelation in the Old Testament*, Oxford, 1946. Besides H. Wheeler Robinson there are a number of other authors who have contributed to the study of the idea of "corporate personality;" some have been independent of the English exegete; others have followed in his vein. Among those who have treated individual-social problems in the spirit of H. Wheeler Robinson, without, however, depending on him, we can cite: S. Mowinckel, *Psalmenstudien I. Awän und die individuelle Klagepsalmen*, Oslo, 1921; *Psalmenstudien II. Das Thronbesteigungsfest Jahväs und der Ursprung der Eschatologie*, Oslo, 1922; *Psalmenstudien V. Segen und Fluch im Israels Kult und Psalmdichtung*, Oslo, 1925; J. Pedersen, *Israel. Its Life and Culture, I-II*, Copenhagen, 1946 (cf. the approbation of H. Wheeler Robinson in *ET* 48 (1936-7) 153; J. Hempel, *Gott und Mensch im AT* (*BWANT III*, 2), Stuttgart, 1936[2] (1926); *Das Ethos des AT*, l.c., chap. 2 — "*Collectivism and Individualism.*" Other authors recognize a certain literary connection with the English pioneer; for example, O. Eissfeldt, *Der Gottesknecht bei Deuterojesaja*, Halle, 1933, 12-24 (H. Wheeler Robinson is quoted on page

Let us begin by determining the exact meaning of the adjective "corporate." Manifestly it refers to the noun "corporation." And by a corporation we commonly mean "a moral body legally authorized to act as a single individual, a kind of artificial person." In actual practice the notion "corporation" presupposes that "an entire group, its past, present and future members might function as a single individual through any of those members conceived as representative of it." [29] This representation must be considered in a thoroughly practical way. It is not merely a question of a juridical and abstract figment of the imagination which would stress the "as if" but of a real physical connection between the representing member and the body. Very often the unity of the group rests on a blood-bond or a common ancestor. The term "corporate personality," then, expresses two things: first of all, that a single individual is truly corporate, that is to say, functionally identified with a community; secondly, that despite this "corporate" characteristic he remains an individual person (be it only in his deportment). If we wish to set forth precisely the implications of the double aspect—corporate and personal—of the notion of "corporate personality" we can do so in the following characteristics spelled out by H. Wheeler Robinson.

13); *The Ebed-Jahve in Isaiah in the Light of the Israelite Conception of the Community and the Individual, the Real and the Ideal*, in *ET* 44 (1932-3) 261-8; A. Stanley Cook, *The Old Testament. A Reinterpretation*, Cambridge, 1936; R. Aubrey Johnson, in *The Labyrinth* (ed. by S. Hooke), 1935, 73-111; *The One and the Many in the Israelite Conception of God*, Cardiff, 1942 (cf. the review of H. Wheeler Robinson in *JTS* 45 (1944) 156-7; *The Vitality of the Individual in the Thought of Ancient Israel*, Cardiff, 1949; *Sacral Kingship in Israel*, Cardiff, 1955; G. E. Wright, *The Biblical Doctrine of Man in Society*, London, 1954.

29 H. Wheeler Robinson, *The Hebrew Conception*, l.c., 49; according to J. Pedersen, *Israel I-II*, l.c., p. 49, every community is conceived on the basis of a family, issuing from a common ancestor, the source of unity. The prophets speak to the "clan" of Israel (Mi. 2:3; Jer. 8:3: *mishpâhâh*), which has its place among the "clans" of the other people (Am. 3:2); the leader of a community is a "father;" members of the clan are the "sons" (cf. The *"Rechabites, sons of Yonadab"* in Jer. 35:18 or the "house of the wicked" in Is. 31:2).

1. "Corporate personality" has an extension going beyond the present moment in both the past and the future.

2. It is an eminently real concept which transcends the purely literary or ideal personification, making the group a real entity entirely actualized in each of its members.

3. The idea is extremely "fluid" in the sense that the human mind passes quickly back and forth (sometimes quite unconsciously) from the individual to the collectivity and *vice versa*.

4. Finally the "corporate" idea persists even after the development of a new individualistic emphasis within it.

Let us examine these four points one after the other.

1. The first characteristic of the "corporate personality" presupposes that the group in question is not limited to a single moment in time but extends to the past and the future. This extension is verified first of all in the family group. On the one hand this group includes, at the level of the present moment, the ancestors and the members already dead; on the other hand from the viewpoint of the ancestor, it takes in advance all future members. This idea is evident in the well known expression "to be gathered to his kinsmen" (Gn. 15:15: the promise made to Abraham; 25:8: the death of Abraham; cf. 25:17; 35:29) or the expression "to be gathered to my people." (Gn. 49:29: Jacob; Nm. 27:13: Moses) There is probabaly question of common burial in the family tomb as can be inferred from 1 K. 25:1: "And Samuel died, and all Israel was gathered together, and they mourned for him, and buried him in his house of Ramatha." (Cf. also 3 K. 2: 34 for Joab; or Jer. 31:15: "Rachel mourns her children.") Those who die do not leave the family group but on the contrary rejoin it by returning to their ancestors. The Hebrew phraseology is very perceptive at this point. The Hebrew term for kin is *ammim* (Gn. 17:14; Ex. 30:33). But *ammim* is the plural of the word *am* "people." Both "kin" and "people" suggest a very close solidarity between the individuals composing the two groups. The expression "to be gathered to his *ammim*" has a parallel in Gn. 49:33, where the Hebrew singular is translated "to be gathered to his people." Both refer to both the living and the dead.

The inclusion of the common ancestor—and therefore of the group—with the future members, especially in the male descendants, is common in the Old Testament. The "people" perpetuate the ancestor. When the prophet Amos says: "Hear this word, O men of Israel, that the Lord pronounces over *you*, over *the whole family that I brought* up from the land of Egypt" (Am. 3:1) and when his contemporary Osee says that "the Lord has a grievance against Israel: he will punish Jacob for his conduct" since "he supplanted his brother" (Os. 12:3-4), these prophets are identifying very plainly the living members of the Chosen People with their predecessors and their ancestor. Although dead for a long time, these latter survive in their race.

The extension of the duration of the corporate group, we must note well, does not diminish the value of the individual person but on the contrary rather highlights the extreme importance of the individual ancestor. The concept of "corporate personality" always implies in one way or another the influence of a great personality who stands at the origin of the group and who "actualizes" it through the course of history. In the complex reality of what has come to be called a "corporate personality," it is this individual person who is to be recognized above all. The Israelite mind is so convinced that the community grows out of the expansion of an individual that it tends to conceive each group—the family, the clan, the nation—as the participating extension of an initial concrete personality. Even if attention is directed from the very first toward the group, its close unity is explained only by the presence of a single person, sometimes fictitious but most often real, who is behind it to sustain it or to unify it. In every way the community acts like an individual person, even if there is no individual person who represents it and acts in its name (as is often the case). In the absence of such a person, we shall speak of a secondary application of the concept of "corporate personality."

Since the "corporate personality" can extend itself for such a long duration, it is fitting to distinguish two subdivisions of the concept, which are not as disparate as they might seem at first. The unity of the corporate group can be due either to the predominance of a single individual who puts his mark on it or to the prolonged influence of an ancestral individual from whom the group originates. The former case—the community is united by a single individual—holds true more when thinking of a given moment in time; among contemporaries a group has a tendency to express itself in a single individual. We can speak then of the contemporaneous aspect of the "corporate personality" or of the "horizontal pattern of the leader." On the other hand, when we see things according to the biblical concept of time,[30] and when we realize how a given individual contains beforehand a present or future community and lives on in it, we emphasize rather the extension of the individual personality, and we can speak of the anticipative or prolonged aspect[31] or of the "vertical pattern of the ancestor." In both cases it must be noted that at the center of the idea of "corporate personality" one exalts the worth of the concrete and living individual, the preeminent embodiment of the center of influence of a given community. In both cases the "corporate personality" assumes the character of a "father"; he is either the royal *pater familias* who rules over an existing group or he is a patriarchial ancestor whose life is prolonged in a number of generations.[32]

30 According to J. L. McKenzie, *Royal Messianism*, in *CBQ* 19 (1957) 25-52, p. 50, this category implies the conviction that 'the present moment could be conceived as recapitulating the whole past, just as it could be conceived as pregnant with the whole future." At the basis is "a reality which persevered through the succession of events ... This reality was the dynasty of David."

31 Cf. A. V. Ström, *Vetekornet. Studier över Individ och Kollektiv i Nya Testamentet*, Stockholm, 1944, 112. On page 110 of this work the Swedish author remarks very pertinently: "The individual plays a considerable role in a collectivistic civilization; this is especially the case in Israel."

32 Whereas E. Best, *One Body in Christ*, l.c., 56 uses the formula "inclusive personality," B. J. Le Frois, *Semitic Totality Thinking*, in *CBQ* 17 (1955) 315-323, prefers to speak of "totality thinking" (cf. J. Schildenberger, *Vom Geheimnis des Gotteswortes*, Heidelberg, 1950, 149: "ganzheitliches Denken"): "It is because the Semite thinks in totalities that he sees in the individual the whole species manifesting itself; with him a typical, concrete individual stands for the collective group; the first one of the dynasty or line of rulers can embody in himself the entire dynasty or line." See also B. J. Le Frois, *The Woman Clothed with the Sun (Ap. 12). Individual or Collective?*

If we emphasize the "individual" component of the two-pronged concept of "corporate personality," we do so for the purpose of correcting somewhat the classical exposition of H. Wheeler Robinson. The originator of the expression "corporate personality" was indeed influenced by the scientific thought of his day. He accepts as his own the famous words of W. Robertson Smith: "A kin was a group of persons whose lives were so bound up together, in what must be called a physical unity, that they could be treated as parts of one common life. The members of one kindred looked on themselves as one living whole, a single animated mass of blood, flesh and bones, of which no member could be touched without all the members suffering."[33] The neighbor is spoken of as "your own" (Is. 58:7); and St. Paul speaks of the Jews as "those who are my flesh" (Rom. 11:14).

In approving a theory according to which it is necessary to deal with a "defective sense of individuality"[34] in pre-exilic Israel, the English scholar is of the opinion that primitive religion and legislation concerned themselves not with the individual man as such but with members of a tribe, a clan, or a family. The individual is looked upon "as merged in the larger group of family or clan or nation."[35] In order to prove this collectivistic thesis, H. Wheeler Robinson appeals to the Gabaonite vendetta in 2 K., chapter 21 or to the allegory of the woman of Tekoa in her complaint to David: "The whole kindred rising against thy hand-

(An Exegetical Study). Rome, 1954, 245-254. K. Stern, The Third Revolution New York, 1954, 267, uses the formula "individual experiences with an achetypical character" (quoted by B. J. Le Frois, l.c., p. 317).

33 W. Robertson Smith, The Religion of the Semites,² pp. 273-74. Cf. Kinship and Marriage in Early Arabia, p. 40, by the same author: "The whole kindred conceives itself as having a single life, just as in the formula 'our blood has been spilt' it speaks of itself as having one blood in his veins."

34 J. K. Mozley, Ruling Ideas in Early Ages, 87.

35 H Wheeler Robinson, The Christian Doctrine of Man, Edinburgh, 1913², 27; The Religious Ideas of the OT, London, 1949⁸, 87; A. S. Peake, The People and the Book, Oxford, 1925, 376; H. Wheeler Robinson, Redemption and Revelation, London, 1944³, 149; Inspiration and Revelation in the OT, Oxford, 1946, 81.

maid, saith: 'Deliver him that has slain his brother, that we may
kill him for the life of his brother; whom he slew, and that we may
destroy the heir. And they seek to quench my spark which is left,
and will leave my husband no name, nor remainder on the earth.' "
(2 K. 14:7) He derives a further argument from a whole series
of institutions and practices which imply the domination of the
individual by the group:[36] the curse which denies the rights of
the innocent and condemns him mercilessly to death; the levirate
law which implies the identity of the individual with his dead
brother (Dt. 25:5); the discretionary absolutism of the father of
a family in killing or offering his children for sacrifice (Gn. 22:
Abraham and Isaac; Gn. 42:37: Ruben and his two sons; Jg. 11:
29: Jephte and his daughter); the punishment of descendants
because of the sins of the fathers (Ex. 20:5: three generations;
4 K. 9:26: "the blood of Naboth and the blood of his children").
All the preaching of the prophets on sin and suffering "flows from
the idea of corporate personality."[37] According to H. Wheeler
Robinson there exists a real contamination through sin which
surpasses a purely juridical responsibility, and which shocks our
modern mentality brought up as it is on an individualistic morality.[38] Deftly the English exegete remarks that the Israelite religious
conscience is quite different from the individualistic Protestant
attitude but comes, from one viewpoint, to Catholicism and the
"Brotherhood" movements of the present time.[39]

   In spite of this rather obvious collectivistic emphasis, the
studies of the British scholar almost instinctively return to the
right track when he directs his attention to the sanctioning of an
entire group because of *the crime of an individual,*[40] or when he
recalls the prophetic notion of the "remnant," that small group
which represents the entire nation and leads it to its fulfillment.

36   H. Wheeler Robinson, *The Christian Doctrine of Man,* l.c., p. 28-31.
37   H. Wheeler Robinson, *The Religious Ideas of the OT,* l.c., 163.
38   *Ibid.,* p. 164.
39   *Ibid.,* p. 185.
40   H. Wheeler Robinson, *The Christian Doctrine of Man,* l.c., 8. On
     page 30 Robinson changes the perspective again when he believes
     that he can conclude from the story of Jos. 7 that "the solicitude of
     Yahweh tends rather to Israel than to the individual Israelites."

"On that day the remnant of Israel, the survivors of the house of Jacob, will no more lean upon him who struck them." (Is. 10:20; cf. 6:13; 4:3; 7:3; 28:5) The English exegete also makes use of the many passages of the Bible in which Israel is treated as a single person (cf. Ps. 128:1). Among other formulas he uses the formula of blessing pronounced by the priests: "This is how you shall bless the Israelites: Say to *them*: The Lord bless you, (singular)and keep you (singular)." (Nm. 6:23) The "you" in this case refers to Israel as a whole and not to individual members of the race. Such is the meaning also in other passages where there is an abrupt change from the singular to the plural. For example: "Out of Egypt I called *My Son*. The more I called *them*." (Os. 11: 1. cf. Dt. 9:1; Ex. 23:17) Despite the multiplicity and diversity of its members, Israel has a very personal consciousness of itself.

Sometimes H. Wheeler Robinson realizes full well the real significance of the individual as a corporate personality. If the nation is one, even to becoming a single psychic whole, it is so because it is concentrated in and entirely present in a single representing personality. The history of Israel has this striking characteristic: the free play given to individual initiative. "There is an equally remarkable series of prominent personalities guiding Israel's life and thought from within... Owing to its relatively narrow compass and concentrated position, the whole nation could be reached, and its life shaped, by the influence of one man." [41]

With good reason the British author emphasizes what he calls "the socialization of the individual experience." [42] This happens

---

41   H. Wheeler Robinson, *The Religious Ideas*, l.c., 20-21. In *The Hebrew Conception of Corporate Personality*, the English author quotes (p. 55) the qualification given to the Semites by the celebrated T. E. Lawrence, *The Seven Pillars of Wisdom*, 157: "the race of the individual genius."

42   H. Wheeler Robinson, *The Social Life of the Psalmists*, in D. C. Simpson, *The Psalmists*, Oxford, 1926, 67-87, p. 85. In another book, *The Old Testament, Its Making and Meaning*, London, 1937, 137, the same author speaks of what he calls "the expansiveness" of the psalms: in these compositions personal religion is revealed as capable of blossoming out into a national, not to say, universal consciousness.

when the deed of a single individual acquires a representative value and is then transferred to the group with which this person is associated. In *Daniel* 7 we pass from a single person, the "Son of Man" (Dn. 7:13), to a group, "the holy ones of the Most High" (Dn. 7:18). Psalm 21 contains a mixture of individual (verses 7, 19, 26) and collective traits. Certain statements are plainly individual: *"My* God, *my* God, why have you forsaken *me?* . . . From *my* mother's womb you are *my* God . . . *My* throat is dried up like baked clay . . . I can count all *my* bones . . . They divide *my* garments among them." But verse 5 speaks of *"our* fathers," and Isaia 44:1-2 speaks of Israel herself being formed from the womb. The "bullocks" of verse 13 and the "dogs" and "the pack of evildoers" of verse 17 refer to a group rather than to an individual.

In treating of Jeremia the English exegete reveals the depth of his thought. Speaking of the "corporate individualism" of this prophet, he explains: "This does not mean an individualism in sharp antithesis to the previous 'corporate personality,' but rather an emphasis on the individual within the group, and an emphasis that springs from the personal fellowship with God which this prophet experienced in such a marked degree." [43]

It is evident that in the thought of the originator of the "corporate personality" concept the emphasis on the individual in the midst of the corporate group does not cease to grow. In spite of this we have the impression that the individual aspect of the two-pronged idea of "corporate personality" is even more marked than the inventor of the expression believes. We can cite a great number of interesting cases in which the import of the representing individual is rather strongly indicated. When Goliath defies the Israelite army, he uses the following words: "Choose out a man of you, and let him come down and fight hand to hand." (The Hebrew has: "Make a pact [*beru* from the verb *bârâh*] with a man, etc."). (1 K. 17:8) In the opinion of the Philistine giant, the Israelites have so intimately identified themselves with their

---

43 H. Wheeler Robinson, *The OT*, l.c., 99. The terms of this explanation show quite clearly that, for H. Wheeler Robinson, the idea of "corporate personality" is sufficiently pliable to allow a more or less large emphasis on the individual.

champion who comes forth in their name that the victory or defeat depends quite simply on him. Contrariwise, when the Philistine is beaten, his countrymen take to flight (1 K. 17:51), because they have been effectively and corporately defeated by David.⁴⁴

The first Israelite leaders—a Gideon or a Jephte—admirably adapted themselves to the solidaristic character of the social organization, which imitated the psychic whole of a single soul. They concentrated in their individual persons all the psychic powers of the group. Their position is exactly of a corporate personality, that is to say, of an individual whose acts have repercussions on all his followers.⁴⁵

In the final analysis, the individual is never closed off to himself but remains continually in contact with the group of which he forms part (even though this group takes in the past and the future as well as the present). It is precisely this union with the group which enables the individual to assume his proper value. "The individual is regarded as a center of power which extends far beyond the contour of the body and mingles with that of the family and the family property, the tribe and the tribal possessions, or the nation and the national inheritance, to form a psychical whole, and, what is more, such a psychical whole has an extension in time as well as in space, so that the mystic bond which unites society may be conceived retrospectively as regards its ancestors and prospectively with regard to future generations."⁴⁶

2. A second note of capital importance for the correct understanding of the idea of "corporate personality" has to do with the *real* character of this idea. It is not simply a question of establishing a more or less close relationship between an individual and a collectivity within a given group, but of being aware that the two aspects of "corporate personality" are bound together by a physical and real bond. Rather than thinking of the two elements as possessing an external and "juridical" solidarity, we must realize that the group and the individual together make one single total reality. In fact, we are concerned here with a point of

44   J. Pedersen, *Israel*, l.c., 38.
45   *Ibid.*, p. 40.
46   R. Aubrey Johnson, *Sacral Kingship in Israel*, Cardiff, 1955, 2.

view, a manner of thinking, which does not at all agree with our philosophical perspective that we have inherited from Aristotle. We must accustom ourselves to thinking at one and the same time of the two aspects of "corporate personality" as together forming one reality and one single psychic whole.[47]

Even when we are dealing with a secondary use of the concept of "corporate personality" as in Ez. 16 (Israel as the adultress) or Ez. 23 (Ohola and Oholiba) or in Is. 54:1 (the spouse) or even in Dn. 7:13 and 27 ("the son of man" representing the "holy people of the Most High"), the description reveals such concrete touches that the representing figure very often appears in a real light. To the eyes of Isaia the ravaged countryside and beseiged Jerusalem are symbolized by an individual man who is covered "from the sole of the foot to the head" with "wounds and welts and gaping gash, not drained, or bandaged, or eased with salve." (Is. 1:5-6) Gomer, the unfaithful wife of Osee, *is* the nation, of which she is a living image and a representative summing up. (Os. 2)

All this imagery would be inconceivable if the entire group were not really present in a given individual. To understand this, it is necessary to appeal to the thesis of dynamic identification (not the same as static identity) of the group with the individual: "The whole is entirely in the individual and *vice versa*."[48]

This thesis applies first of all to the family community upon which the Israelites model every other association of individuals, whether it be natural (through birth) or artificial. All those who are members of the family group are concrete representatives of this living whole. The ancient Hebrews were convinced that the family is wholly in each single member with all its blessings, all its substance, and all its responsibility. In all truth, the individual *is* the family, because the latter expresses itself so clearly in him.[49] As the soul is completely in each part of the body,

---

47 J. Pedersen, *Israel, l.c.,* p. 26 remarks, with good reason, that this "psychology of the Hebrews" is thoroughly constant throughout history. Cf. the recent book of T. Bomen, *Das Hebräische Denken im Vergleich mit dem griechischen,* Göttingen, 1954,[2] 57.

48 J. Pedersen, *Israel,* l.c., p. 55.

49 *Ibid.,* p. 276.

so the entire group is completely in each individual who forms part of it.[50]

In a certain sense the close cohesion characteristic of the family is found in the other communities which are formed of individual Israelites. There is, first of all, a kind of community of place: Nobe, "the city of the priests" was put to the sword by Saul, "both men and women, children, and sucklings, and ox and ass, and sheep." (1 K. 22:19) When the ark of God arrived in Accaron, the Accaronites cried out: "They have brought the ark of the God of Israel to us, to kill us and our people." (1 K. 5:10). [The French text used by the author has the first person singular throughout instead of the first person plural.] All the inhabitants of Accaron are, so to speak, present in, and represented by, the individual person who speaks in the first person singular.

This idea of the dynamic identification of the family with one of its members does not in any way lessen the value of the individual; on the contrary, it presents him endowed with the special character and peculiar spirit of the community.[51] For our modern mentality the starting point is most frequently the individual. By joining several individuals we arrive at a society or group. For the ancient Israelites the collectivity is presupposed from the very first, not as an abstraction or more or less artificial personification, but as a tangible and controllable reality. The species, which really exists, is revealed in the individuals: a Moabite is not an individual with such or such personal qualities who comes from a country called Moab. Rather he is a concrete manifestation of the national Moabite type which already includes (one might say before any individuation) the characteristic traits to be found in each Moabite individual. When the king of Moab and the king of Edom negotiate, it is really the Moabite nation and Edomite nation that are revealed in their words and deeds.[52] Similarly, the Hebrew patriarch—Abraham, Isaac, or Jacob—is the Israelite type, and by that very fact the concrete representation of the Chosen Nation. In general the individual is a form, a

50 *Ibid.*, p. 277.
51 *Ibid.*, p. 57.
52 *Ibid.*, p. 110.

specimen, a participation of the type.[53] From which it follows that the individual never acts solely for himself; all that he does, the family does. For together they form an organism so closely united that no part can be separated from the others as an independent entity.[54] Conversely, the "great I" of the family, of the tribe, or of the people does not simply consist in the addition of all the individual members. On the contrary it remains always this single reality, living in all the individual members, whom it creates and keeps in existence. This reality is embodied preeminently in specially chosen individuals such as the ancestors, the mother of the tribe, the king, even the divinity (who in the ancient Oriental world belonged to the group of its people).[55] This interpenetration of the individual and of the group explains the close parallelism between their individual psychology and their conception of society. Man's own psychological consciousness being the only one he knows from within, he is almost inevitably drawn to express his views of society in terms of that psychology. The ancient Hebrews were no exception to this law. But whereas we have learned to distinguish, even to analyze, the content of our consciousness, they remained at that stage where they unqualifiedly affirmed the real presence of the group as a whole in the individual.

The perceptive reader will have observed many times by now that this interpenetration, not to say this dynamic identification, of the individual with the group, recalls readily the terminology created by the French Sociological School of Lucien Lévy-Bruhl and Emile Durkheim. As a matter of fact, on many occasions the defenders of the idea of "corporate personality" have sought help from the theory of "primitive mentality." [56] The Norwegian scholar Sigmund Mowinckel, for example, is definitely convinced that the

53 *Ibid.*, p. 111.
54 *Ibid.*, p. 271.
55 J. Hempel, *Gott und Mensch im AT* (*BWANT III*, 2) Stuttgart, 1926; 1936², 190.
56 H. Wheeler Robinson, *The Hebrew Conception*, l.c., p. 53.—Cf. S. Mowinckel, *Psalmenstudien II. Das Thronbesteigungsfest Jahväs und der Ursprung der Eschatologie*, Oslo, 1922, 225: "All the ancient Orient is rooted in the soil of primitive 'prelogical' thought."

mentality of ancient Israel differed little from that which is common to all "primitives." In both cases the "great I" of society is concentrated in some mystic fashion in a single representative; this "collective I"—a term which Mowinckel thinks unfortunate[57] —is apparent especially in the figure of the king, "the ideal incorporation of the popular soul." This is true not only conceptually but also in a mystical-real sense.[58] Several times the Norwegian exegete takes care to note that "according to primitive ideas" the "representative does not mean the same thing as in our modern idiom. He *is* truly that which he represents; all are present in him." [59]

It will, perhaps, be interesting to investigate a bit this thesis of the French scholars in order to see if the concept of "corporate personality" has been tainted by it to such an extent that it will have to be catalogued as *passé*.

Emile Durkheim is of the opinion that the individuals of a given social group act in concert not because their desires *resemble one another* but because they are really identical. There is truly a common identical intention which is imposed on the individual members as the obligatory ideal. All psychological consciousness in the individual is reduced to a manifestation of this common mentality.[60] In this sense "the individual soul" is nothing but a portion of "the collective soul" of the group.[61]

Nonetheless, the French sociologist recognizes that "the anonymous force which is at the basis of cult" is incarnated "in an individual whose personality it assumes." The individual—in the eyes of Durkheim—is only the "*mana* individualized";[62] but on the other hand, "the impersonal forces emitted from the collectivity cannot assert themselves without being incarnated in the con-

---

57 S. Mowinckel, *Psalmenstudien II*, l.c., p. 300: "this somewhat unfortunate expression."
58 *Ibid.*, p. 301, with note 1.
59 *Ibid.*, p. 100.
60 R. E. Peck - E. W. Burgers, *Introduction to the Science of Sociology*, Chicago, 1928, 33.
61 E. Durkheim, *Les formes élémentaires de la vie religieuse*, Paris, 1925², 378.
62 *Ibid.*

sciousness of individuals where they are individualized." [63] In making this concession Durkheim must logically admit that "even in the most primitive societies, there are generally some men whose important social role singles them out to exercise a directing influence on the religious life." [64]

However, the French scholar tries to safeguard his point of view by saying that these privileged individuals form a very small minority in the given group. He refuses to identify individuation, individual status, with the "personality," the chosen individual who leads the group: "A person is not only a single subject who is distinguished from the others; he is besides, and especially, a being to whom is attributed a relative autonomy in relation to the milieu with which he is immediately in contact." [65] This relative autonomy is extolled as a "creation" of society. It is society—in the opinion of Durkheim— that discovers in its leading members "the principal aspirations which are at work in it, as well as the means of satisfying them." [66] It is evident that the mind of the French sociologist vacillates between two poles: at one time he bows to the evidence and accepts the value of the individual, but shortly thereafter he bases this value on the collective and anonymous forces of the group.

The same vacillation of thought characterizes Lucien Lévy Bruhl. On the one hand this scholar thinks that "the individual is to be thought of only as an element of the group of which he forms part and which alone is a true unity." [67] But almost without stopping he adds: "According to the more or less important place which it occupies in the group, this element has greater or less representative standing." [68] Nonetheless, as with Durkheim, the value of the individual rests entirely on the fact that he is "more or less the bearer of the mystic force or of *mana*." [69] The leader himself only incarnates, and, so to say, per-

63   *Ibid.*, p. 382.
64   *Ibid.*, p. 61, note 1.
65   *Ibid.*, p. 388.
66   *Ibid.*, p. 304.
67   L. Lévy-Bruhl, *L'âme primitive*, Paris, 1927, 129.
68   *Ibid.*
69   *Ibid.*, p. 130.

sonifies the social group: "He is equivalent . . . to the group it-self." [70]

The primitives, says Lévy-Bruhl, scarcely think of the in-dividual in himself. The individual really doesn't exist for them except in so far as he is one of the group. "A native Maori," writes the French sociologist, "identifies himself so completely with his tribe that in speaking of it he never fails to use the first person. When recalling a battle which took place perhaps ten generations ago, he will say, 'I defeated the enemy there.' " [71]

This "common individuality," [72] this quasi-identity of the members of a group, is explained, according to Lévy-Bruhl, by what is called "the primitive mentality." It "considers all beings and all objects homogeneous, that is to say, participating either in a common essence or in the same ensemble of qualities." [73] In the mind of primitive man "it is not precisely the individual or the group (species) which is thought of; but both at the same time, the one in the other." [74] The sociologist refers to the Platonic idea,[75] to the archetypes of the philosophers,[76] and especially to totemism. An extremely close solidarity unites the animals of the same species; because they have issued from a common totemic ancestor, their individuality remains relative. They are in fact only "multiple and transitory expressions of the one single and imperishable essence." [77] The "patriarch" of the beavers is "a type of the genus of the personified species in which the indivi-duals, the younger brothers, participate, and which makes them what they are." [78] The animal in turn is indistinguishably con-fused with man, and the individual human being is considered on the same level as an individual animal. If the individual animal

70 *Ibid.,* p. 286.
71 *Ibid.,* p. 71
72 *Ibid.,* p. 99.
73 *Ibid.,* p. 6.
74 *Ibid.,* p. 60.
75 *Ibid.,* p. 61.
76 *Ibid.,* p. 66.
77 *Ibid.,* p. 62.
78 *Ibid.,* p. 66, quoting P. Lejeune, S. J., *Nouvelle-France,* Paris, 1635, 46.

is completely absorbed in the species, the individuals of primitive groups—so Lévy-Bruhl holds—are similarly confused and absorbed in their respective groups. We have here a specific application of the famous "law of participation," according to which, because of a mystic bond between them, "the image *is* the model."[79]

In still another sense—in the opinion of Lévy-Bruhl—the individual must be conceived as a true "place of participation,"[80] that is to say as the point of insertion of multiple influences: the ancestors, the totem inanimate nature (the earth, the rocks, the flowers), the living and the dead of his clan, etc. The French scholar thinks that "in the thought of the primitives . . . the individuality of each does not stop at the periphery of his person; the frontiers are undecided, poorly determined, and even variable according to how much of the mystic force or of *mana* the individuals possess.[81]

Lévy-Bruhl points out an imposing number of these "appurtenances,"[82] which make up a veritable "extension of the personality."[83] He mentions hair on various parts of the body, nails, foot-prints, echoes, the remains of the meal, clothes saturated with sweat, home made objects, one's reflection or shadow. According to Lévy-Bruhl there is such a "participation" between these appurtenances and the individual that it amounts to "a kind of identity."[84]

In order to throw some light on this condition, Lévy-Bruhl falls back upon his well known thesis about the "pre-logical" character of primitive mentality. According to the data of sensible perception and objective experience, for the primitive as well as for us, his sweat . . ., his footprints, his clothes, the tools he has used, all his external appurtenances are external to his person;

79 L. Lévy-Bruhl, *Les fonctions mentales dans les sociétés inférieures,* Paris, 19289, 80.
80 L. Lévy-Bruhl, *L'âme primitive,* l.c., p. 251.
81 *Ibid.,* p. 133.
82 *Ibid.,* p. 134, for the term.
83 L. Lévy-Bruhl traces the expression to J. Van Wing, S. J., *Etudes Bakongo,* Louvain, 1920, 129.
84 L. Lévy-Bruhl, *L'âme primitive,* l.c., p. 185.

this must not be ignored. But he experiences them to be no less, and imagines them to be no less than integral parts of his own individuality. This conviction is thoroughly in possession of his thought." [85]

This "pre-logical" character of the primitive thought patterns is revealed—according to Lévy-Bruhl— in a number of habits. The individual *is*, in a certain sense, his tribal companion. In case of sickness a certain diet is prescribed for the sick person and for all his household.[86] Incest on the part of a couple "brings for the entire clan terrible evils, droughts, famines, sterility of the women." [87] In the collective punishments, "the innocent and the guilty are not separated; they are mixed together in the unity of the group." [88] To say that an individual dies is to say that he is going to take his place, according to his rank, among the dead members of the group. [89] The primitive mentality tends to look upon a future event, whose certainty is vouched for by mystic reasons, as already present. [90]

We know that the "postulate of sociological method" which includes the "primitives" in an "indistinct mob whose movements are faultlessly assured by the interplay of collective thought," [91] was subjected to a number of severe criticisms. In the ninth edition of his work on *The Mental Functions in Inferior Societies*, Lévy-Bruhl decided to correct and shade his thought as follows: "In calling it (the mentality of lower types of societies) pre-logical, I wish only to say that it is not obliged, as we are, to abhor contradiction above all. It's first concern is to obey the law of participation. Thus oriented, it does not delight unreasonably in contradiction (that would make it ordinarily absurd for us) but

85   *Ibid.*, p. 187.
86   *Ibid.*, p. 96.
87   *Ibid.*, p. 121, according to J. Van Wing, *Etudes Bakongo*, l.c., p. 175.
88   *Ibid.*, p. 121.
89   *Ibid.*, p. 387.
90   L. Lévy-Bruhl, *La mentalité primitive*, Paris, 1925[4], 374. Cf. pp. 520-21: "Often the future event, if considered as certain, and if it provokes a strong emotion, is considered as already present."
91   O. Leroy, *La raison primitive. Essai de réfutation de la théorie du prélogisme*, Paris, 1927, 55.

it is not concerned with avoiding it either. Frequently it is simply indifferent to it. That is what makes it so difficult to follow." [92]

With still more precision, the French author reveals the basis of his thought in a posthumous writing (he died on March 12, 1939): "Concerning the 'pre-logical' character of the primitive mentality, I have for the past tawenty-five years been watering down my understanding of it; the results which I have now come to concerning this matter makes this evolution definitive, *causing me to abandon completely a poorly established hypothesis* ... The logical structure of the mind is the same in all known human societies ... (It is true that) the primitive mentality accepts incompatibilities without blinking an eye (I used to say contradictions, which seemed to imply logical conditions which do not exist in reality) ... (Sometimes) the ordinary man, in exceptional circumstances, without thinking, takes the attitude characteristic of the primitives .... In everything that has to do with everyday experience, transactions of every sort, political life, economic life, use of numbers, etc. they (the primitives) act in a way which implies that they use their faculties in the same way as we do." [93]

The attacks against the "idea of pre-logical thought" (even when restricted to "mythical" thought or "religious" thought) were particularly violent concerning the immanence of the group in the individual or the relations of the man with his group. Lévy-Bruhl seems sometimes to forget the essential dialectic between the individual and society. Surely the individual man can and must be considered as "a member of a body," and this social solidarity has in the more inferior societies "a more organic and vital character than in our societies." [94] But on the other hand several critics inveigh against "the inexorable tyranny of the group.[95] Even in the midst of highly organized groups there is still room for consciously individual behavior. It is true that the primitive scarcely think of an individual as such; but has one the right to conclude that "an

92 Paris, 1928[9], 79.

93 Cf. *"Les Carnets de Lucien Lévy-Bruhl,"* in *RPh* July-September 1947, 257-81, pp. 258, 260, 265-66, 280. On the last page "prelogisme" is qualified as a "gratuitous hypothesis."

94 L. Lévy-Bruhl, *La mentalité primitive,* l.c., 465.

95 P. Radin, *Primitive Man as Philosopher,* New York, London, 1927, 36.

individual only exists in so far as he participates in his group or in his species?"[96]

Not a few factors in the behavior of "savages" discredit the extreme view that denies the existence of an individual conscious life among them. W. McDougall enumerates several: the existence of individual names (even though secret), private property, private rites; individual vengeance (alongside the group vendetta), vanity and pride, competition in games or in legerdemain, technical or artistic accomplishments.[97] A French critic calls attention to "the influence of leaders, of sorcerers, of priests among the non-civilized on styles of art, language and religion, customs and habits," and he concludes: "The individaul, even in the most primitive civilizations, is not always swallowed up in the mass ... Skills, myths, rituals, and codes ... have not come into existence spontaneously. The primitive societies have had their geniuses, whose impetus the group has only assimilated ... The individual in savage societies makes his presence felt not only when he reacts occasionally against social and religious prescriptions by his lifelessness or flight, or when he brings a variety of talents to his group, but also when he affirms his personality more vigorously by creating or modifying the rules and beliefs ... When these non-civilized peoples attribute their institutions to mythical heroes, there is no reason to arbitrarily deny this testimony."[98]

Other students of primitive civilizations verify "evident signs of social discrimination": "The primitive," writes Robert Lowie, "is not an imbecile. He is prompt to observe and appreciate individual differences which, in the same way as an inevitable biological phenomenon, appear in all groups, even the most primitive (as Marett very rightly notes)."[99] The American philosopher alludes to individual prowess in time of war, shamanism, riches, the existence of castes, etc. Even some experts of the French sociological school, such as H. Hubert and M. Mauss are forced to

96 L. Lévy-Bruhl, *L'âme primitive*, 229.
97 W. McDougall, *The Group Mind. A Sketch of the Principles of Collective Psychology with the Attempt to Apply to the Interpretation of National Life and Character*, Cambridge, 1920, 72.
98 O. Leroy, *La raison primitive*, 1.c. 58-59.
99 R. Lowie, *Traité de sociologie primitive*, Paris, 1935, 332.

recognize that "revelation by magical means (in Australia) is normally produced by isolated individuals and not by a group. It is a social phenomenon which is produced only by individuals. It is often provoked by the individual who thinks himself fitted to become a magician and has business with other magicians or has predetermined nervous dispositions."[100] Paul Radin, for his part, protests against the widely held opinion that all investigations of primitive cultures should necessarily begin with the assumption that there is nothing beyond the collective consciousness.[101] As a matter of fact, the influence of the group on the individual is by no means irresistible. There remains always an element which is not fashioned or created by the group; namely, personal initiative.

The initial error under which Lévy-Bruhl labored (and which he admitted at the end of his life) has been denounced by more than one critic. It consists in this that the French sociologist began by setting up too neat a distinction between the so-called primitive and the self-styled civilized person. It is an error, says McDougall, to think that the mental life of every civilized man follows a purely rational and logical trend: "It is not true, then, that we are logical individuals, while savages are wholly pre-logical in virtue of the dominance among them of the collective mental life ... The truth rather is that, whenever emotion qualifies our intellectual operations, it renders them other than purely and strictly logical."[102] And the English philosopher does not hesitate to conclude: "The interval between the modern man of scientific culture and the average citizen of our modern states is far greater than that between the latter and the savage."[103]

An observation of Oliver Leroy points in the same direction: "Among savages as among civilized people, society is made of an amorphous mass which is directed by vigorous personalities in direct proportion to the state of the average intellectual activity of its members."[104]

100   H. Hubert and M. Mauss, *Mélanges d'Histoire des Religions*, Paris, 1929², 171.
101   P. Radin, *Primitive Man as Philosopher*, l.c., 36.
102   W. McDougall, *The Group Mind*, l.c., 75.
103   *Ibid.*, pp. 75-76.

Paul Radin, in turn, makes as "a conviction slowly forced upon me from my observations and contact with a number of aboriginal tribes" the following significant observation: "Among primitive peoples there exists the same distribution of temperament and ability as among us. This I hold to be true in spite of all the manifest differences in the configuration and orientation of their cultures."[105] The same author affirms that the "primitive perceives very plainly the distinction between social reality and individual reality. Although he participates in both of them at the same time,[106] they do not have in his eyes any common measure. In fact they follow entirely separate and independent paths.[107]

The almost identical manner of carrying out primitive vendettas and modern collective reprisals in time of war is rather delicately noted by Robert Lowie. We would be wrong, thinks this author, to conclude, from the way in which civilized nations engage in war lump together the guilty with the innocent, that in the mind of civilized men "the individual is indistinguishable from the group."[108] This example of a false conclusion based on a perfectly true observation shows the danger of hasty generalizations. There are collective undertakings among all peoples, even among all individuals. That is an undeniable fact. But that must never prevent us from recognizing the complementary fact. Everywhere, in primitive organizations as well as in civilized societies, the more gifted individuals are behind new movements, whether they be religious, social, or technical. The setting up within the group of select organs to maintain unity and cohesion in the group is not the effect of an impersonal force at the service of the collective conscience. It is due to the fact that the sentiments and views which prevail in the community, even if it is "primitive," find their definitive and efficacious expression among individuals who are competent to supply it.[109]

104 O. Leroy, *La raison primitive*, l.c., 58.
105 P. Radin, *Primitive Man as Philosopher*, l.c., 5.
106 *Ibid.*, p. 37.
107 *Ibid.*, pp. 42 and 61.
108 R. Lowie, *Traité de sociologie primitive*, l.c., 390.
109 Often the "leader" is the symbolic projection of the community ideal; cf. K. Young, *Social Psychology*, New York, 1946, 249; E. Faris,

From what has been said, we can expect two things almost *a priori*. On the one hand, it is possible to observe "primitive" actions even in the most advanced civilized nations. Such actions, however illogical they seem to be, are perfectly compatible with the normal use of reason. On the other hand, we must recognize a common basic structure of the human mind whether we are dealing with real "savages" or with would-be civilized persons. Concerning the question at hand, that of the continual interaction between the individual and his social milieu, we must keep in mind that it presents an eternal problem: "The individual and the community are never juxtaposed without affecting one another; it is always a question of the two complementary poles of the total life of man."[110] In stating and solving this eternal problem, inherent to human nature, the only difference between the "primitive" attitude and the modern attitude is that the former "lives" and "realizes" intensely the union of the two poles whereas the latter possesses a lively reflex consciousness of the "two ends of the chain." Whereas the "primitive" asserts from the very first and concretely the coexistence, even the interpenetration of the individual and society, the modern distinguishes two aspects, only to reunite them later on through an appropriate intuitive thought pattern.

The analysis which we have just made shows how baseless it would be to press too forcibly the idea of the "primitive" behavior of the ancient Hebrews. Perhaps we have accepted too readily the theories maintaining that the individual is completely absorbed

The Nature of Human Nature, New York, 1937[2], 31-32; F. W. Jerusalem, *Über den Begriff der Kollektivität und seine Stellung im Ganzen der Soziologie*, in KVSW II, 1 (1922) 47-53, p. 50; A. Bertholet, *Dynamismus und Personalismus* (A collection of popular lectures 142), Tübingen, 1930, 18-19. Primitive mentality exalts aggressive individuals such as Achilles, Gilgamesh, or the heroes of the *Niebelungen,* because in that way it pictures to itself its own leaders. As G. LeBon shows in *Psychologie des foules*, Paris, 1939[1], 94, accidental groupings such as crowds presuppose the influence of an outstanding individual; "In human crowds the leader plays a considerable role; his will is the nucleus around which opinions form and identify themselves."

110   R. Lockner, *Deskriptive Pädagogik*, Reichenberg, 1927, 103.

in the group. Perhaps we have betrayed a bit of simplicity in the way we have used such ready made terms as "law of participation,"[111] "extension of personality,"[112] even "belongingness."[113] In any case several recent authors have voiced their objection—with good reasons, it seems to us—against the idea of a pronounced primitivism in Israel. All that can be said is that here and there one finds traces or remnants.[114] As is so frequently the case, the truth is probably between the extremes. Since we have shown that "primitive" reactions are not necessarily or uniquely the mark of the non-civilized, we can say, if we wish, that such "primitive" reactions are found, if one wishes, "sublimated in the Old Testament ideas."[115]

3. In the third place we must not lose sight of the fact that the idea of "corporate personality" includes what H. Wheeler Robinson calls a great "fluidity." This does not at all mean that it is vague or difficult to pin down. Rather it means that there is a continual oscillation or fluctuation between the two poles of the idea: the individual and society. Sometimes the group is in the forefront

111 H. Wheeler Robinson, *The Hebrew Conception*, l.c., p. 53.

112 R. Aubrey Johnson, *The One and the Many*, l.c., p. 103. The author refers (as does L. Lévy-Bruhl himself) to J. Van Wing, *Etudes Bakongo*, l.c., p. 129. In his essay Johnson applies the idea of "the extension of personality" to Yahweh himself (which H. Wheeler Robinson thinks "somewhat unguarded": Cf. *JTS* 45, 1944, 156-7n.); he is thinking especially of "the spirit of the Lord" (Jg. 6:34; 14:6, 19; 1 K. 10:10) or of His "word" (Is. 55:10; 1 K. 3:11; Ez. 12:23-28), or of His "name" (Nm. 6:22-27; Ps. 19:54), even of His "angel" (Gn. 16:7-14; Jg. 6:11-24) or of the ark (Nm. 10:35; Ps. 67:2; 1 K. 4:5-8).

113 R. Aubrey Johnson, *The Vitality of the Individual in the Thought of Ancient Israel*, Cardiff, 1949, 7-8. The author refers explicitly to L. Lévy-Bruhl and is of the opinion that all the *"belongings"* can be identified purely and simply with the individual. In fact, the individual expresses himself therein fully each time.

114 G. E. Wright, *The Biblical Doctrine of Man in Society*, London, 1954, 24.

115 H. Wheeler Robinson, *The Hebrew Conception*, l.c., 53. The author compares the taboos of holiness, or the symbolic magic, which, according to him, underlie the "prophecy in act."

of our attention; sometimes the individual is. This fluctuation is possible because of the physical and concrete character of the "corporate personality." Each man and each woman is *at one and the same time* a determined personality, living at a given moment of time, and a concrete personification of the group. We can compare the abrupt shift from one to the other to what takes place in a psychological pattern. In a simple design of cubes arranged according to perspective, the eye is at one time drawn to a retreating figure, and at another time to a projecting figure. The transition from one to the other is made without effort or even awareness. Because of the intimate union of the individual and the social in ancient Israel, the shift from one to the other is not only easier but also more normal.

We can certainly draw attention to the oneness of the individual person as he develops in the group, but we must also admit that the Hebrew mind, without in any way forcing the issue, passes from this truth to the other; namely, that the individual person is at the same time (by a reverse pattern of thought) a corporate extension of the group.

A wealth of examples will illustrate the great ease with which the mind passes from the collective "I" to the many persons who compose it. On the occasion of the unfortunate negotiations with the king of Edom, the messengers speak at one time of "your brother Israel," (Nm. 20:14) and at another time of "us," which is, moreover, identical with "our fathers." (cf. verse 15) But despite the promise: *"We* will go straight along the royal road without turning to the right or to the left, until *we* have passed through your territory" (Nm. 20:17), Edom (in virtue of the "corporate personality" of its king?) replies: *"You* (singular in the original) shall not pass." (Nm. 20:18, 20) In the last speech of Moses in the Book of Deuteronomy, the same switch from the plural to the singular is used: *"You* (plural have seen all the Lord did in the land of Egypt before your very eyes ... the great testing *your* (singular in the original) own eyes have seen." (Dt. 29:1-2)[116]

---

116 R. Aubrey Johnson, *The One and the Many*, l.c., p. 11, shows how the "messenger" is an "extension" of his master, with whom he identifies himself (Gn. 44:10: the words of the steward refer rather

We find this same interchange of the singular pronoun with the plural pronoun when the legislator addresses the people. The community as well as the individual is constantly in his mind. "The individual who is indicated by the singular "you" of the Hebrew laws must be considered as the leader or representative of a group rather than as an individual properly speaking." Such is the opinion of H. Cazelles.[117] This alternating movement of thought, passing readily from the group to the individual and *vice versa,* is characteristic of certain psalms. For example, Ps. 102 in which the singular "my" is used in verses 1-5 and the plural "our" in verses 10-14; Ps. 129 in which verses 1-2 are in the singular, whereas verse 8 speaks of Israel; Ps. 136 in which verses 1-4 and verse 8 are plural, and verses 5-6 are singular.

In recent times a rather plausible explanation of the phenomenon of oscillation (which unites the individual Israelite and the Chosen People even while contrasting them with each other) has been proposed. "It can no longer be argued (as once was done)," writes a recent commentator on the *Book of Daniel,* "that the Hebrews stressed the importance of the community because their thinking was too undeveloped for them to attach importance to the life of the individual. Their emphasis on the life of the community no doubt owes something to the primitive stage of human culture, but it owes far more to their religious grasp of our human situation." [118] It is certain that the formation of the Chosen People is the central act of God in the Old Testament. God revealed to the community of the "children of Israel" its election, its task, and its destiny. The individual finds his true life when he accepts his vocation in this community.[119] This presupposes that the individual hears the Word which God addressed to the group as addressed to him personally. Instead of being an insignificant

---

to the master: "The one with whom it is found shall be *my* slave."); cf. also Jg. 11:12-13; 4 K. 9:18.

117   H. Cazelles, *Loi israélite,* in *DBS V,* 497-530, p. 510.

118   E. W. Heaton, *The Book of Daniel, Torch Bible Commentary,* London, 1956, 242.

119   G. E. Wright, *The Biblical Doctrine,* l.c., p. 18. Cf. S. W. Baron, *Histoire d'Israel. Vie sociale et religieuse* (Collection Sinai I) French Translation, 1956, 182.

element of the tribal group, he must, on the contrary, receive the divine precepts freely with all his heart and with all his soul, and with all his strength. (Dt. 6:5) The fact that the Law applies to the individual as well as to the Chosen People as such, shows that "man and society are not opposing concepts but are involved in one another... Rather than being lost in the social group, he is instead found in it, attaining his true selfhood by sharing its purposes and partaking of its well-being (*shalom*)." [120]

The reversibility of these two complementary aspects of the two-pronged idea of "corporate personality" is based ultimately on the undeniable fact that "the whole group could function through, or be seen in, any of its members. He was regarded realistically as the representative of the group, without any special delegation to the office." [121] It is one of the glories of the Hebrew genius (or rather an evident disposition of divine Providence) that it knew so well how to maintain the unity of the individual and the group while referring with equal facility to either the representative individual or the group which he represented.[122]

4. A fourth aspect of "corporate personality" can be deduced logically from the two preceding ones. If this concept has a concrete realism and a dialectical reversibility of its two component parts, it follows that the community aspect will never be lacking even in the periods of extreme individualism, as at the

120   G. E. Wright, *The Biblical Doctrine*, l.c., p. 51. Cf. W. Hobhouse, *The Church and the World in Idea and in History* (Bampton Lectures 1909), London, 1911, 20: "True religion must always have both its individual and its corporate side .... Each human soul must appropriate the truth and make its personal response .... But a bare individualism is inadequate. True religion is also social and corporate."

121   H. Wheeler Robinson, *Redemption and Revelation*, London, 1944³, 258.

122   Cf. the formula of A. Stanley Cook, who wrote in 1925 in the *Cambridge Ancient History*, III, 493: "An individual or a specific group may be regarded as the true embodiment or representative of the many, so that not only can singulars and plurals interchange, according as one thinks of the unity or the multiplicity of a group, but Hebrew thought refers with equal facility to a representative individual as to the group he represents."

time of Jeremia (31:33-34), Ezechiel (37:40-49), or Joel (3:1-2; cf. Nm. 11:29).

The prophets always preached in the midst of all the Israelites, but their message was directed to the "remnant" of Israel, that is to say, too its more worthy representatives. The new covenant, announced Jeremia, in which the beginning of personal and individual religion is proclaimed, is made with the "house of Israel." (Jr. 31:33) The words of Ezechiel proclaiming individual retribution are particularly significant: "Therefore I will judge you, *house of Israel, 'each'* according to his ways." (Ez. 18:30; cf. 14:7-8) As the retribution, so the sin had been collective and individual at the same time: "As for you (plural), *house of Israel*, thus says the Lord God: Come, *each one* of you, destroy your idols: Then listen to me, and never again profane my holy name with your gifts and your idols." (Ez. 20:39) In his turn Zacharia tells his listeners in the name of Yahweh: "Render true judgment, and show kindness and compassion toward *each other.*" (Za. 7:8) In the psalms individual piety goes hand in hand with the very obvious consciousness of belonging to a group which surpasses the individual (the God-fearing, Israel, all humanity). This consciousness might be compared "to the pedal notes of the organ, ready to give body and substance to whatever be the melody." [123] In fact, all the psalms, even the most personal ones, are potentially psalms of intercession, since they are basically representative. Always, the one represents the many, and the many pray and praise God through the mediation of the one. Israel has a very acute consciousness of the simultaneity of the collectivity and the individual. If the group envelops, upholds, even surpasses the isolated individuals, these same individuals manifest, express, and even create the feeling of solidarity. The "I of the psalms" is at one and the same time all Israel and each individual Israelite. Only the context determines which holds the upper hand in the thought and in the language of the psalmists. [124]

We could use a great number of texts to show that all through the history of Israel (after the exile as well as before), "the God

123   H. Wheeler Robinson, *Inspiration and Revelation in the OT.* Oxford, 1946, 264-5.

124   *Ibid.*, pp. 83 and 264.

of Israel would show his mercy upon his people." (cf. Jud. 7:4)
But other texts, no less numerous, show that the total concept
of "Israel" is embodied at all the great turning points of history
in individual persons acting in the name of the nation; the
patriarchs, the kings (sons of God), prophets (Amos, Jeremia),
a priest, an outstanding layman, a woman (Gomer, the wife of
Osee), the Macabean martyrs.[125] Esdras, as leader of the people,
is conscious of divine protection of his person: "And I being
strengthened by the hand of the Lord my God, which was upon
me." (Esd. 7:28) But the same words apply to his countrymen:
"The hand of our God is upon *all* that seek him in goodness; and
his power and strength and wrath upon all them that forsake
him." (Esd. 8:22)

An objective examination of the battery of texts (cf. Chapter
2)—texts which cover the full sweep of Jewish history—will
supply the best answer to the usual objection: the concept of
"corporate personality" is applicable only to the "nomadic" part
of Israelite history. For from one end to the other we will find
that this fundamental concept is taken for granted and that its
atmosphere is all-pervading.

125   Cf. J. De Fraine, *Individu et Société*, l.c., pp. 463-75.

2

The Concept of "Corporate Personality" in the Texts of the Old Testament

In the preceding chapter we discussed the meaning that modern exegesis gives to the idea of "corporate personality." In this one we wish to show by an extensive analysis that this idea is widespread in the Old Testament and that it takes into account the various nuances which the biblical text contains.[1]

Let us begin by repeating our nominal definition: "The group could be thought of as functioning through an individual member, who for the time being so completely represented it that he became identical with it... There was a fluidity of thought which seems strange to us, whereby the speaker could pass from the community to the individual who represented it, and from the individual back to the community, without any apparent consciousness of the transitions."[2]

On closer investigation it becomes evident that we must distinguish two types of "corporate personality." The first (which seems to be the primary meaning of the term) emanates from the concrete individual and considers him in so far as he is

1 H. Wheeler Robinson, *Hebrew Psychology*, in: S. A. Peake, *The People and the Book*, Oxford, 1925, 353-382, p. 378. It is not our intention to give a profound exegesis of the texts quoted, but only to give a backdrop for the concept we are studying.

2 H. H. Rowley, *The Rediscovery of the O.T.*, Philadelphia, 1946, 216; cf. also by the same author, *The Faith of Israel*, 1956, 118.

"corporate" (whether that be in relation to time—the ancestor—
or whether it be in relation to space—the royal *pater familias*).
The second (which seems to be the secondary meaning) focuses
attention on the community in so far as it is summed up concretely in one individual. The first type emphasizes the "expansiveness" of the individual; the second underscores the concrete unity
of the group. We may compare the former to the diastolic beat
of the heart and the latter to the systolic beat.

If we stick to the formal meaning of the idea "corporate
personality," the historical reality of the individual concerned
is not of great moment. The individual ancestor may be fictitious
or he may be historical. In any case, the individual and the group
form one single, concrete, physical reality. Moreover, the Bible
emphasizes the irreplacable value of the individual in the bosom
of the community, especially—as we have already seen—because
of the religious Covenant. For this reason we begin our examination of the texts by taking the passages which illustrate the "corporate personality" of real individuals. Among these we will choose
examples from both the horizontal (*pater familias*) and the vertical
(ancesor) patterns. After that we will consider the secondary
meaning of the concept of "corporate personality," especially in
the case where the community acts as though it were a single
individual.

Within our over-all plan we would like to divide the different
groups and communities mentioned in the texts under different
biblical themes. In order to determine the exact meaning of these
themes and to determine their precise reference to the problem of
the "corporate personality," we will survey the four major divisions
of the Old Testament canon:

a) The Pentateuch
b) The Historical Books (the early prophets of the Jewish
   canon)
c) The Prophets (the later prophets of the Jewish canon)
d) The Sapiential Books.

The purpose of our investigation is twofold: to show the
presence of the concept of "corporate personality" from one end
to the other of biblical literature; to establish as detailed a "proof"
as possible by giving an appropriate phenomenological description.

Chapter two will be concerned with the *general* themes in which we think we have discovered a corroboration of the concept of "corporate personality." Chapter three will be devoted to the study of six specialized themes, namely:

a) Adam (theme of the ancestor)
b) The king (theme of the *pater familias*)
c) The prophets (theme of the "father" in the general sense)
d) The servant of Yahweh (theme of the "father")
e) The Son of Man (theme of the union of the group in a single individual)
f) The "I of the psalms" (theme of the concentration of the group)

In chapter four we will add a seventh specialized application: (the theme of the *"pater familias"*) in the doctrine of the Mystical Body of Christ.

In a general way the detailed examination of the texts of the Old Testament (according to the order of the four subdivisions of the canon) will furnish us with the following nine general themes: Within the *horizontal* pattern of the *expansive* aspect of the term there are three general themes: 1) the "father of the family" and *his household,* 2) the beneficial influence of the representing individual, 3) the harmful influence of the representing individual. Within the *vertical* pattern of the *expansive* aspect of the term, there are three others: 4) the ancestor and his descendants, 5) the beneficial influence of the "fathers" on their "children," 6) the harmful influence of the "fathers" on their "children." Within the *unitive* aspect of the term there are three more general categories: 7) the identity of name for a clan and for a person, 8) the concretization of the people in one single person, 9) the legal "thou" referring to the entire nation.

Before beginning the study of the nine categories, it will be useful to give a schema of the present chapter in which each of these themes will be considered.

    1. "Corporate personality" in its *expansive* aspect
        A. The horizontal pattern (the "father of the family")
            1) the father of a family and his household

        2) the beneficial influence of the representing individual
        3) the harmful influence of the representing individual
    B. The vertical pattern (the ancestor)
        1) the ancestor and his descendants
        2) the beneficial influence of "fathers" on their "children"
        3) the harmful influence of "fathers" on their "children"
  2. "Corporate personality" in its *unitive* aspect
        1) the identity of name for a clan and for a person
        2) the concretization of the people in an individual person
        3) the legal "thou" referring to the entire nation

THE FIRST THEME

The Father of a Family and His Household

The Old Testament has a distinct consciousness of the place of the individual in the familial society. The strictly monarchical structure of the patriarchal family is well known. The "father," the object of a profound veneration because of his power to bestow a blessing or a curse (cf. the blessing of Noe: Gn. 9:23), makes final decisions regarding marriages (Gn. 24:1 Abraham; Gn. 28:1 Isaac), decrees the eventual sale of children (Ex. 21:7), even condemns them to death. (Gn. 34:24 Juda and Thamar; 42:37 Ruben). In general the individual Israelite is never restricted unduly; such limitation might provoke an unnatural solipsism. Yet the individual normally develops in the "home."

Without a doubt "the family must be considered as a community of spirit as well as a community of body, as an identity of personalities as well as the fleshy unity of the race,[3] as a desired collectivity as well as a forced solidarity."[4] But such a "con-

---

3 E. Dhorme, *L'évolution religieuse d' Israël*, I, Brussels, 1937, 266.
4 J. De Fraine, *Individu et Société*, in *Bb* 33 (1952), 1.c., 458.

spiratio animorum" is inconceivable for an ancient Israelite unless the family is a unique whole strongly structured. W. Robertson Smith, even though he exaggerates, puts his finger on a vital point when he describes each family as "one living whole, a single animated mass of blood, flesh and bones, of which no member could be touched without all the members suffering."[5] To our way of thinking that might be a simple metaphor; but for the Orientals of former times the line of demarcation between the metaphorical and the literal was not so tidily marked. Very often figures of speech and symbols were treated as realities.

The organized solidarity of the family presupposes a concrete idea of the bond of the flesh: Incest is prohibited because the sister of the father is the flesh of the father, and the sister of the mother is the flesh of the mother (Lv. 18:12-13), even one's own flesh. (Lv. 20:19) Near relatives are referred to by the expression "of the same flesh." (Lv. 18:6) The brothers of Joseph refuse to kill the future patriarch because "he is our brother, our own flesh." (Gn. 37:27) Laban says to his nephew Jacob: "You are indeed my flesh and bone." (Gn. 29:14)

The sacred bond of common origin is expressed by the term *baith,* "the household." The close cohesion of the family group is due to the "father of the family," who guarantees the unity of the home, for the term used for "the family" is precisely *bét 'âb,* "the household of the father."

The texts of the Old Testament show convincingly that the "family" shares so fully in the lot of the "father" that it is customary to designate the "household" by the father, and *vice versa.* To illustrate this statement, we will run through the four great divisions of the Old Testament, one after the other.

1. *The Pentateuch*

The Pentateuch, both in its narratives and in its legislative parts, amply attests to the close association between the "father" and his "household."

a) THE NARRATIVES

The just Noe will be able to enter the ark taking "your sons,

5   W. Robertson Smith, *The Religion of the Semites,* Edinburgh, 1889, 255.

your wife, and your sons' wives with you." (Gn. 6:18) In doing
so the "father" saves "all his household." (Gn. 7:1) The same
things happens to Lot who receives this command from the angel:
"Have you anyone else here? Sons-in-law, sons, daughters, or
anyone you have in the city, take them out of the place; for we
are about to destroy this place." (Gn. 19:12) It must be noted
that even though his wife and his two daughters were saved together
with him, the biblical text speaks only of leading him in the 16th
verse: "led *him* forth, and set *him* outside the city." Evidently, Lot
is the corporate representative of his household.

The patriarch Abraham is rewarded if "his household" does
good: "Indeed, I have chosen him, that he may charge his sons
and his *household* after him to observe the way of the Lord, doing
what is good and right, so that the Lord may fulfill *for Abraham*
what he has promised him." (Gn. 18:19) When Pharao took
Sara, the wife of Abraham, "the Lord struck Pharao *and his
household* with great plagues." (Gn. 12:17) When a similar event
took place in Gerara, king Abimelech was warned by Yahweh in
a dream: "But if you do not restore her, know that you will surely
die, you *and all that are yours.*" (Gn. 20:7) But Abraham interceded for Abimelech and God "cured Abimelech and his wife
and maidservants, and they bore children. For the Lord had closed
the wombs of Abimelech's *household* because of Sara, the wife
of Abraham." (Gn. 20:17-18) It is evident from this passage
that the king of Gerara determined to a certain extent the lot of all
those who were subject to his patriarchal and familial authority.
This conclusion is strengthened by the fact that before making an
alliance with Abraham, the king demanded this oath from Abraham: "Swear to me by God that you will not deal falsely with me
nor with my children nor with my descendants." (Gn. 21:23)
Descendants and children are evidently an "extension of the
principal personality.

The story of Jacob offers other examples pointing to the same
conclusion. First of all there is the phrase which, in order to
designate the entire family, links together very closely the members
of a matriarchal family. As Joseph approaches his brother Esau,
he prays, "Save me from my brother Esau; for I fear that he is
coming to kill me and all my family." (The French translation

speaks of killing "the mother with the children.") (Gn. 32:12)
Another incident so identifies Jacob with his "household" that
when the patriarch speaks of "me" he is referring to his family
as well as to himself. After the extermination of the Sichemites
by Simeon and Levi, he fearfully tells them: "I have but few
men; if they unite against *me* and attack me, *my family and I will*
be destroyed." (Gn. 34:30) Again, after the return to Palestine,
Jacob says "to his *family* and to all who were with him": "Do
away with the strange gods you have among you, purify yourselves . . . Let us be on our way to Bethel." (Gn. 35:2) The
common danger of famine strengthens the solidarity of the sons
of Jacob. Juda says to his father: "Let the boy go with me, that
we may . . . save from death both you and ourselves, as well as
our *children.*" (Gn. 43:8) Finally when Joseph makes himself
known, he sends this message to his father: "Come down to me,
and do not delay . . . I will provide for you there, that you, and
your household, and all who belong to you may not be impover-
ished." (Gn. 45:9, 11)

These few examples not only show us that the father of the
family determines in some way the lot of his family but also tends
to identify in some way the house with the individual father, to
the extent that whatever happens to one happens to the other. It
is this extreme fluidity in the presentation of this first theme
which links it up with our notion of "corporate personality."

b) THE LEGISLATIVE SECTIONS

In the different laws the "household" is constantly being associated, indeed identified in some way, with the individual. Instead
of a purely juridical solidarity or of a somewhat extrinsic association, there is question of a living and concrete reality.

In the decalogue the sabbath rest extends to the entire family
as to a unified whole: "But the seventh day is the Sabbath of
the Lord, your God. No work may be done then either by you, or
your son or daughter, or your male or female slave, or your beast,
or by the alien who lives with you." (Ex. 20:10; Dt. 5:14; cf.
Lv. 25:6: "While the land has its sabbath, all it produces will
be food equally for you yourself and for your male and female
slaves, for your hired help and the tenants who live with you.")

This stereotyped enumeration underlines the fact that the family is considered as a unit in treating of the sabbath (decalogue and Deuteronomy) or the sabbatical year (sacerdotal legislation).

Deuteronomy offers several cases where the individual Hebrew is considered to be the center of influence of the "household." The first speech of Moses ends on this hortatory note: "You must keep his statutes and commandments which I enjoin on you today, that *you and your children* after you may prosper, and that you may have long life on the land that the Lord, your God, is giving *you* forever." (Dt. 4:40) The law concerning the place of worship provides for the liturgical celebration held in common: "You shall make merry before the Lord, your God, *with your sons and daughters,* your male and female slaves, as well as with the Levite who belongs to your community." (Dt. 12:12) The same formula is found in Dt. 16:11 in the singular: "In the place which the Lord, your God, chooses as the dwelling place of his name, you shall make merry in his presence together with your *son and daughter,* your male and female slave, and the Levite who belongs to your community, as well as the alien, the orphan and the widow among you." (cf. also Dt. 16:14) The slave who of his own free will desires to remain in the family he has served is permitted to do so: "If, however, he tells you that he does not wish to leave you, because he is devoted to *you and your household* ... he shall then be your slave forever." (Dt. 15:16) The turn of thought here would seem to indicate that the master takes in also the entire "household." The "you" in whose presence the slave finds contentment is the family circle. Certain religious meals (for example, that at which the first-born of cattle and sheep is offered to God and eaten) are to be taken in common, "in the presence of Yahweh": "Year after year you and your family shall eat them before the Lord, your God, in the place he chooses." (Dt. 15:20; cf. 14:26) The pious king of Dt. 17:14-20, who does not give in to pride before his brethren, *together with "his descendants* will enjoy a long reign in Israel." (Dt. 17:20) In chapter 29 of Deuteronomy mention is made of those who have taken part in the Covenant: "Your chiefs and judges, your elders and officials, and all of the men of Israel, *together with your wives and children."* (Dt. 29:10)

The very same ideas are found in the priestly legislation. The priests, that is to say, "Aaron and his sons" (Lv. 8:2, 6, 14, 18, 22, 31, 36; 9:1; 10:6, 22) are to offer sacrifices both in their own names and in the name of the entire community. In the report of the beginnings of the ceremony for the "Day of Atonement," we read: "Aaron shall bring in the bullock, his sin offering to atone *for himself and for his household."* (Lv. 16:6, 11) A few verses later we read that the offering is for *"himself and his household,* as well as for the whole Israelite community." [6] (Lv. 16:17; cf. verse 24: "for himself and for his people") From this quotation we can see that the high priest (here designated by the name of Aaron) not only acts *for the benefit* of his people but *in their place.* He represents them and sums up in himself the desire for expiation felt by the entire family and national group. Yahweh hurls this terrible threat against those who dare to adore Moloch: "I myself will set my face against *that man and his family* and will cut off from their people *both him and all* who join him in his wanton worship of Moloch." (Lv. 20:5) Here once again the evildoer is thought of as the representative of his "family" and draws punishment upon them. Freedom for a slave during the Jubilee Year means also freedom for his family: *"He, together with his children,* shall be released from your service and return to his kindred and to the property of his ancestors." (Lv. 25:41)

The texts which we have just quoted permit us to draw the following conclusion. The intimate association (equal to a dynamic identification) between the father and his "household" is based in the last analysis on the inherent unifying and representational role of the father. (cf. Gn. 32:11, where Jacob says after his return from the land of Edom: *"I* have grown into two camps"). We have here, then, the twofold aspect of "corporate personality": a select individual dominating the corporate group which he represents and vivifying it by his strong and profound influence.

2. *The Historical Books*

The historical books frequently give examples of the intimate union between the "father" and his family or "household." Very

---

6 Cf. Lv. 16:34: "Once a year atonement shall be made for all the sins of the Israelites." Each priest represents the people of God and can

often this intimate union is evident in the "household's" close sharing of the "father's" fate, particularly if it is inauspicious.

What is done to descendants, is done equally to the father. In his famous apologue Joatham sees in the murder of the sixty-nine Gedeonites the infamous treatment of his father Gedeon-Jerobaal: "If you have dealt well with *Jerobaal and with his family,* and if you have treated *him* as he deserved." (Jg. 9:16, 19) One is impressed with the strong identification between *"Jerobaal and his family"* and "Jerobaal." Similarly, to kill the posterity of Jonathan would be to suppress "the name of Jonathan." (1 K. 20:16, cf. 1 K. 24:22)

The kingship which belonged to the "house of Saul" was taken away from his line (2 K. 3:10); whereas David is chosen in place of Saul "and all his house." (2 K. 6:21)

The ark's presence with Obededom the Gethite brought blessings upon all his house: "And the Lord blessed Obededom *and all his household"* (2 K. 6:11) "and all that he had." (2 K. 6:12; cf. 1 Par. 13:14)[7] Ethai, the faithful servant of David, determines to remain with the exiled king, "with all the men that were with him, and the rest of the people." (2 K. 15:22) Those who try to get Mathathias, the father of the Machabees, to apostatize promise him: *"Thou and thy sons* shall be in the number of the king's friends, and enriched with gold, and silver, and many presents." (1 Mac. 2:18) But the old Jewish patriarch replies proudly: *"I and my sons and my brethren* will obey the law of our fathers." (1 Mac. 2:20) A number of heroic Jews, encouraged by this demonstration of bravery, take refuge in the desert. "They abode there, *they had their children, and their wives,* and their cattle, because afflictions increased upon them." (1 Mac. 2:30)

The three persons whom we have just spoken of—Obededom the Gethite, Ethai, and Mathathias—were able to exert a favor-

on the basis of that (functionally and to a limited extent) be considered as a corporate personality.

7   Compare this with the blessing Gabelus pronounced over the young Tobias: "The God of Israel bless thee, because thou are the son of a very good and just man, that feareth God, and doth almsdeeds. And may a blessing come upon thy wife and upon your parents." (Tob. 9:9)

able influence on those around them because of their privileged position as "fathers of the family." The descendants, the women, and the children are simply "extensions" of the *pater familias,* who form with him a single concrete whole and as a result ordinarily are subject to a fate identical with his.

Very often, on the other hand, the "father of the family" exerts a baneful influence on his subordinates. The ephod which Gedeon set up in the city of Ephra in the midst of the clan of Abiezer "caused the ruin of Gedeon and *his family."* (Jg. 8:27) The whole family suffers because of the irreligious act of the father. The Ephraimites, whom Jephte had not invited on his expedition to fight the Ammonites, threaten him with dire reprisals: "We will burn your house over you." (In the French: "We will burn *you and your house."*) (Jg. 12:1) Micha, the Ephraimite, in trying to get back from the men of Dan his "god" receives this warning from them: "Let us hear no further sound from you, lest fierce men fall upon *you and you and your family* lose your lives." (Jg. 18:25)[8]

The terrible fate that will befall Heli of Silo will befall all his family also: "Behold the days come, and I (Yahweh) will cut off *thy* arm, and the arm *of thy father's house,* that there shall be an old man in thy house." (1 K. 2:31) A short time later Samuel reports the words of Yahweh: "In that day I will raise up against Heli all the things I have spoken *concerning his house."* (1 K. 3: 12) The person of the high priest of Silo is so closely tied in with his "household" that what happens to one affects the other.

The history of David contains several interesting pertinent details. He sought refuge in the cave of Odollam, and "when *his brethren and all his father's house* had heard of it, they went down to him thither." (1 K. 22:1) The young leader had to fear the wrath of Saul not only for himself but for all those who were near to him. The priests of Nobe, who had lent David assistance, were the object of Saul's fierce hatred. The king calls for Achime-lech, the son of Achitob, with "all his father's house, the priests that were in Nobe." (1 K. 21:11) Accused of treachery, Achime-

---

8 The expression is found again in the incident in the *Book of Daniel* 14:29, where the angry Babylonians threaten their king: "Hand Daniel over to us, or we will kill *you and your family."*

lech answers Saul: "Let not the king suspect such a thing against
his servant, *or anyone in all my father's house,* for *thy servant*
knew nothing of this matter, either little or great." (1 K. 22:15)
Nonetheless, Saul, immediately condemns all of them to death:
"Dying thou shalt die, Achimelech, *thou and all thy father's house."*
(1 K. 22:16) As a matter of fact, not only were the eighty priests
put to death at once by Doeg the Edomite but "Nobe the city of
the priests he smote with the edge of the sword, both men and
women, children, and sucklings, and ox and ass, and sheep with
the edge of the sword." (1 K. 22:19) From this it can be seen
that the acts of the high priest, who "consulted the Lord for him
(David), and gave him victuals, and gave him the sword of
Goliath the Philistine" (1 K. 22:10), had a repercussion on all
the priests, in fact on the priestly city itself. In the person of
Achimelech all "the priests of Yahweh" offered help to Saul's
rival. (1 K. 22:17)

When David wished to seek the good graces of Nabal of Carmel, he sent ten messengers to him with this instruction: "Go up
to Carmel, and go to Nabal, and salute him in my name with
peace. And you shall say: 'Peace be to my brethren, and to thee,
and *peace to thy house,* and peace to all that thou hast.' " (1 K.
25:6) Because of Nabal's persistent refusal to accept David's
offer of friendship, David decides to attack him and to teach
him a lesson. In the meantime, however, Abigal, the wife of Nabal,
learns from the servants that "evil is determined against thy
husband, and *against thy house."* (1 K. 25:17) David had sworn
not to leave "any that belong to him till morning." (1 K. 15:22)
Unhesitantly Abigal throws herself at the feet of David to beg
mercy for her husband. David listens to her entreaties, but cannot
refrain from commenting: "Otherwise as the Lord liveth the
God of Israel . . . if thou hadst not quickly come to meet me, there
had not been left to Nabel by the morning light any male." (1 K.
25:34)

As a punishment for his sin of taking the wife of Urias, God
tells David that "the sword shall never depart *from thy house."*
(2 K. 12:10) The remaining story of David is told from this
viewpoint. A continuing chain of misfortunes befalls the king,
and it is from his own family (Absalom) that he has the most
to suffer.

The execution of Joab removes guilt from the house of David. Solomon declares as much in these words: "Thou shalt remove the innocent blood which hath been shed by Joab, from me, and from the house of my father." (3 K. 2:31) On Joab, however, "and upon the head of his seed forever" the guilt falls. (3 K. 2:33) Contrariwise, the kindness of David in regard to Miphiboseth, the infirm son of Saul, is acknowledged by Miphiboseth: "For *all of my father's house* were no better than worthy of death before my lord and king; and thou hast set me thy servant among the guests of thy table." (2 K. 19:28) Here David skirts the law which considered it altogether normal to expiate the crime of the father on the sons.

The *Books of Kings* mention numerous cases of palace revolutions in which "the entire family" of the fallen king is massacred. In the name of Yahweh, the prophet Ahias had proclaimed: "I . . . will cut off from Jeroboam every male . . . and I will sweep away the *remnant of the house of Jeroboam,* as dung is swept away till all be clean." (3 K. 14:10) Similarly Baasa slew the son of Jeroboam, Nadab, and *"left not so much as one soul of his* seed, till he had utterly destroyed him." (3 K. 15:29) In turn Yahweh prepares to "cut down the posterity of Baasa, and *the posterity of his house."* (3 K. 16:3) Zambri killed Ela, the son of Baasa, and "slew *all the house of Baasa,* and left not one male, and all his kinsfolk and friends." (3 K. 16:11) Jehu, in turn, "slew all that were left of the house of Achab in Jezrahel, and all his chief men, and his friends, and his priests, till there were no remains left of him." (4 K. 10:11; cf. 3 K. 21:21; 4 K. 9:7-9) Later still, in the kingdom of Juda, Athalia, having heard of the death of her son Ochozias, "slew all the royal seed" (4 K. 11:1) of *"the house of Joram."* (2 Par. 22:10) Perhaps all these bloody measures can be explained by a fear that all the members of a family had been privy to the misdeed; but they still presuppose a more or less reasoned conviction of the identity between father and family, an identity in which the former lives on, and in which he represents the family.

In the later historical books this same baneful influence of the father on the whole family perdures. Aman, the son of Amadathi, conspiring against the Jewish people; Esther prostrates herself before Assuerus, the Persian king, begging him for her

own life and for the life of "my people." (Est. 7:4) She is convinced of the solidarity between herself and her people: "For we
are given up, I and my people, to be destroyed, to be slain, and
to perish." (Est. 7:4) Assuerus listens to the pleas of his wife
and authorizes the Jews "to stand for their lives, and to kill and
destroy all their enemies *with their wives and children* and all
their houses, and to take their spoil." (Est. 8:11) After the
vindication of Mardochai, Aman, together with "his sons" (Est.
9:25) or *"all his kindred"* (Est. 16:18) is hanged. Threatened
by the Syrian armies, Judas Machabeus encourages his followers:
"They come against us with an insolent multitude and with pride,
to destroy *us,* and *our wives, and our children,* and to take our
spoils. But we will fight for our lives and our laws. And the
Lord himself will overthrow them before our face; but as for you,
fear them not." (1 Mac. 3:20:22) One readily gets the impression
from this late text that each individual really represents his "household."

All these texts which we have discussed seem to suggest, with
more or less force, that the individual is ordinarily not thought
of except as accompanied by, or perhaps completed by, the entire
family group. The picture of Elcana, the father of Samuel, presenting himself each year at the sanctuary with *"all his household"*
(1 K. 1:21) illustrates this idea very well. The individual Israelite
implicates his entire "household" in everything he does, whether
it be good or bad. The good fortune of the father has its repercussions on all his family; on the other hand, his humiliation, his
sin, his misfortunes implicate all those whom he represents or,
perhaps more correctly, all those he bears in some way in his own
personality. Could there be any better way of expressing graphically
the idea that the "father of the family" is frequently considered a
"corporate personality?"

3. *The Prophetic Books*

The prophets frequently associate the father of the family with
his "household." Sometimes this association works to the welfare
of the family. Jeremia, for example, wishing to exhort king
Sedecia to hand himself over to the Babylonians, tells him in the
name of Yahweh: "Thus says the Lord God of hosts, the God

of Israel: If you surrender to the princes of Babylon's king, you shall save your life; this city shall not be destroyed with fire, and *you and your family shall live."* (Jer.38:17)

More frequently, however, it happens that a sort of collective punishment falls upon the "household" of the evil-doer. Amos makes the following prediction to Amasia, the priest of Bethel: "Your wife shall be made a' harlot in the city, and your sons and daughters shall fall by the sword; your land shall be divided by measuring line, and you yourself shall die in an unclean land; Israel shall be exiled far from its land." (Amos 7:17; compare Jer. 20:6: "You Phassur, *and all the members of your household* shall go into exile. To Babylon you shall go, you and all your friends; there you shall die and be buried, because you have prophesied lies to them.") Although these priests are differentiated from their families in so far as they are individuals, they are joined with them in punishment because the families are in a sense an "extension" of their personality.

Isaia reminds Achaz, the Davidic king, of the punishment Yahweh had threatened through the mouth of Nathan (2 K. 7: 14b): "The Lord shall bring upon you and your people and *your father's house* days worse than any since Ephraim seceded from Juda. (This means the king of Assyria.")) (Is. 7:17)

Jeremia in his invectives against the false prophets declares in the name of Yahweh: "If a prophet or a priest or anyone else mentions 'the burden of the Lord,' I will punish that man *and his house."* (Jer. 23:34)

The accusers of Daniel are thrown into the lion's den together with their families: "The king then ordered the men who had accused Daniel, *along with their children and their wives,* to be cast into the lion's den." (Dn. 6:25) Similarly the priests of Bel, convicted of fraud, are seized together with "their wives and their children." (Dn. 14:21)

The prophet Habacuc paraphrases the words: "You have devised shame for your *household"* with the following: "forfeiting *your own life."* (Ha. 2:10) It would be difficult to express more clearly the deep conviction that the "household" is in some way identified with the father of the family.

When Abraham desires to receive favorable treatment from the Egyptians because of his wife Sara, he urges her in this wise: "Say you are my sister, so that *I* may be treated well *on your account,* and *my life may be spared for your sake.*" (Gn. 12:13) Evidently Sara is able to obtain the good graces of the king for herself and for her "family." [11] The same patriarch is heard by Yahweh when he begs mercy for the inhabitants of Sodom and Gomorrha.[12]

The intercession of Abraham recalls that of Moses at the time of the battle against the Amalecites: "As long as Moses kept his hands raised up, Israel had the better of the fight." (Ex. 17: 11)[13] The great leader is strongly convinced that he forms a single unit with his people. Yahweh in fact had told him: "Now, go and lead the people whither I have told you. My angel will go before *you* (singular) ... I will punish *them* for their sin." (Ex. 32:34) Moses in turn asks Yahweh: "For how can it be known that we, your people and I, have found favor with you, except by your going with us? Then we, *your people and I,* will be singled out from every other people on the earth." (Ex. 33:16) The functional identity between Moses and the people he leads is so great that Yahweh is able to say: "Here, then, said the Lord, is the covenant I will make. Before the eyes of all your (sing.) people I will work such marvels as have never been wrought in any nation anywhere on earth, so that *this people among whom you* (sing.) *live* may see how awe-inspiring are the deeds which I, the Lord, will do at *your* (sing.) side.'" (Ex. 34:10) One is surprised at the strong identification between Moses and the people. That which Yahweh does for Moses, He does for the people. So

11 The expression *bigelalekâ* ("because of you") is found elsewhere; cf. Gn. 30:27 (Jacob) or Gn. 39:5 (Joseph).

12 K. Galling, *Vom Richteramt Gottes,* in *DT* 6 (1939) 86-97, p. 91 refuses to recognize "that there is in Gn. 18:23 ff. a request by Abraham for the people of Sodom." The text, however, expressly says: "I have chosen him, that he may charge his sons and his household after him to observe the way of the Lord, doing what is good and right, so that the Lord may fulfill for Abraham what he has promised him."

13 Consider also the power of Moses's intercession in the episode of the "bronze serpent." (Nm. 21:7: "prayed for the people")

much are the two thought to be identified that Yahweh is able to say: "Write down these words (of the covenant), for in accordance with them I have made a covenant with *you* and with Israel." (Ex. 34:27) There is no denying that in reality Moses and Israel are separable, yet so great is the unity between the two that Moses is enabled to exercise a profound influence on the group. Precisely in that does one observe the concrete and fluid notion of a "corporate personality."

2. *The Historical Books*

Throughout their history the Hebrews recognized the indissoluble bonds uniting the acts of certain individuals to the fate of the entire community. Likewise they recognized that the destiny of the community (or one of its subordinate groups) depended greatly upon the acts of certain individuals. There is a solidarity of good, in virtue of which the acts of an individual can be the source of a collective well-being.

In answering the prayer of Josue before Gabaon, Yahweh was really listening to Israel also: "Never before or since was there a day like this, when the Lord obeyed the voice of a man; for the Lord fought for Israel." (Jos. 10:14) Together they formed an indestructible unit which Yahweh wished to bless.

The vital solidarity in good is also evident in the case of Rahab, the prostitute of Jericho. As a reward for the services she had rendered the Israelites, this woman had requested of Josue's messengers: "Swear to me by the Lord that, since I am showing kindness to you, you in turn will show kindness *to my family;* . . . that you are to spare my father and mother, brothers and sisters, and all their kin, and save us from death." (Jos. 2: 12-13) The cord of scarlet string is to indicate the place where the family is gathered together: "Gather your father and mother, your brothers, *and all your family* into your house." (Jos. 2:18) After the fall of the city, "the spies entered and brought out Rahab, with her father, mother, brothers, and all her kin. *Her entire family* they led forth . . . Josue spared her with her family and all her kin." (Jos. 6:23-25) Like Rahab, the spy who had shown them how to get into Bethel was spared by the house of

Joseph: "But they let the man and *his whole clan* go free." (Jg. 1:25)

The close union between the group and its representative is exemplified in the actions of two great Israelite leaders, Josue and Jephte. On the occasion of the stealing of contraband material from Hai, Josue intercedes for Israel: "Alas, O Lord God, why did you ever allow *this people* to pass over the Jordan, delivering *us* into the power of the Amorrites, that they might destroy us?" (Jos. 7:7) There can be no doubt that the leader identifies himself with his people. Similarly despite his common birth, Jephte identifies himself so completely with the people whom he commands that he says to the king of the Ammonites: "What have you against *me* that you come to fight with me *in my land?*" (Jg. 11: 12; cf. verse 19). For "should we not possess all that the Lord, our God, has cleared out for *us?*" (Jg. 11:24) Jephte concludes: "I have not sinned against you, but you wrong *me* by warring against *me*. Let the Lord, who is judge, decide this day between *the Israelites* and the Ammonites." (Jg. 11:27) Is the last mentioned "me" to be understood of the leader or of the people? It is difficult to say. But it is undeniable that there is an identity between Jephte and the people. When Jephte complains to the Ephraimites, it is evident that he is referring to himself as much as to the Israelites: "My soldiers and I were engaged in a critical contest with the Ammonites. I summoned you, but you did not rescue *me* from their power. When I saw that you would not effect a rescue, I took my life in my own hands and went on to the Ammonites, and the Lord delivered them into my power. Why, then, do you come up against *me* this day to fight with *me?*" (Jg. 12:2-3)[14]

14 Several times a "leader" is identified or identifies himself with those under him. The Gabaonites, who desire to live in peace with Israel, submit themselves to Josue, saying: "We are your servants" (Jos. 9:8); but, according to Jos. 9:6 they speak "to him (Josue) and the men of Israel." Esdras feels himself one with his sinful brothers: "My God *I* am confounded and ashamed to lift up *my* face to thee, for *our* iniquities are multiplied over *our* heads, and *our* sins are grown up even unto heaven." (Esd. 9:6; cf. Esd. 10:6: "He (Esdras) ate no bread, and drank no water; for he mourned for the transgression

After his consecration Saul receives the promise that he and all his "father's house" would receive the wealth of Israel. (1 K. 9:20) In this case the individual, having become king, passes on his blessing to all who form part of his patriarchal family (even though he is not the father in the flesh). The future victor over Goliath will be covered with blessings: "And the man that shall slay him, the king will enrich with great riches, and will give him his daughter, and will make *his father's house* free from tribute in Israel." (1 K. 17:25)

The pious widow Judith is conscious of her role as instrument and of her intimate union with her people. Before killing Holofernes, she prays thus: "Strengthen *me,* O Lord God of Israel; and in this hour look on the works of *my* hands, that as thou hast promised, thou mayest raise up *Jerusalem* thy city; and that I may bring to pass that which I have purposed, having a belief that it might be done by thee." (Jud. 13:7) The fate of the entire people rests in the hands of this lone woman. Without doubt she acts as the representative of the holy nation which, in some way, is encompassed in her.

3. *The Prophetic Books*

There are a number of texts in the prophets in which the interplay between the individual and the collectivity tends to set off the role of the individual, who by influencing the group in some way dominates it.

For example, the power of intercession of an individual is

of them that were come out of the captivity.") Nehemias, in turn, confesses the sins of the people: "O Lord God of heaven, let thy ears be attentive, and thy eyes open to hear the prayers of thy servant, which *I* pray before thee now, night and day, for the children of Israel thy servants. And *I* confess the sins of the children of Israel, by which they have sinned against thee: *"I and my father's house have sinned."* (Neh. 1:6; cf. 5:14: "I and my brethren") The zeal of the Machabees is described as follows by Simon, the high priest and ethnarch of the Jews, in his exhortation to the frightened people: "You know what great battles *I* and my brethren, and the house of my father, have fought for the laws, and the sanctuary, and the distresses that *we* have seen." (1 Mac. 13:3)

brought out in this text from *Jeremia*: "Roam the streets of
Jerusalem . . ., to find even one who lives uprightly and seeks to be
faithful, and I will pardon her!" (Jer. 5:1) True it is that the
prophet seems to say something different in the following text,
but it must be remembered that the words of the text are by
way of exaggeration: "Even if Moses and Samuel stood before
me, my heart would not turn toward this people." (Jer. 15:1)
The prophet wishes to emphasize the unalterable decision of
Yahweh to punish the obstinate people, who, even if the prophets
were to intercede for them, would not change their hard hearts.

The prohetic notion of the "remnant," so frequently mentioned
in the writings of the prophets,[15] also points to the concentration
of the vitality, and one might say, of the piety and the virtue
of the respective groups. Entire Israel is summed up in the benefits
from the weak nucleus of the "remnant" which can at times be
condensed into one person.

4. *The Sapiential Books*

The idea of a specially chosen individual exercising great influence over his group finds echoes even in the Wisdom Books.

The author of the *Book of Sirach* extols Joseph in these terms:
"The *leader* of his brothers, the support *of his people*." (Sir.49:
15) (The text as given in the French is not found in the C.C.D.
translation). He shows thereby the importance of the representing
individual for the welfare of his brethren who find their "support"
and their well-being in his person. We find here—although a bit
vaguely—the pattern of the "corporate personality" of the king
which we will treat in the following chapter.

An unbiased examination of the preceding texts and an effort
to understand them in the light of our provisional definition of
"corporate personality" shows how such a concept explains the
coexistence of an outstanding individual with a group which

---

15   W. E. Müller, *Die Vorstellung vom Rest im A.T.*, Liepzig, 1939,
33: "The remnant is bearer of the existence of the people." Cf. Is.
4:3; 10:20-21; 11:11, 16; 28:5; 37:32; 46:3; 60:21: Jer. 23:3; 31:7;
42:15, 19; 50:20; Ez. 6:23; 14:22; Amos 5:15; Mi. 4:7; 5:7; So.
3:13; Za. 8:11; Jl. 2:32.

benefits from his influence. True enough, the group never co-incides statically with the individual as such. But the Israelite mind perceived not only the individual but also the intimate bond between the group and the individual. This bond was the source of the well-being for the group. This well-being is not a hazy and distant effect of the union but the direct result of a close identification with the well-being of the individual who is the source. The image of a spring, always bubbling over yet always giving of itself, gives some idea of the influence of the representing individual on the group. This vital influence is one of the most characteristic elements of the notion of "corporate personality."

THE THIRD THEME

The Harmful Influence of the Representing Individual

Whereas in modern legal codes "there is no juridical responsibility except that based on *personal* culpability," [16] ancient Oriental law admitted of collective responsibility. For modern jurists "responsibility" is synonymous with "imputability." "Responsibility has as its primary condition guilt, and as its result a certain necessity for *satisfaction* on the part of the evil-doer." [17] But according to ancient Semitic law every transgression appears malicious; every mistake, an offense; all satisfaction takes on the characteristics of a punishment.[18] Such a viewpoint begets a much more frequent application of penal responsibility, which ignores the intention and scarcely distinguishes between accidental harm and deliberate harm, or between harm due to direct intention or to imprudence.

Moreover, the oldest form of penal responsibility is collective responsibility. Whereas "responsibility (in the modern sense of individual responsibility) is one of the fundamental postulates

16   F. De Visscher, *Le régime romain de la noxalité*, 1947, 29.
17   *Ibid.*, p. 39.
18   Cf. L. Husson, *Les transformations de la responsabilité. Etude sur la pensée juridique*, Paris, 1947, 333.

of justice for us,"[19] the Semitic codes (we now know of at least six which predate the Old Testament; they date from 2050 to 1350 B.C.) have no qualms about collective retribution. The Old Testament has not escaped this characteristic of ancient Oriental law.

At the beginning of all known ancient codes, collective responsibility falls upon the social group to which the culprit belongs, even though the other members had no part in his deed. This does not mean to imply the individual culpability of the other individuals (at least not always) but rather their physical bond with the evildoer. This latter is punished through the reparation imposed on the group. As the owner, he endures the "ruler's punishment." Collective reparation as the result of collective responsibility, far from presupposing automatically collective guilt, sometimes merely demands passive acceptance of the sanction. Several times in the biblical text we find examples where a community is expressly declared innocent, but assumes nonetheless the punishment for the crime committed by a single member. In such cases one always finds some physical and material bond which joins the group and the culpable individual.

At other times, however, we must carefully observe the meaning of the Old Testament texts. Not infrequently the text mentions a truly collective culpability: either the entire community is declared (truly) culpable because of the crimes of a single member (through an eminently real "fiction"), or the entire community has truly participated in the wrongdoing (for example, practicing idolatry as a group). Another possibility is when an innocent person atones for the group which is truly guilty, or for a group which must simply bear responsibility.

There are, then, over and above individual culpability (the individual crime begets individual responsibility) three other distinct juridical situations:

a) Collective responsibility: a group, closely tied to the guilty individual, is juridically obliged to "answer" for the crime by passively assuming the punishment.

b) Collective culpability: the entire group is in a *state* of

19   J. Harvey, *Collectivisme et Individualisme*, in: *Sc. Eccl.* 10 (1958) 167-202, p. 174.

c) Individual responsibility: an innocent person can take on wrongdoing (or as a group is guilty of the same wilful act); in the latter case collective responsibilty is obvious.
the punishment flowing from individual culpability, collective culpability, or collective responsibility.

It is interesting to note, from our point of view, the role which the culpabale individual plays in the midst of his community. This role establishes him in the full sense of the term as a "corporate personality." While remaining distinct from the community, he affects it *at the same time* and causes it to partake of either the culpability or the responsibility of his acts. Because of the concrete and physical simultaneity of the two points of view (the individual and the collectivity) there is a constant interaction between the two, in the sense that the mind passes readily from one to the other. And this is precisely a property of the idea of "corporate personality."

The presence in the Old Testament of this emphasis on community justice along the lines of "corporate personality" does not at all indicate the absence of individual culpability or individual responsibility in the biblical texts. Rather, the "modern" attitude develops as Israelite law evolves. The first step, beginning with a rather generalized collective responsibility (where the solidarity, at least passive, is complete), consists in limiting the collective retribution to a single day (called a day of judgment) or in restricting the degree of relationship beyond which the collective retribution cannot extend. Later on comes the recognition of the group's (whether familial or of another kind) right to disassociate itself from the accused, leaving him to receive his own punishment. In almost all ancient Oriental codes of law, the time arrives when pecuniary compensations, at first voluntary and later fixed by law, serve as punishment.[21]

The biblical text gives us valuable indications of continuing battle against the idea of collective responsibility. The following dialogue between Joseph, the viceroy of the king of Egypt, and his brother Juda, when the former discovers his cup in the sack

20   *Ibid.*, p. 175 n. 20: the author quotes CH (the code of Hammurabi) aa. 116, 210, 230.
21   J. Harvey, *Collectivisme et Individualisme*, l.c., p. 176.

of Benjamin, is an example: "Juda replied, '. . . . God has discovered *the guilt of your servants.* We are indeed the slaves of my lord, *both we and the one with whom the cup was found.*' 'Far be it from me to act thus,' said Joseph. *'The one* with whom the cup was found shall be my slave; *as for the rest,* go in peace to your father.' " (Gn. 44:16:17) A similar attitude is manifest in the narration of the rebellion of Core. At the moment of the rebellion, Moses and Aaron pray to God in these significant words: "O God, God of the spirits of all mankind, will *one man's sin* make you angry with *the whole community?"* (Nm. 16:22) This protest against a widespread view is confirmed in the Deuteronomic Code: "Fathers shall not be put to death for their children, nor children for their fathers; only for his own guilt shall a man be put to death." (Dt. 24:16; cf. 4 K. 14:6) This prescription of the Deuteronomic Code presupposes the divine precept: "Understand, then, that the Lord, your God, is God indeed, the faithful God . . . who repays with destruction *the person* who hates him; he *does not* dally with such a one, but makes him *personally* pay for it." [22] (Dt. 7:9-10; It is well to compare this passage with Dt. 5:9-10 or Ex. 20:5-6 which mirror the collectivistic point of view of the Mosaic age.)

Despite the tendency of biblical law to evolve toward the notion of individual responsibility as we know it today, we see everywhere traces of the opposite point of view; namely, of a collective responsibility, and even a collective culpability.

1. *The Pentateuch*

Occasionally the Torah gives examples of a real collective culpability. According to Johannes Hempel there is question of an almost magical contamination: [23] "Precisely in so far as

22 Convinced that *Deut.* is identical with the code found by Josia in
     622, Harvey, l.c., p. 179, supposes that, under the influence of the
     prophets Osee and Amos "the collectivistic conception of penal
     justice became intolerable." This is true only for some special texts;
     the collectivistic conception will still be maintained for a long time
     afterward. Moreover, Harvey quotes several examples of a "return to
     collectivism" (for example, Is. 39:7; Jer. 22:18-30; Is. 14:21).
23 J. Hempel, *Das Ethos des AT* (ZAW Bhft 67), Berlin, 1938, 51; cf.

he is a member of the communal 'big *I,*' the culpable individual is coresponsible for the fate of the group to the extent that he represents it." [24] In other places, although the guilty act was the act of individuals, "root that would bear such poison and wormwood" (Dt. 29:17), the culpability of these individuals extends to the entire community. Such is the opinion of Hempel.[25] Because of the act of Achan, the entire people are spoken of as having "violated the covenant." (Jos. 7:11)

A number of typical and explicit examples will show how such ideas pervaded past ages.

a) NARRATIVES

The story of Abimelech of Gerara as told in the *Book of Genesis* is a case in point. He inveighs against Isaac who had falsely told him that Rebecca was his sister: "Why did you do this to us? How easily *someone* could have lain with your wife, and you would have brought guilt upon *us!*" (Gn. 26:10) The sin of a single resident of Gerara would have affected in some way all the citizens. By performing one sinful act, the individual contaminates the entire group to which he belongs, and which is summed up in him.

When Moses discovers the heinous crime of the "golden calf," he holds his brother Aaron responsible: "What did this people ever do to you that you should lead them into so grave a sin?" (Ex. 32:21), for "Aaron had let the people run wild." (Ex. 32:25) The sin of Aaron, the religious leader, is the beginning of (one might almost say the summation of) the collective sin of the people. When the sons of Aaron, Nadab and Abiu, "offered up before the Lord profane fire, such as he had not authorized, fire, therefore, came forth from the Lord's presence and consumed them." (Lv. 10:1-2) But over and above that, the entire community is subject to God's ire, as Moses tells Aaron and his sons: "Do not bare your heads or tear your garments, lest you bring not only

by the same author, *Gott und Mensch im AT* (*BWANT III,* 2), Stuttgart, 1936², 142.

24 J. Hempel, *Gott und Mensch,* l.c., pp. 190-91.
25 J. Hempel, *Das Ethos,* l.c., p. 52.

death on yourselves but God's wrath also *on the whole community*. Your kinsmen, *the rest of the house of Israel,* shall mourn for those whom the Lord's fire has smitten." (Lv. 10:6; cf. Nm. 16: 22, where the emphasis on the individual is even more obvious) The evil deed of the two "sons of Aaron" affects the community as such; their personal sin becomes, in the eyes of Yahweh, a collective blot.

The story of Phinees the priest also points up the solidarity in evil. His courageous stand against the idolatry offered to Baal-Phogar brings upon him the praise of Yahweh: "Phinees, son of Eleazar, son of Aaron the priest, has turned my anger *from the Israelites* by his zeal for my honor among them; that is why I did not put an end to the Israelites for the offense to my honor." (Nm. 25:11) In a smaller way the Madianite woman whom Phinees killed encompasses in a concrete way (rather than a coldly juridic way) all her fellow country men. That is why Yahweh gives the order to strike the Madianites without distinction: "Treat the Madianites as enemies and crush them, for *they* have been your enemies by their wily dealings with you as regards Phogar and *as regards their kinswoman Chozbi."* (Nm. 25:16-18) The action of the Madianite seductress, seemingly personal in its responsibility, takes on a collective aspect. Or, to put it in another way, a characteristic of all the Madianites is manifested ("made present") in the act of the individual Madianite.

Most frequently, however, it is not a question of collective culpability (whether real or through contamination) but simply of collective responsibility, the culpability of one bringing with it punishment for the group which is ontologically joined with him.

The one who stole the cup of Joseph, the viceroy of Egypt, is readily recognized as the person at fault. Nonetheless, in a sense he determines the fate of the inocent brothers. That is what the latter have in mind when they say to Joseph's steward: "If it is found with anyone of us, he shall die, and we will be my lord's slaves." (Gn. 44:9) Even though innocent, the brothers find no responsibility in accepting a punishment. Theirs is indeed much lighter than that of their guilty brother; but because of the bonds which unite them to him, they are responsible with him in the sense that they have a passive obligation to "answer" for the crime by undergoing a certain punishment.

The rebels Dathan and Abiram were punished "with *their wives and sons and little ones*" (Nm. 16:27) even though the latter were completely innocent. An entire city is to be destroyed because of certain good-for-nothings who rashly suggest idolatry. (Dt. 20:13)

The purpose of the vendetta, as explained in the following text of *Numbers,* is perhaps the desire to put and end to contamination through blood: "Since bloodshed desecrates the land, the land can have no atonement for the blood shed on it except through the blood of him who shed it." (Nm. 35:33) If we understand the word "land" in the concrete sense of "people," the meaning is this: the murderous blood continues to infect the community (much like an infection) unless equilibrium is once again established and the infection arrested by the *Lex Talionis.*

b) LEGISLATION

The baneful influence exercised by an evil individual in a community obliges the religious society to "root out" that person from "his people." (Ex. 31-14) In a sense the community is the sphere within which the contagion of sin spreads; the community therefore has the obligation to "purge the evil from your midst." (Dt. 13:5)

This wicked person may be one who is uncircumcised (Gn. 17: 14); one who eats leavened bread during the feast of the Passover (Ex. 12:15, 19); one who anoints a layman with holy oil (Ex. 30:38); an unclean person who eats the flesh of the thanksgiving sacrifice (Lv. 7:20; cf. Nm. 19:20); one who slaughters outside the camp (Lv. 17:4); one who practices sexual abominations (Lv. 18:29); one who eats a thanksgiving sacrifice on the third day (Lv. 19:8); an incestuous person (Lv. 20:17); one who without reason fails to offer the Passover sacrifice (Nm. 9:13); one who reviles the Lord by sinning wilfully (Nm. 15:30); the prophet who advocates idolatry (Dt. 13:6); one who dares pervert the cult (Dt. 17:7); one who disobeys the priest or the judge (Dt. 17:12); one who spills innocent blood (Dt. 19:13);

the unjust witness (Dt. 22:21); the adulteress (Dt. 22:24); one who kidnaps a fellow Israelite. (Dt. 24:7)

It is noteworthy that these prescriptions are found in all strata of Israelite legislation: the laws of the Exodus, the Deuteronomic and the sacerdotal codes. Throughout the long evolution of biblical law, one finds the same idea regarding the possible transfer of legal stain—culpability or responsibility—from one individual to the entire community. It is to root out this contagion that it is necessary to do away with the evil person. This would seem to prove the close cohesion of the group. The honor of the family, even of the nation, is bound up with each individual evil act. According to *Deuteronomy* 22:21, the woman found guilty of adultery must be stoned "because she committed a crime against Israel by her unchasteness in her father's house." [26] For at the moment of her sin she represents in some way all her kin. It is precisely this note which sets off her corporate role and makes her—functionally and to a lesser degree than some others—a "corporate personality."

2. *The Historical Books*

The historical books likewise have their examples of collective responsibility, and even of collective culpability.

The most interesting example for our purposes is that of Achan. (Jos. 7) On the occasion of the taking of Jericho, "the Israelites violated the ban. Achan, son of Charmi, son of Zabdi, son of Zara of the tribe of Juda (one definite individual), took goods that were under the ban, and the anger of the Lord flared up against *the Israelites*." (Jos. 7:1) Here it is manifestly a question of collective culpability, (transferred imaginatively yet somewhat realistically), for Yahweh declares that since "*Israel* has sinned" and "violated the covenant which I enjoined them" (Jos. 7:11) it is necessary that "you remove from among you

---

26 According to G. Von Rad, in *ThW* (Kittel) III, 357, 1. 13, the formula *beyisrá'él* would signify "against Israel," that is to say against the community unified by the Yahwistic cult or by the sacred amphictyony (von Rad refers to Jg. 20:10, the crime of Gabaa, or to Jos. 7:15, the story of Achan).

whoever has incurred the ban." (Jos. 7:13) Moreover there is a double collective responsibility. When the culprit has been found, he *"shall be destroyed by fire with all that is his."* (Jos. 7:15) Achan committed a crime in Israel (Jos. 7:15) and thereby brought upon all the people a state of collective culpability. This is indicated in the words of Josue: "The Lord bring upon you today the misery with which you have afflicted us!"[27] (Jos. 7:25) Moreover, by the same act Achan brings evil upon the limited circle of his family, for responsibility rests not only on himself but also on "his sons and daughters, his ox, his ass and his sheep, his tent, and all his possessions." (Jos. 7:24) When Josue speaks to him in the singular: "The Lord bring upon *you* (singular) today the misery!" (Jos. 7:25), he no doubt has in mind Achan and all his family. The singular "you" includes all members of the family, as, in a certain sense, it included all Israelites.[28]

The woman of Thecua, who appeared before King David to plead the cause of her son whom her family wished to kill because he had murdered his brother, freely acknowledges the collective responsibility (if not the culpability) of the family: "Upon me, my lord, be *the iniquity; and upon the house of my father."* 2 K. 14:9)

Many times chance strikes an individual an evil blow, and

27 H. H. Rowley, *The Faith of Israel,* London, 1956, 106 makes this excellent comment: "One individual's failure of duty may involve a whole community in disaster and suffering."

28 E. F. Sutcliffe, *Providence and Suffering in the Old and New Testaments,* London, 1953, 62 n. 4 cites the opinion of E. Power (Cath. Comm. on Holy Scripture # 231 b), who, on the basis of Jos. 7:25 LXX, believes that Achan was put to death alone. In that case Jos. 7:24 would be an ancient interpolation. As a matter of fact Jos. 22:20 compares the case of Achan ("Did not wrath fall upon the entire community of Israel? Though he was but a single man, he did not perish alone!") with the individualistic acts of the Transjordanian tribes who had built an altar of their own without informing the other Israelites. This act is interpreted by the delegation of the "sons of Israel" as an act of idolatry, which will have evil consequences for all Israel: "You are rebelling against the Lord today and by tomorrow he will be angry with the whole community of Israel." (Jos. 22:18)

an entire group, perfectly innocent, suffers the disastrous consequences. The individual himself may be largely blameless. Because of her marriage to Samson, the Philistine wife of the Judge
suffers threats of terrible reprisals. When her banquet companions
force her to coax the key to the riddle from Samson, they say to
her: "Coax your husband to answer the riddle for us, or we
will burn *you and your family.*" (Jg. 14:15) The sons of Jechonia,
who did not take part in the rejoicing of the men of Bethsames
upon the return of the ark, were severely punished: "And he slew
of the people seventy men ... And the people lamented, because
the Lord had smitten the people with a great slaughter." (1 K. 6:
19) Striking an important segment of the nation is tantamount
to striking the entire people, even though the people as such were
innocent. The indeliberate failing of Jonathan in breaking the
vow that Saul had made in the name of all the people not to eat
until evening prevented the king (and all the people with him)
from receiving the anticipated divine oracle. (1 K. 14:38-39)
Although Jonathan's responsibility is negligible (according to our
standards wholly absent), his action has an effect upon the entire
group.

3. *The Prophetic Books*

The *prophets* readily admit that individuals "became an
occasion of sin to the house of Israel." (Ez. 44:12) We will consider several examples in the next chapter when we consider the
king. (chap. 3, §2)

4. *The Sapiential Books*

Various sapiential books express the principle that the evil
of an individual can redound to others. One need think only of the
saying: "In woman was sin's beginning, and because of her we all
die." (Sir. 25:23) The same author recalls the case of the impious
king Jeroboam who "should not be remembered, the sinner who
led Israel into sin, who brought ruin to Ephraim and caused
them to be exiled from their land." (Sir. 47:24)

All the biblical texts we have cited portray a lively consciousness of the considerable influence for evil which can follow from
an individual act. At all times, and even today, Jews consider

themselves mutually responsible. This feeling has had a special keenness in their psychology because of the extreme solidarity that binds them together. The sin, perhaps even the shortcoming, of an individual can bring disaster and suffering to an entire community, precisely because the mutual responsibility is so intense. Here we have two significant aspects of the idea of "corporate personality": on the one hand, the individual is always a member who works and suffers in intimate union with the group; on the other hand, he has a signal significance for his group in that he is capable of directing or at least influencing its destiny.

THE FOURTH THEME

The Ancestor and His Descendants

The coexistence of the twofold aspect—community and individual—of a particular group receives a typically Israelite expression in the fact that an individual is prolonged in a group which comes after him and whose existence is dependent upon him.[29] This idea of the survival of the individual in his descendants makes up the "vertical pattern" of "corporate personality." According to this vertical pattern of the idea, "the tribal ancestor lives in all those who descend from him, generation after generation; he *is* the living tribe just as are the other members who come from him; the ancestor dies only when the tribe dies out."[30]

1. The Pentateuch

This "pattern of the ancestor" runs through both the narratives and the legislation of the Pentateuch.

29 O. Eissfeldt, *Der Gottesknecht,* l.c., 15: "They (the tribal father or the tribal mother) not only belong to the past, but they continue to live on in the community produced by them and are partakers, yes, bearers of their fates."

30 H. S. Nyberg, *Smärtornas man. En studie till Jes.* 52: 13-53:12, in SEA 7 (1942) 5-82, p. 68.

a) THE NARRATIVES

It underlies the opposition between the descendants of the serpent and those of the woman in Gn. 3:15. The fecundity promised to our first parents is to be a "multiplication,'" an expansion into a large family of human beings: "Be fruitful and multiply; fill the earth and subdue it." (Gn. 1:28) The "seed" of the woman is an "extension" of herself, just as the "seed" of the serpent is basically the same as the serpent himself, that is to say, evil personified.

The concept of the patriarchal ancestor shows very well how an entire group derives, in some way or other, from one individual. Jabel, the son of Lamech, "was the forerunner of those who dwell in tents and have flocks." (Gn. 4:20) Jubal was "the fore-runner of all who play the harp and flute." (Gn. 4:21) Thubal-cain, in turn, was "the forerunner of those who forge vessels of bronze and iron." (Gn. 4:22) These three "ancestors" are the original types which are repeated in their descendants (even the fictional ones).

The covenant negotiated by Yahweh with Noe includes both the ancestor and his descendants: "I will establish my covenant *with you, and with your descendants* after you; and with every living creature that is with you." (Gn. 9:9-10) The sacred writer spontaneously associates the descendants with their ancestor, because for him they are but two aspects of the same psychic unity, which in evolving remains fundamentally the same.

This concept of a tightly unified totality is at the basis of all the genealogies. (Cf. Gn. 10: Nm. 1-4, 26; 1 Par. 1-9; Esd. 2; Neh. 7:11) In chapter ten of *Genesis,* all the people living in the environment of the sacred writer are considered to be part of the descendants of the sons of Noe. (Gn. 10:1) These different nations are the extension in time of the first ancestors, even when the progeny is not in any way based on physical generation, as is the case with *Tharsis* (a city), "descendant of Javan" (Gn. 10:4); or *Mesraim* (a country: Egypt), "descendant of Ham" (Gn. 10:6); or Caphthorim (Crete), "descendant of Mesraim" (Gn. 10:13); or finally Sidon (a city), "descendant of Canaan." (Gn. 10:15) The metaphor of physical generation suggests that a tight bond unites these peoples because of their respective conections with the three sons of Noe.

Sem, in his turn, appears as "the father of all the descendants of Eber" (Gn. 10:21) and the sons of Sem are catalogued "according to their families and their languages, in their countries, by their nations."[31] (Gn. 10:31) But the ancestor *par excellence* of the Israelite people, the one in whom the real and eternal substance of this people is manifested for the first time in its relations with God is Abraham.[32] (Jos. 24:3) From the first moment of his calling, this patriarch is pictured as an individual who exercises a profound influence on the Chosen People. Yahweh promises Abraham: "I will make a great nation of you; I will bless you, and make your name great, so that you shall be a blessing." (Gn. 12:2) Blessing Abraham is the same as blessing the people, and through the intermediary of the people "all the nations of the earth."[33] (Gn. 12:3)

The patriarchal exploits spontaneously link the "race" with the ancestor. The great importance which the "fathers" assume in Israelite thought indicates that they are looked upon as the foreshadowing of the "children" who follow them. Abraham is the "father" and the "ancestor" because Yahweh said to him: "This is my covenant with *you*: You shall be the *father* of a multitude of nations ... I will make you exceedingly fruitful; I will make nations of you, and kings shall descend from you. I will establish my covenant between you and me *and your descendants after you* throughout their generations, as a perpetual

---

31 We can compare the "heads of the ancestral clans" of Ex. 6:25.

32 H. Wheeler Robinson, *Inspiration and Revelation in the Old Testament,* Oxford, 1946, 151: "The nation is not only represented by, but is summed up in, its ancestors ... God deals with the race through its ancestor."

33 *Ibid.,* p. 151. The same promise is repeated after the sacrifice at the place called Yahweh-yireh: "I swear by myself, says the Lord, since you have done this and have not withheld your only son, I will indeed bless *you,* and will surely multiply your descendants as the stars of the heavens, as the sands of the seashore." (Gn. 22:16-17) In Gn. 24:7 Abraham speaks not of himself but of his *descendants* as the recipients of the promised land; cf. also Ex. 32:13.

covenant, that I may be a God *to you* and *to your descendants after you*." (Gn. 17:5-7)[34]

The phrase "you and your descendants after you" (Gn. 17:9) is repeated frequently. Isaac becomes the heir of the promises: "I will establsh my covenant *with him* as a perpetual covenant *for his descendants after him*." (Gn. 17:19) A bit later Yahweh appears to Isaac and tells him: "Do not go down into Egypt, but dwell in the land which I shall point out to you ... I will be with you and bless you; for I will give all these lands *to you and to your descendants*." (Gn. 26:3-4; cf. 26:24)

When Jacob is about to leave for Phaddan-Aram, Isaac, his father, calls him and says to him: "May God Almighty bless *you*, and make you fruitful; may he multiply you so that you become many nations. May he bestow on you, and your descendants also, the blessing of Abraham." (Gn. 28:3-4) During the vision of the ladder, Jacob receives the same blessing from Yahweh himself: "I am the Lord, the God of Abraham *your* father and the God of Isaac. I will give *you and your descendants* the land on which you lie. They shall be as the dust of the earth. *You* (singular) shall spread abroad to the west, to the east, to the north, and to the south; *in you and in your descendants*, all the nations of the earth shall be blessed." (Gn. 28:13-14; cf. 32:13; 35-12; 46:3; 48:4) We shall note not only the close union between the descendants and the patriarch but also the stark realism with which the union is expressed. "You (singular) shall spread abroad to the west, etc." indicates that Jacob himself is present in his descendants.[35] In Ex. 19:3 the descendants are called simply "the house of Jacob."

---

34 Cf. Gn. 18:18: "Abraham shall surely become a great and powerful nation."

35 Cf. Gn. 35:11-12: "God said to him (Jacob), 'I am God Almighty. Be fruitful and multiply; a nation and many nations shall spring from you; kings shall stem from you. I will give you the land which I gave to Abraham and Isaac; this land will I give *also to your descendants*'"; or Gn. 46:3: "I will make you a great people"; or Gn. 48:4: "He (God) blessed me and said, 'I will make *you* fruitful and numerous; I will make *you* many nations, and I will give this land to your descendants after you *as a possession for all time*.'"

Alongside the great patriarchs, the Bible speaks of other "ancestors" who live on in a great posterity. To Agar, the Egyptian mother of Ismael, the angel of the Lord promises: "I will so multiply your posterity that it shall be too many to count." (Gn. 16:10; cf. 21:13) The Ismaelites are Ismael multiplied, as Yahweh proclaims to Abraham in the sacerdotal text: "As for Ismael, I have heard you. I will bless him and make him fruitful and multiply him exceedingly. He shall become the father of twelve princes, and I will make him a great nation." (Gn. 17:20)[36] The wish for Rebecca is significant: "May you, sister, become a thousand times ten thousand." (Gn. 24:60) One could hardly express more explicitly the identity between the descendants and the ancestor who is perpetuated in them.

After having listed the descendants of "Esau, father of the Edomites," the sacred author concludes: "These are the descendants of Esau, and these are their chiefs. Esau is Edom." (Gn. 36: 19) Esau is identified with his sons, the Edomites, for "Esau is Edom." (Gn. 36:1, 8)

The blessing which Jacob gives to Joseph (really to his children, especially Ephraim and Manasse) is equally characteristic: "May ... the angel who has delivered me from all evil bless the boys *that my name* and the name of my fathers Abraham and Isaac *be preserved through them;* and may they grow in numbers on the earth." (Gn. 48:16; cf. also 19)

We might also cite the case of Moses. When Yahweh turns away from the Israelites, he says to Moses: "Let me alone, then, that my wrath may blaze against them to consume them. Then I will make *of you a great nation.*" (Ex. 32:10)[37]

b) LEGAL PASSAGES

In several places in the biblical legislative codes we find the same concept about the close union between an ancestor and his

36 Cf. Gn. 25:16: "These were the sons of Ismael and these are their names according to their villages and encampments; twelve princes according to their tribes."

37 Previously it was a question of the "son of the slave-girl", namely Ismael, who will become "a great nation." (Gn. 21:13, 18) The *Book of Genesis* mentions other ancestors; for example, the incestuous son

descendants. For example, in the sacerdotal legislation the "sons of Aaron" are often simply "the priests." (Ex. 30:21; Lv. 6:9, 18; 10:14; Nm. 3:10, 48, 51; 4:15, 27; 8:19; 18:1) The fact that these "sons of Aaron" must fulfill certain functions in conformity with a "perpetual ordinance" (Lv. 7:34; 24:3, 9) seems to imply the idea of an extension of Aaron in time.

We find similar phrases for other individuals. For example, speaking of Phinees, Yahweh says: " I hereby give *him* my pledge of friendship, which shall be for *him and for his descendants* after him the pledge of an *everlasting* priesthood." (Nm. 25:13) It is as though the priest Phinees himself performs the function of priesthood throughout the ages.

Frequently the sacerdotal laws, in so far as they are a "perpetual ordinance" are promulgated "for your descendants wherever they may dwell." (Lv. 3:17; 6:11; 7:36; 10:9; 23:14, 21, 41; 24:3; Nm. 10:8; 15:15; 18:23) Sometimes the wording is even more expressive and more solemn as in Ex. 27:21: "This shall be a perpetual ordinance for the Israelites throughout their generations." This formula recalls certain others: for example, from the *Book of Numbers*: "This is an inviolable covenant to last forever before the Lord, for you and your descendants." (Nm. 18:19); or from *Deuteronomy*: "Both what is still hidden and what has already been revealed concern us and our descendants forever." (Dt. 29:28) All three of these quotations imply the idea of a profound solidarity, even of identification, between the same peoples down through the ages. As a matter of fact Yahweh is always mindful of "the covenant I made with their forefathers, whom I brought out of the land of Egypt under the very eyes of the Gentiles, that I, the Lord, might be their God." (Lv. 26:45) In the "sons" Yahweh sees in some way the ancestors with whom he made the covenant. This identity between the living members and the deceased members of the Chosen People is set in the limelight by the divine precept regarding Hebrew slaves: "Since

of Lot: "he is the father of the Moabites of the present day" (Gn. 19:37), or the twins, Esau and Jacob, whom Rebecca carries in her womb. Regarding these latter Yahweh tells Rebecca: "Two nations are in your womb; two peoples shall stem from your body." (Gn. 25:23)

those whom I brought out of the land of Egypt are servants of mine, they shall not be sold as slaves to any man." (Lv. 25:42; cf. 25:55)

2. *The Historical Books*

The two facets of the ancestor theme (the ancestor is continued in his descendants, and the ancestor encompasses within himself all future members of his group) are both continually emphasized in the historical books.

Certain phrases betray a deep conviction regarding the survival of the ancestor in his descendants. Hebron remains "the heritage of the Cenezite Caleb, son of Jephonne, to the present day" (Jos. 14:13) long after the death of Caleb. *Deuteronomy* tells us why: "For to him (Caleb) *and to his sons* I will give the land he trod upon." (Dt. 1:36) All evidence points to the fact that the children form one psychic whole with their forefathers: "I will bring him (Caleb) into the land where he has just been, and his descendants shall possess it." (Nm. 14:24)

Because he had killed seventy sons of his father Gedeon, Abimelech must die in the flower of his youth: "Thus did God requite the evil Abimelech has done to *his father,* in killing *his seventy brothers."* (Jg. 9:56) Killing the brothers is tantamount to harming the father.

Ruth, as well as Rebecca, (Gn. 24:60) received a blessing which indicates that the numerous posterity of the wife of Booz was looked upon as a continuation of herself: "May you do well in Ephratha, and win fame in Bethlehem." (Rt. 4:11)

The pact of friendship which united Jonathan and David is perpetuated in their descendants. Jonathan declares: "Go in peace, and let all stand that we have sworn both of us in the name of the Lord saying: The Lord be between me and thee, and between my seed and thy seed *forever."* (1 K. 20:42)

Curses against an individual extend to his entire posterity. David heaps reproaches against Joab the murderer of Abner: "May it (the blood of Abner) come upon the head of Joab, *and upon all his father's house;* and *let there not fail* from the house of Joab one that hath an issue of seed, or that is a leper, or that holdeth the distaff, or that falleth by the sword, or that wanteth bread." (2 K. 3:29; cf. 3 K. 2:33) The severed head of Isobeth, son of Saul, proves to David that "the Lord hath revenged my lord the king this day of Saul and *of his deed.*" (2 K. 4:8) To kill the son of a dead father is to "leave my husband no name, nor remainder upon the earth" and to "quench my spark which is left." (2 K. 14:7)

King Saul, who massacred a number of Gibeonites, appears to the eyes of the survivors as "the man who crushed *us* and oppressed *us* unjustly." (2 K. 21:5) Because Saul is dead, seven of his sons (in reality two sons of a concubine and five grandsons) will be punished in his place. (2 K. 21:6) In a sense Saul survives in them and is punished in them. A similar idea is evident in the story which sings the mercy of God to the impious king Achab. When this king of the northern kingdom repents. Elias receives this word from Yahweh: "Hast thou not seen Achab humbled before me? Therefore, because he hath humbled himself for my sake, I will not bring the evil in his days, but in his son's days will I bring the evil *upon his house.*" (3 K. 21:29) Two generations later Jehu "slew all that were left of the house of Achab in Jezrahel, and all his chief men, and his friends, and his priests, till there were no remains left of him." (4 K. 10:11) The usurper "slew *all that were left of Achab* in Samaria, to a man, according to the word of the Lord, which he spoke by Elias." (4 K. 10:17 referring to 3 K. 21:21) Killing the "survivors" is tantamount to killing the ancestor, even if this ancestor was forgiven in his own right as an individual.

When evil falls upon a given individual, his descendants feel the consequences. It is as though a contagion perdures through the ages. The prophet Eliseus foretells his greedy servant Giez: "The leprosy of Naaman shall also stick to thee and *to thy seed forever.*" (4 K. 5:27) The "blood of Naboth" and the blood *of his children"* is linked together in 4 K. 9:26.

3) *The Prophetic Books*

The prophets frequently allude to the continuity between the people and their ancestor. For Isaia "the God *of the house of*

Jacob" is identical with Him "who redeemed Abraham" (Is. 29: 22), for "Abraham" *is* "the house of Jacob" in which he perdures. (cf. Is. 65:9: "From Jacob I will bring offspring.")

When Osee describes the perversity of the Israelite people, he links it with that of their eponymous ancestor: "The Lord has a grievance against Israel: he shall punish Jacob for his conduct, for his deeds he shall repay him. In the womb he supplanted his brother, and as a man he contended with God." (Os. 12:3-5) The nation, descendant of the patriarch, has inherited the wickedness of the ancestor. (Os. 5:2) The identical kind of resistance to the Lord proves the identity of the nation wtih its ancestor.[38] Or, to put it another way, the guilty father survives in the evil nation.[39] Amos sees Israel as the single patriarchal family that Yahweh "brought up from the land of Egypt." (Amos 3:1; cf. Jr. 31:33; Ez. 20:5)

What is true of the Chosen People in general is also true of particular groups. Isaia sees a close connection between "seeing his descendants" and "a long life." (Is. 53:10) Jeremia identifies the begetting of children with multiplying one's own person. (Jer. 29:6)[40]

Parents are blessed or punished in the person of their descendants. Yahweh assures us through Jeremia that *"never* shall there fail to be a descendant of Jonadab, Rechab's son, standing in my service. (Jer. 35:19) Contrariwise, Rachel "dies" in her great great grandchildren (Jer. 31:15), and the race of a king is exterminated or cast out with its ancestor. (Jer. 22:28) To "strip *Esau"* is tantamount to bringing about the ruin of his *"sons, and brothers, and neighbors"* (Jer. 49:10); to "hate *Esau"* is to make "his mountains a waste, his heritage a desert for jackals." (Mal. 1:3) Yahweh punishes the false prophet Semeia the

---

38 Cf. Is. 43:27: *"Your first father* (Jacob) sinned; your spokesmen rebelled against me till I repudiated the holy gates, put *Jacob* under the ban, and exposed *Israel* to scorn."

39 J. Hempel, *Gott und Mensch,* l.c., p. 142. Hempel speaks of a kind of contamination of stain and of curse.

40 On the other hand, anyone who remains "without children" is one who "will never thrive in his lifetime!" (Jer. 22:30)

Nehelamite: "I will therefore punish Semeia, the Nehelamite, *and his offspring*. None of them shall survive among this people to see the good that I will do to this people." (Jer. 29:32) Jeremia invokes a curse upon his enemies and their "offspring": "So now, deliver their children to famine, do away with them by the sword. Let their wives be made childless and widows." (Jer. 18:21)

4) *The Sapiential Books*

These books occasionally speak of the descendants as the normal fulfillment of the ancestor, who lives on in them.

To have "neither son nor grandson among his people, nor any survivor where once he dwelt" (Jb. 18:19) is looked upon as the height of misfortune. On the other hand, "a father's blessing gives *a family* firm roots, but a mother's curse uproots the growing plant." (Sir. 3:9)

The *Book of Proverbs* makes frequent mention of the same thoughts: "When a man walks in integrity and justice, *happy are his children after* him!" (Prs. 20:7) "Those who are just shall escape." (Prv. 11:21) The happiness of the just will be incomplete unless "you shall know that your descendants are many, and your offspring as the grass of the earth." (Jb. 5:25)[41]

The just Noe "left to the world a future for his race." (Wis. 14:6) Godly men generally find that "their family endures, and their hopes are never shattered." (Sir. 44:13) "Abraham, father of many peoples, kept his glory without stain: . . . For this reason, God promised him with an oath that in his descendants the nations would be blessed." (Sir. 44:19-21) Aaron and his offspring (Sir. 45:21, 25), Phinees and his descendants (Sir. 45: 24), David and his race (Sir. 45:25), Caleb and his offspring (Sir. 46:9)—all are blessed with a similiar blessing. Each ancestor is bound firmly with his descendants.

41   On the other hand, a man crushed by misfortune is not concerned any longer about his posterity; such is the thought of Job: "You prevail, O Yahweh, once for all against him and he passes on; with changed appearance you send him away. If his sons are honored, he is not aware of it; if they are in disgrace, he does not know about them." (Jb. 14:20-21)

Whereas the uprightness of a father brings blessings to his children, the wickedness of a mother brings misfortune to her children. The children of an adulterous woman "will not take root; her branches will not bring forth fruit." (Sir. 23:25)[42] "The children of adulterers will remain without issue, and the progeny of an unlawful bed will disappear ... For dire is the end of the wicked generation." (Wis. 3:16, 19)

Certain actions of parents bring in their wake horrible but inevitable results for the children: "Their heritage is lost to sinners, children and want abides with their descendants." (Sir. 41:6) Solomon in giving in to lust and idolatry "brought dishonor upon *your reputation,* shame on your marriage, wrath upon *your descendants."* (Sir. 47:20)[43]

All these themes are found also in the *Book of Psalms.* Evildoers are punished in their children: "May the Lord consume *them* in his anger; let fire devour them. Destroy their fruit from the earth and their *posterity* from among men." (Ps. 20: 10-11) On the other hand, whereas evil strikes both parents and children, the good fortune of the ancestor is transmitted to his offspring. Of "the man who fears the Lord" it is said: *"He* abides in prosperity, and *his descendants* inherit the land." (Ps. 24:13) "Happy the man who fears the Lord ... His posterity shall be mighty upon the earth." (Ps. 111:2) The uprightness of the just finds its reward in the happiness of the children: "Neither in my youth, nor now that I am old, have I seen a *just man* forsaken nor his *descendants* begging bread. All the day he is kindly and lends, and his *descendants* shall be blessed." (Ps. 36:25:26) The blessing of the just man is to "see your children's children." (Ps. 127:6; cf. 146:13) "Watch the wholehearted man, and mark the upright; for there is a future (*posterity* in the French translation) for the man of peace." (Ps. 36:37)

---

42. Cf. also Sir. 40:15: "The root of the godless is on sheer rock; or they are like reeds on the riverbank."

43 In spite of this "profanation" of his "race" occasioned by Solomon: "he (God) gave to Jacob a remnant, to David a root from his own family" and "He does not uproot the posterity of his chosen one." (Sir. 47:22)

THE FIFTH THEME

The Beneficial Influence of the "Fathers" on Their "Children"

When we understand the term "father" in a wider sense than that of direct physical generation, we have the meaning that is often found in the Bible. Frequently the sacred writers speak of the influence these "fathers" (in a wider sense of "forefathers," "members of past generations") have on their "children."

1. *The Pentateuch*

Especially in certain legal passages of the Pentateuch do we find expression of this enduring and beneficent bond between the "fathers" and their distant "descendants."

The promise which God made to the "fathers" applies to the "sons." This is evident from the stereotyped formula of the promise: "When the Lord, your God, has brought you into the land of the Chanaanites, which he swore to *you and to your fathers.*" (Ex. 13:11; cf. 32:11; 33:1)

But it is especially *Deuteronomy* which emphasizes the bond between the generations. In dealing with the great hope for the approaching conquest of the Promised Land, it views all these events as the accomplishment of Yahweh's salvific will for his people: "The Lord, your God, has given this land over to you. Go up and occupy it, as the Lord, *the God of your fathers,* commands you." (Dt. 1:21; 6:18; 7:12; 8:1; 10:11; 11:21) What is most significant for our study is that this people of God embraces not only the patriarchs, the original recipients of the Promise, but also their posterity, the Israelites who are now preparing to conquer Chanaan: "Go now and occupy the land I swore to your fathers, Abraham, Isaac and Jacob, I would give to them and to their descendants." (Dt. 1:8; 6:10; 9:5, 27; 34:4) Yahweh's completely gratuitous love of predilection extends to all generations of the Chosen People: "Yet in his love *for your fathers* the Lord was so attached to them as to choose *you, their descendants,* in preference to all other peoples, as indeed he has *now* done." (Dt. 10:15; cf. 4:37)

The divine promise made to the "fathers" about the Promised

Land applies with equal force to the "sons": "And that you may have long life on the land which the Lord swore to your fathers, he would give *to them and their descendants.*" (Dt. 11:9) For as Moses recalls in his commentary on the decalogue: "Your ancestors went down to Egypt seventy strong, and now the Lord, your God, has made you as numerous as the stars of the sky." (Dt. 10:22)

The goodness of Yahweh is unending; it is he who initiates the love between himself and the people: "The Lord, your God, will circumcise your hearts and *the hearts of your descendants,* that you may love the Lord, your God, with all your heart and all your soul, and so may live." (Dt. 30:6) Upon the acceptance of this offer of love ests the welfare of future generations: "Choose life, then, that *you and your descendants* may live, by loving the Lord, your God, heeding his voice and holding fast to him." (Dt. 30:20) It is evident that there is a close solidarity between the generations; the members of the Chosen People have a deep consciousness of the effect of their acts and of their virtuous life on the anonymous multitude of future members. It is this deep conviction of being members one of another, even in the distant future, which underlies the "corporate" character of each individual. Whenever any person is viewed in the light of belonging to the psychic whole of the "fathers and their descendants," that person has a function to fulfill: he in turn becomes a "father" and a "corporate personality" (even though it be on a very reduced scale).

In the minds of the priestly compilers, there exists also a certain functional identity between the living members and the deceased members of the Chosen People. Even when He is dealing with the living, Yahweh remembers always the covenant he had concluded with the early generations whom He had led out of Egypt. (Lv. 25:42, 45, 55) Very probably we are here dealing with a religious sublimation of a sociological bond. The deep-seated unity of the Chosen People is due to a divine vocation, which reinforces the already existing physical union with the "fathers."

2. *The Historical Books*

We find in the historical books some traces of this generalized theme of the "fathers." Israel is the "descendants of Abraham" (Ps. 104:6), God's friend *forever."* (2 Par. 20:7) The same divine love embraces the ancestor and those whom he bears within himself *in germine:* "Remember forever his covenant: the word which he commanded to a *thousand generations*: the covenant which he made with Abraham, and his oath to Isaac." (1 Par. 16:15-16) Mindful of his commitment to the "fathers," Yahweh delivers His people from their enemies: "And now let us cry to heaven, and the Lord will have mercy on us, and will remember the covenant of our fathers, and will destroy this army before our face this day." (1 Mac. 4:10)

One of the greatest sources of blessing for the entire Israelite people during the course of its history was the Davidic kingdom. These words taken from among the last of David: "Neither is my house so great with God, that he should make *with me an eternal covenant,* firm in all things and assured" (David is not denying the existence of the covenant but rather pointing out that it comes from the bounteous love of God) (2 K. 23:5) recall the terms of the celebrated prophecy of Nathan: "The Lord foretelleth to thee, that the Lord will make thee a *house* ... I will raise up *thy seed after thee,* which shall proceed out of thy bowels, and I will establish his kingdom." (2 K. 7:11-12; cf. 1 Par. 28:7; 2 Par. 7:18) The great king understood very well the import of the divine promise: *"Thy house* shall be faithful, and *thy kingdom forever* before thy face, and thy throne shall be firm *forever"* (2 K. 7:16), for he begins his thanks in these words: "But yet this hath seemed little in thy sight, O Lord God, unless thou didst also speak of the house of thy servant *for a long time to come!"* (2 K. 7:19) The perpetuity of the kingdom is pictured under the form of a lamp. (3 K. 11:36; 15:4) Many times Yahweh remembers the promise made to David and to the dynasty of the great king in favor of all Juda: "But the Lord would not destroy Juda, for David his servant's sake, as he had promised him, *to give him a light, and to his children always."* (4 K. 8:19; 4 K. 19:34; 20:6, 2 Par. 21:7) The Davidic line—the corporate extension of the illustrious ancestor— exerts a benign influence upon all the members of the line regardless of the time of their existence.

3. *The Prophetic Books*

There are also some interesting references to the "fathers" theme in the prophets. *Isaia* 61 proclaims that the "covenant I will make with them" consists in this that "their descendants shall be renowned among the nations, and their offspring among the peoples; all who see them shall acknowledge them as a race the Lord has blessed." (Is. 61:8-9)[44]

The prayer of the prophet Michea recalls to Yahweh the promises he made to the "fathers": "You will show faithfulness to Jacob, and grace to Abraham, as you have sworn to our fathers, from days of old." (Mi. 7:20) In showing favor to the contemporary Israelites of the prophet's time, Yahweh is carrying out the promises made to the "fathers" and being kind toward Abraham who lives on in his descendants.

All sacred history shows that Yahweh delights in forgiving every generation of His Chosen People. In giving the land of Chanaan to the Israelites, Yahweh was carrying out the promise made to their forefathers. In the words of Jeremia: "This land you gave them as you had promised their fathers under oath." (Jer. 32:22) After the sufferings of the Exile, Yahweh reestablishes Israel in virtue of the promises made to the "fathers": "The days will come, says the Lord, when I will change the lot of my people (of Israel and Juda, says the Lord), and bring them back to the land which I gave to their fathers; they shall have it as their possession." (Jer. 30:3) We have here the vivid expression of the eternal value of the divine promises. Once made to the "fathers," they remain valid and efficacious for all their descendants.[45]

---

44 Cf. also Is. 65:23: "They shall not toil in vain, nor beget children for sudden destruction; for a race blessed by the Lord are they *and their offspring*." In Is. 66:22 the promise of endurance refers to the "race" and to the "name."

45 The divine promise is formal: "I will bring them back to the land which with my oath I promised to their fathers, to Abraham, Isaac, and Jacob." (Bar. 2:34)

The "new heart" which Jeremia promises in the name of Yahweh is given to the penitent Israelites for "their own good, and for that of *their children after them*" for as Yahweh says, "I will make *with them an eternal* covenant." (Jer. 32:39)

4. *The Sapiential Books*

The *Psalter* also contains the idea of the concrete unity of the Chosen People. This people serves Yahweh because in virtue of "an everlasting covenant" (Ps. 104:10) they are aware of being the "descendants of Abraham, his servants." (Ps. 104:6) When Yahweh "remembered his holy word to his servant Abraham, he led forth his people with joy." (Ps. 104:42) The Chosen People who form the great "house of Israel" must grow always greater: "May the Lord bless you more and more, both *you and your children*." (Ps. 114:14)

The promise that "The children of your (Yahweh's) servants shall abide, and their posterity shall continue in your presence" (Ps. 101:29) is realized pre-eminently in the great king David. But it is likewise true that the pact made with David refers just as much to his royal line and to the people governed by him as to himself. Psalm 88 declares this explicitly: "I have made a covenant with my chosen one, (the Septuagint reads: chosen ones), I have sworn to David my servant: 'Forever will I confirm *your posterity* and establish *your* throne for all generations." (Ps. 88:4-5; verse 37 adds: "His posterity shall continue forever, and his throne shall be like the sun before me.")

THE SIXTH THEME

The Harmful Influence of the "Fathers" on Their "Children"

A profound realization of the continuity of sin from generation to generation always existed in Israel. The "fathers" did more than give "bad example." Their "evil heart" manifested itself and reflected its influence at every turn of national history. Underlying this conception is the concrete unity of the nation which manifests itself at various levels.

1. *The Pentateuch*

One gets the impression that the legislators of the Pentateuch were fully persuaded that an unbreakable bond ties generation to generation. Aware of this, one has less trouble appreciating the motivation behind the Decalogue: "For I, the Lord, your God, am a jealous God, inflicting punishment *for their fathers' wickedness* on the children of those who hate me, down to the third and fourth generation; but bestowing mercy to the thousandth generation, on the children of those who love me and keep my commandments." (Ex. 20:5; cf. Dt. 5:9 and Nm. 14:18) A certain "vertical" (temporal) collective responsibility is here recognized.

The idea of a close solidarity between the past, present, and future members of a community follows from the fact that a priest who marries a woman not belonging to the tribe of Levi degrades his children. (cf. Lv. 21:15) The sin of a single distant ancestor affects all the group of which he is part, even long after his death.

In the minds of the "priestly" redactors, there exists a veritable identity between different generations. The guilt of the different generations is basically one: "Those of you who survive in the lands of their enemies will waste away for their own and their father's guilt." (Lv. 26:39) As a result it is most befitting to confess not only their own sins but also those of their fathers." (Lv. 26:40)

2. *The Historical Books*

The historical books likewise give evidence of a solidarity in evil, even in sin, between generations. It is interesting to note that even when personal responsibility is affirmed: "The Lord will reward everyone according to his justice and his faithfulness" (1 K. 26:23; cf. 3 K. 8:32; 4 K. 17:41), the theme of "the sins of the fathers" is still valid. After the finding of the "Book of the Law" in the temple, king Josias sends the priest Helcias to the prophetess Holda: "Go and consult the Lord for me, and for the people, and for all Juda, concerning the words of this book which is found, for the great wrath of the Lord is kindled against *us,* because *our fathers* have not harkened to the words of this book to do all that is written for us." (4 K. 22:13; cf. 2 Par. 34:21) We see here that the disapproval and anger of God fall upon the present generation because of its close union with its sinful "forefathers." The same thought dominates the Chronicler when he puts these words in the mouth of Ezechias: "Our *fathers* have sinned and done evil . .. therefore the wrath of the Lord hath been stirred up against *Juda and Jerusalem."* (2 Par. 29:6, 8)

The prayer of the blind Tobias sets in bold relief the solidarity of guilt: "Take not revenge of *my* sins, (O Lord) neither remember *my* offenses, nor those of *my parents* . . . For *we* have not obeyed thy commandments, therefore are *we* delivered to spoil and to captivity and death . . . And now, O Lord, great are thy judgments, because *we* have not done according to thy precepts." (Tob. 3:3-4)

A similar thought underlies the confessions of Esdras and Nehemias. The former says: "Our sins are grown up even unto heaven, *from the days of our fathers.* And *we* ourselves also have sinned grievously unto this day, and for our iniquities we and our kings and our priests have been delivered into the hands of the kings of the lands, and to the sword, and to captivity, and to spoil, and to confusion of face, *as it is at this day."* (Esd. 9:7) Nehemias says that "the seed of the children of Israel separated themselves from every stranger; and they stood, and confessed their sins, and the iniquities *of their fathers."* (Ne. 9:2) The leader of the people humbly admits: "Our kings, our princes, our priests and *our fathers* have not kept thy law." (Ne. 9:34)

3. *The Prophetic Books*

In the prophetic books the "sons" quite evidently suffer because of the evil deeds of their "fathers." The "sons" are massacred because of "the guilt of their fathers." (Is. 14:21) "He will not be named forever, that scion of an evil race!" (Is. 14:20)

Very often the prophets proclaim a kind of solidarity in sin. The evils of the "fathers" are visited on their "sons." "Our fathers, who sinned, are no more; but *we bear their guilt."* (Lam. 5:7) All evidence would seem to indicate that we have here the idea of a real transfer of guilt. From *Amos* to *Third-Isaia* the same conviction is apparent. Amos reproaches Juda, "The lies which *their fathers followed* have led them astray." (Amos 2:4) *Third-Isaia* spells out the irrevocable decision of Yahweh: "Lo, before me it stands written; I will not be quiet until I have paid in full *your* crimes and the crimes of *your fathers* as well, says the Lord." (Is. 65:6-7) This verse in particular brings out the point at issue: there is an uninterrupted accumulation of sin with the consequent snow-balling of culpability, which becomes the one collective culpability of the nation.

Even the dyed-in-the-wool defenders of individual retribution, Ezechiel and Jeremia, do not fail to underline the continuity of this sinful attitude. Ezechiel puts this accusation in the mouth of Yahweh: "They (the children of Israel) *and their fathers* have revolted against me *to this very day."* (Ez. 2:3) Jeremia in turn has an acute awareness of the common guilt which has come down from the "fathers" to his contemporaries: "Let us lie down in our shame and let our disgrace cover us, for we have sinned against the Lord, our God, from our youth to this day, we and our fathers also." (Jer. 3:25; cf. 6:21)

Each individual sin is a renewal of the culpability of the fathers: "They (the men of Juda and the inhabitants of Jerusalem) have returned to the crimes of their forefathers." (Jer. 11:10) That is why this champion of a personal and individualistic religion admits freely that Yahweh repays "the fathers' guilt, even into the lap of their sons who follow." (Jer. 32:18) And he does not fear to confess in the name of his contemporaries: "We recognize, O Lord, *our wickedness,* the guilt *of our fathers;* that we have sinned against you." (Jer. 14:20)[46]

46 Obstinacy in sin is grounded in the example of the "fathers"; "We will not listen to what you say in the name of the Lord," say the people who lived in Lower and Upper Eypt (after the fall of Jerusalem). "Rather will we continue doing what we have proposed; we will burn incense to the queen of heaven and pour out libations to her, *as we and our fathers,* our kings and princes have done in the cities of Juda and the streets of Jerusalem." (Jer. 44:16-17) In describing the condition Baruch says: "Justice is with the Lord, our God; and *we, like our fathers,* are flushed with shame even today." (Bar. 2:6) Much later the author of the *Book of Daniel* puts these words in the mouth of his hero: "On account of *our* sins *and the*

4. *The Sapiential Books*

We find in the Wisdom Books a rather lively polemic against the law of solidarity in evil. Certain "wise men" become indignant over this "family retribution" and would like to replace it with a strictly individual responsibility: "May God not store up the man's (the evil man who has worldly possessions) misery for his children; let him requite the man himself so that he feels it." (Jb. 21:19) Basically this fit of indignation, in face of the personal impunity of the wicked one, is accompanied by the conviction that the individual, regardless of how wicked he may be, succeeds in bringing good fortune to his children. The thought is a scandal for the author of the *Book of Job*: "Why do the wicked survive, grow old, become mighty in power? Their progeny is secure in their sight; they see before them their kinsfolk and their offspring." (Jb. 21:7-8) There is a classic reply to this objection which amounts to this: The good fortune which the wicked obtain for their descendants is as ephemeral as it is apparent. Sirach gives this advice: "Desire not a brood of worthless children, nor rejoice in wicked offspring." (Sir. 16:1) The *Book of Wisdom* assures us: "Better is childlessness with virtue; for immortal is its memory." (Wis. 4:1)

The *Psalter* sanctions the universal punishment of perversity perpetuated from "fathers" to their "sons." There is an evident parallelism between the two parts of verse 28 in psalm 36: "Criminals are destroyed, and *the posterity* of the wicked is cut off." On one occasion in the desert Yahweh thought of exterminating the unfaithful Israelites: "Then with raised hand he swore against them to let *them* perish in the desert, to scatter *their descendants* among the nations, and to disperse them over the lands." (Ps. 105:26) Finally, the imprecatory psalms overwhelm the enemy with terrible threats: "May his posterity meet with destruction; in the next generation may their name be blotted out." (Ps. 108:13)

crimes of our fathers, Jerusalem and your people have become the the reproach of all our neighbors." (Dn. 9:16)

THE SEVENTH THEME

The Identity of Name for a "Clan" and for a Person

The two preceding themes—the influence of "fathers" on their "sons" for good as well as for evil—have enlarged the concept of "corporate personality," in this sense that it was no longer a question (as in the first four themes) of a strictly individual personality exercising his influence horizontally or vertically in a given group, but rather of two parts of a *single group*, with one influencing the other. Thus we have departed almost inperceptibly from the first meaning of "corporate personality" and have arrived at what we have called the secondary meaning. This secondary meaning will be studied in depth in the following three final themes.

Although the secondary meaning of the idea of "corporate personality" definitely proceeds from the community,[47] it must be noted that the community is not considered under the aspect of numbers but under the aspect of the strictest unity. Thus it happens that "a group may be considered as a unit; a personal name (designating an individual being) can assume a collective meaning."[48] This identity of name between a determinate group and a well-known individual is the basis of our seventh theme.

1. *The Pentateuch*

Rather frequently the Law (Torah) represents the group by a single person whose name is exactly the same as that of the group.

Such is the case with many clans which are designated by the names of individual persons: the name of the place where Abraham settled, Mamre, is borne by one of the patriarch's allies in his fight against the enemies of Lot. (Gn. 14:13, 24) Here evi-

---

47 T. W. Manson, *The Son of Man*, in *BJRL* 32 (1949/50) 171-193, p. 191: "where the conception of corporate personality is dominant, there is often a tendency to see the corporate personality as embodied in a person."

48 A. Stanley Cook, *The Old Testament. A Reinterpretation*, 1936, 126.

dently a single person designates (and it is therefore tantamount to) a group of warriors.

The guilty cities of Sodom and Gomorra are considered concretely in the guise of a single individual whose "cry rises to heaven." [49] (Gn. 18:20-21: The C.C.D. translation does not bear out this interpretation). The phrase "to Ismael" employed to designate the place where Esau is going to get a wife, refers evidently to the clan of Ismael, and even more remotely to Ismael the ancestor. (Gn. 28:8)

Having narrated Jacob's blessing on his twelve sons, the author of *Genesis* continues: "All these are the twelve tribes of Israel." (Gn. 49:28) But it is certain that references to the fate of the tribes in *Genesis* 49 are intertwined with allusions to the destiny of *individuals*. For example: "The sceptre shall not depart from Juda" (Gn. 49:10) or "Zebulon shall dwell by the seashores" (Gn. 49:13) or "Benjamin is a ravenous wolf" [50] (Gn. 49:27: an allusion to Jg. 3:15; 5:14, 19-29, and perhaps to Saul).

2. *The Historical Books*

It is not rare in the historical books to find one or the other group personified or represented by a single individual. Sometimes the literary aspect of the personification is evident, as when a city is compared to a "mother in Israel." (2 K. 20:19: the city of Abela). More frequently, however, it is necessary to presuppose the existence of definite individuals whose symbolic significance is very plainly marked, in the sense that they accomplish a deed which of itself has a collective significance, or which expresses an attitude of the group.

---

49 The translation of the "Jerusalem Bible" (Paris, 1956, 24): *"against Sodom"* seems a bit forced to us, if it is to be understood, as the reference to Gn. 4:10 would seem to indicate, of the earth crying to heaven for vengeance.—In *RB* 1897, p. 209, the name *Mohammed ibn-Djad,* which is used to designate a person, a clan, and a war cry, is mentioned.

50 The twelve names of the "children of Israel" (Ex. 28:9-10) are inscribed on two cornelian stones on the ephod of the priest Aaron: "Thus Aaron shall bear their names on his shoulders as a reminder before the Lord.'" (Ex. 28:12, 29)

After passing over the Jordan at the ford of Jericho, the twelve tribes led by Josue are instructed to place twelve stones as a sign. This they do through the intermediary of twelve men chosen from their midst. Through the act of these twelve men, "the Israelites" carry out the orders of their leader, Josue. (Jos. 4:2, 4, 8) These twelve men "represent" in a condensed way the twelve tribes which are soon going to make up the amphictyony.

At the beginning of the *Book of Judges,* the Judaites are spoken of as though they were one individual person, but from the context it is evident that the sacred author was thinking of the entire tribe (this is most evident from the change of pronouns from singular to plural): "Juda then said to his brother Simeon, 'come up with *me* into the territory allotted to me, and let *us* engage the Chanaanites in battle. *I* will likewise accompany *you* into the territory alloted to you'" (Jg. 1:3. In verse 9 the Judaites attack the Chanaanites; in verse 10 and verses 17-20 it is simply Juda again who acts). The entire tribe is condensed, as it were, in the representative individual, a leader, or a well-known person as in Jos. 22:13: "They sent ... ten princes, one from every tribe of Israel, each one being both prince and military leader of his ancestral house."[51]

Goliath, the champion of the Philistines, is convinced that he represents, that is to say, encompasses in his person all the life forces of the Philistine people: "Am not I a Philistine, and you the servants of Saul?" (1 K. 17:8) One gets the impression that the expression "a Philistine" might be paraphrased by "the Philistine people," for there is contrast between the *servants of Saul* and the figure of the giant Philistine. This impression is confirmed

51   This is the beginning of the account telling of the erection of their own altar by the Transjordanian tribes of Ruben and Gad. Ten "princes" are sent to reprimand these reputed schismatics. One gets the impression that these ten spokesmen are thought to be the concrete representatives of their respective tribes. The same personification of an entire tribe by the name of an individual is found in Jg. 1:27: Manasse; in Jg. 1:30: Zabulon; in Jg. 1:31: Aser; in Jg. 1:33: Naphthali. The Israelite nation is represented by a singular "me" in the story of the messengers sent to the king of Edom: "Let *me* pass through your land." (Jg. 11:17, 19)

by the fact that at the end of the singlehanded combat, "the Philistines seeing that their champion was dead, fled away." (1 K. 17:51) They are indeed defeated, for he who encompasses them all has been defeated. On the other hand, "he (David) put his life in his hand, and slew the Philistine, and the Lord wrought great salvation for all Israel." (1 K. 19:5)[52]

3. *The Prophetic Books*

We are acquainted with the grandiose personifications of the prophets in which the neighboring countries of Chanaan are designated by names of individual persons. In his "oracle on Egypt" Isaia constantly intertwines the two points of view, for the Hebrew term *mesrayim* can mean either the country or the inhabitants. Sometimes the prophet evidently is thinking of the latter, as, for example, when he says (in the singular): "The courage of the Egyptians (the French translation has Egypt) ebbs away within them, and I will bring nought their counsel; ... The Lord has prepared among them (the Egyptian diviners) a spirit of dizziness, and they have made Egypt stagger in whatever she does, as a drunkard staggers in his vomit." (Is. 19:3, 14) Again when he denounces the weakness of the Egyptian alliance: "The Egyptians (the French translation has Egypt) are men, not God, their horses are flesh, not spirit; when the Lord stretches forth his hand, the helper shall stumble, the one helped shall fall, and both of them shall perish together." (Is. 31:3) Jeremia personifies Egypt: "Egypt surges like the Nile ... I will surge forward," he says, "and cover the earth, destroying the city and its people." (Jer. 46:8 cf. 46:20 for another figure of Egypt: "Egypt is a pretty heifer.")

All the nations around Israel receive oracles from the prophets who address them as though they were persons. Ezechiel receives the divine order: "Say to the Ammonites: Because *you* cried out your joy over the desecration of my sanctuary, the devastation of

---

52   The idea of representing an entire group by a handful of individuals (cf. the idea of the "remnant" in the prophets) occurs again, for example, on the occasion of the struggle between the twelve young men of Benjamin and the guard of David, who was also represented by twelve servants. (2 Kgs. 2:15)

the land of Israel, and the exile of the house of Juda, therefore
I will deliver you into the possession of the Easterners . . Because
Edom has taken vengeance on the house of Juda and has made
itself grievously guilty by taking vengeance on them, therefore
I will stretch out my hand against *you*. I will make *you* plunder
for the nations, I will cut *you* off from the peoples, and remove
you from the lands." (Ez. 25:3-4, 12, 7) (All underlined pronouns are in the singular) The same prophet addresses Tyre
as "the prince of Tyre" and "the king of Tyre" (Ez. 28:2, 12)
and predicts its terrible ruin. The oracle against Moab in Is. 16
presupposes an extremely vital conception of the unity of this
neighboring people: "We have heard of the pride of Moab, how
very proud he is with his haughty, arrogant insolence that his
empty words do not match." (Is. 16:6, cf. 12: "Though Moab shall
be seen tiring himself on the high place, entering his sanctuary
to pray, it shall avail him nothing.") Za. 9:5 describes the
impression the fall of Tyre will have on other nations: "Ascalon
shall see it and be afraid; Gaza also; she shall be in great pain;
Accaron too, for her hope shall come to naught."

We could multiply examples, but those already given are
sufficiently clear. The prophets had a very clear idea of the
ambivalence of the names of the countries, which designated not
only the geographic country (as with us) but also the inhabitants
thereof, often united under the rule of a "king." The divine oracles
are addressed to all the people who are conceived of as a single
individual. We conclude, therefore, that we have here a basis
for speaking of a "corporate personality," at least in the secondary
sense.

4. *The Sapiential Books*

We find in the sapiential literature the same identification between the name of a clan (or country) and an eponymous individual. Besides the well known example of Jacob-Israel (cf. Ps.
13:7; 52:7; 77:71; 104:23; 147:19; Sir. 24:8; 44:22), we can
cite Ps. 79:2: "O guide of the flock of *Joseph*," or the enumeration
of Ps. 82:8-9: "Gebal and Ammon and Amalec, Philistia, with
the inhabitants of Tyre; the Assyrians, too, are leagued with
them; they are the forces of the sons of Lot." Ammon (Gn. 19:38)

and Amalec (1 Par. 1:36) are certainly names of persons. The juxtaposition of Sisara and Madian (Ps. 82:10) suggests that Madian is the name of a clan as well as the name of an individual. (cf. 1 Par. 1:33)

THE EIGHTH THEME

The Concretization of a People in an Individual Person

It is a well known phenomenon of the sacred books that the entire Chosen People is treated by Yahweh and by the Israelites themselves as a single person. A series of individual images underline the concrete, one might almost say physical, character of this unity. This concrete note often reveals the concretization of the group in a real individual person who supports it and carries its hopes.

1. *The Pentateuch*

Now and then, the Torah personifies the Chosen People under the form of "the son of Yahweh." The parallel drawn between this "son" and the "first-born" of Pharao (Ex. 4:23) leaves little doubt about the concreteness of this idea. In the mind of Yahweh— so Israel believes—it is a question of a unity truly comparable to that of a single individual.[53]

53 O. Eissfeldt, *Der Gottesknecht bei Deuterojesaja*, Halle, 1933, 14: "The Israelite is, therefore, his people, a unit, an individual, a unit produced by the tribal father and maintained as such in him continuously." In a similar vein A. Lods, *Les antécédents de la notion d'Eglise en Israël et dans le Judaïsme*, in *Origine et nature de l'Eglise*. Lectures given at the Faculty of Protestant Theology, Paris, 1939, 7-50, p. 49: "The Semite is profoundly convinced that the collectivity forms a kind of living being more real than the individuals who compose it" (Lods refers to Jgs. 9:2 in which Abimelech says to the Sichemites: "You must remember that I am your own flesh and bone." We might refer also to 2 Kgs. 19:44: "The men of Israel

This basically realistic idea of the unity of the Chosen People explains a number of incidents of sacred history. After the events of Mara, Moses says to the people: "If *you* really listen to the voice of the Lord, your God," he told them, "and do what is right in his eyes: if *you* heed his commandments and keep all his precepts, I will not afflict *you* with any of the diseases with which I afflicted the Egyptians; for I, the Lord, am *your* healer." (Ex. 15:26. All pronouns underlined are in the singular.) God here deals with His people (who form a collectivity much as did the Egyptians who were struck by the plagues) as with a single person. This divine attitude is justified because the unity of the "sons of Israel" is based on their election and on the divine covenant as much as, if not more than, on the solidarity of the primitive clan.

The same idea of a people unified by divine initiative is vividly expressed in the complaint of Moses: "Was it I who *conceived* all this people? Or was it I who *gave them birth,* that you tell me to carry them, like a foster father carrying an infant?" (Nm. 11:12) Despite this touching description of the people as an individual infant, the great lawgiver was evidently thinking of the collectivity for he says: "Where can I get meat to give to all this people? For *they* are crying to me, 'Give us meat for our food.'" (Nm. 11:13) *Deuteronomy* speaks of the nation as of a single individual whom Yahweh "created" (Dt. 32:6) "guarding them as the apple of his eye. As an eagle incites its nestlings forth by hovering over its brood, so he spread his wings to receive them and bore them up on his pinions." (Dt. 32:10-11) These images give concrete evidence of the personal relationship which Yahweh desires to have with the Chosen People,[54] who are really

answered the men of Juda, and said: 'I have ten parts in the king more than thou, and David belonged to me more than to thee. Why hast thou done *me* a wrong, and why was it not told *me* first, that I might bring back *my king?*' "

54   These individual relationships are pushed to the extreme in the extravagant theory proposed by H. S. Nyberg, *Studien zum Hoseabuche,* Uppsala, 1935, 27: the unity of the Israelite people would be due to the fact that the God of a group (a "people," *'âm,* a collectivity of similar beings) is also the parent God (*'âm*) of this group. Accord-

one—as an individual man is one—in the eyes of its heavenly "Father."

Sometimes the symbolism is stated in so many words. The Hebrew hagiographer knows full well that Yahweh carries his people *"as* a man carries his child all along your journey" (Dt. 1:31) or that Yahweh disciplines his children *"as a man* disciplines his son." (Dt. 8:5) Besides, the profound conviction about the intimate union of each individual with the whole nation comes to the fore continually. To realize this we need only refer to the well known profession of faith in *Deuteronomy*: "Then you shall declare before the Lord, your God, 'My father was a wandering Aramean who went down to Egypt with a small household and lived there as an alien. But there he became a nation great, strong and numerous.'" (Dt. 26:5) According to the context this is an individual profession of faith, but the individual is completely identified with the group, even with its deceased members, and the group expresses itself through him: "When the Egyptians maltreated and oppressed *us,* imposing hard labor upon *us, we* cried to the Lord, the God of our fathers." (Dt. 26:6-7)

The description of the return of the exiles is also very instructive. It is pictured as the fate of a single human being. "Provided that you and your children return to the Lord, ... the Lord, your God, will change your lot; and taking pity on *you,* he will again gather *you* from all the nations wherein he has scattered *you.* Though you may have been driven to the farthest corner of the world, even from there will the Lord, your God, gather *you;* even from there will he bring *you* back. The Lord, your God, will then bring you into the land which *your* fathers once occupied, that *you* too may occupy it, and he will make *you* more prosperous and numerous than *your* fathers." (Dt. 30:3-5) (All the underlined pronouns are singular in form.)

ing to Nyberg, "The group in so far as it is an historical collectivity is the mother whom the God has married." As a matter of fact the unity of the Israelite nation depends less on a "naturalistic" religiosity which implies necessary relationships with the divinity, than on a free spiritual choice. In the last analysis it is based on the salvific event of the Exodus (cf. Ex. 13:8; 20:2; 23:15; Dt. 5:1, 15; 16:1,3,12; Jg. 2:1; 4 Kgs. 17:36; Ps. 80:1; Ag. 2:5; Amos. 2:10; 5:25).

The constant oscillation between the collectivity of the entire nation and the individual, who is so dear to a personalist conception of religion, is evidenced in the constant interchange between the singular and plural pronouns. In the canticle sung by "Moses and the Israelites" (Ex. 15:1) the poet begins with the singular pronoun: *"I* will sing to the Lord, for he is gloriously triumphant; . . . *My* strength and *my* courage is the Lord, and he has been *my* savior. He is *my* God, I praise him; the God of my father. I extol him." (Ex. 15:2) All the while it is evident that the poet has in mind "the people you (Yahweh) redeemed." (Ex. 15:13, 16) "You brought *them* in and planted *them* on the mountain of your inheritance." (Ex. 15:17)[55]

The same abrupt transition from the corporate singular to a true collectivity shines forth, for example, in the episode of the negotiations with the Edomites: "From Cades Moses sent men to the king of Edom with the message: 'Your brother Israel has this to say: You know all the hardships that have befallen *us.*' " (Nm. 20:14) But the king "answered him, 'You (singular) shall not pass through here." (Nm. 20:18, 20: cf. Nm. 21:22; Dt. 2:27-29)

We can well wonder whether this oscillation between the singular and the plural would be possible if the ancient Hebrews had not been definitely convinced of the existence of the people as a single reality which is summed up in a single representative.

---

55 Even if this last verse is a later addition, it is interesting to note that the interpretation which it ultimately received agrees very well with the "corporate" character of the initial "I." We can observe the same transposition in the *Book of Lamentations;* the fifth lamentation interprets the apparently individual lament (of Lam. 1) as referring to the community: "The joy of *our* hearts has ceased . . . over this *our* hearts are sick, at this *our* eyes grow dim." (Lam. 5:15, 17) Cf. H. Wheeler Robinson, *The Old Testament. Its Making and Meaning,* London, 1937, 143: "The 'individual lament' is, however, based on the conception of 'corporate personality,' which enables the poet to pass from his own personal sorrows to those of the particular group or the whole nation"; the individual concerned here is "representative and summary of all their sorrows."

2. *The Historical Books*

We find certain indications in the historical books which permit us to suppose that the personification of an entire group by a single individual was not unknown.

We have already spoken of the identity of the name of a clan or of a tribe with that of a human person. (cf. Jg. 1:3: "Juda then said to his brother Simeon." Also Jg. 20:23: "Shall I again engage my brother Benjamin in battle?")

In the story of Gideon we get the impression that "Madian" is a single person: "When the Israelites had completed their sowing, Madian, Amalec, and the Cedemites would come up." (Jg. 6:3); "Thus was Israel reduced to misery by Madian." (Jg. 6:6) Yahweh promises his judge Gideon: "I shall be with you, and you will cut down Madian to the last man." (Jg. 6:16); "By means of the three hundred who lapped up the water I will save you and will deliver Madian into your power." (Jg. 7:7) Madian is compared (in the dream of the Madianite) to a tent which is struck and felled by a loaf of barley bread (symbolizing Israel). (Jg. 7:13) At the end of the campaign Madian was "brought into subjection by the Israelites; no longer did they hold their heads high." (Jg. 8:28)

Jephte, the Galaadite, is "son of Galaad" (Jg. 11:1); the district is personified. The same phenomenon is verified in "my brother Benjamin" in Jg. 20:23, 28. Although there is question of the entire tribe of Benjamin, Yahweh promises: "Tomorrow I will deliver *him* into your power." (Jg. 20:28)

The unity of the Chosen People is portrayed vividly. After the outrage at Gabaa, "All the Israelites came out *as one man*: from Dan to Bersabee." (Jg. 20:1) Goaded on by Saul the Israelites "went out as one man" against the Ammonites, who attacked Jabes Galaad. (1 K. 11:7) Following the victory over the Ammonites, "all the people went to Galgal, and there they made Saul king before the Lord." (1 K. 11:15)

The famous prayer of Esther gives us a marvelous idea of the destiny of the people of Israel: "Thou, O Lord, didst take Israel from among all nations, and our fathers from their predecessors, to possess them as an everlasting inheritance." (Est. 14:5)

Contrariwise, some nations are destined for extermination, such, for example, as Amalec, about which God gives Saul the following orders: "Now therefore go and smite Amalec, and utterly destroy all that *he* hath. Spare *him* not, nor covet anything that is his; but slay both man and woman, child and suckling, ox and sheep, camel and ass." (1 K. 15:3)

3. *The Prophetic Books*

Especially in the poetical compositions of the prophets do we find verifications of the group being represented under the traits of an individual human person.

In the eyes of the prophets divine election refers particularly to the entire nation, conceived under the figure of a single being. We can recall the image of a "child" (Os. 11:1; Jer. 31:9, Mal. 3:10) or of the "vine" (Is. 5:7; 27:3; Os. 10:1; Jer. 2:21; 5:21; 6:9; 12:10; Ex. 17:6; 19:10; Ps. 79:15) or of the "first fruits" of the harvest (Jer. 2:3) or of the "flock" (Jer. 10:21; 23:1; Ez. 34; Is. 40:11; Mi. 5:3) or of "my own special possession." (Mal. 3:17)

All these figures are intended to express the deep unity of the people descended from Jacob-Israel and set apart by the favor of the Lord of the Covenant. This people, in its entirety, is neither an abstraction (which would have to be considered "in itself," that is to say, apart from the concrete individuals) nor a personification (which would be an artificial device to reduce the multiplicity to a unity) nor a universal idea (which would exist only in the mind), but rather the very reality with which each individual identifies himself. The history of salvation is truly one, as is the nation. The history of the nation, in turn, is reflected in the history of the different individuals. At every moment the nation is present in its various members, which explains the tendency of the prophets to hypostatize the people as though they were dealing with one individual. Since Yahweh said to Sion: "You are my people" (Is. 51:16; cf. 10:24: "O my people who dwell in Sion"; also Is. 3:12), it is only natural for the Israelite prophets to describe the people under the figure of a single person.

Very often this figure is that of a woman, who appears sometimes as a fiancée, sometimes as an unfaithful wife, and sometimes as a mother. There is no doubt about the oneness of this figure, and the allegorical application to Israelite history is no less obvious.

The image of the "virgin Israel" (Jer. 18:13) or of the "daughter Sion" (Is. 1:8; 10:32; 16:1; 37:22; 52:5; 62:11; Jer. 4:31; 6:2, 23; 13:21; Amos 5:2; Mi. 1:13; 4:8, 10, 13; So. 3:14; Za. 2:14; 9:9) casts a bright light on the unity of the nation, particularly from the point of view of salvation. Other nations also are personified: the "virgin daughter Babylon," dethroned, and condemned to take millstones and grind flour (Is. 47:1; cf. Jer. 51:33) or the "virgin daughter of Egypt" who multiplies remedies in vain (Jer. 46:11; 19:24; Ex. 30:18) or "you (the daughter) that dwell in Dibon" (Jer. 48:18) or the "daughter of Edom (Lam. 4:21-22) or the "rebellious daughter" (Amon) (Jer. 49:4) or Sodom, "your sister Sodom." (Ez. 16:48) In all these cases we have in all probability more than a simple literary device; these different peoples are considered so much a unity by Yahweh and his prophets that they think of them as individuals.

The Israelite nation is first of all described under the image of a fiancée. Osee in particular makes use of this figure: "I will espouse you to me forever; I will espouse you in right and in justice, in love and in mercy; I will espouse you in fidelity, and you shall know the Lord." (Os. 2:21-22) The same imagery is found in other prophets. Jeremia puts the following in the mouth of Yahweh: "I remember the devotion of your youth, how you loved me as a bride, following me in the desert, in a land unsown." (Jer. 2:2) Ezechiel says in the name of Yahweh: "Yet I will remember the covenant I made with you when you were a girl, and I will set up an everlasting covenant with you." (Ez. 16:60)

Frequently the prophets accuse the "daughter of Sion," the fiancée, or the spouse of Yahweh, of infidelity and adultery. Isaia cries out: "How has she turned adulteress, the faithful city, so upright! Justice used to lodge within her, but now, murderers." (Is. 1:21) Jeremia expresses the divine chagrin: "Does a virgin forget her jewelry, a bride her sash? Yet my people have forgotten me days without number." (Jer. 2.32) The same prophet castigates his hearers with the following biting accusations: "Your adulteries, your neighings, your shameless prostitutions; on the hill in the highlands I see these horrible crimes of yours. Woe to you, Jerusalem, how long will it yet be before you become clean!" (Jer. 13:27)

The idolatry of the two kingdoms, Israel and Juda, is constantly depicted under the figure of sacred prostitution. According to Jeremia: "She (Israel) has gone up every high mountain and under every green tree she has played the harlot ... Her traitor sister Juda was not frightened; she too went off and played the harlot." (Jer. 3:6, 8) Ezechiel uses the same imagery in his allegory of the two sisters Ohola and Oholiba. (Ez. 23) Despite their realistic descriptions, the prophets realize very well that they are speaking to the community of "the house of Jacob," to "all the clans of the house of Israel" (Jer. 2:4), to "the descendants of the house of Israel." (Jer. 23:8) With the greatest ease Jeremia passes from the figure of "rebel Israel" (Jer. 3:11) to that of "rebellious children." (Jer. 3:14, 19, 22) The many individual sins constitute one single reality, since he is dealing with the people as an historical unity. Throughout its entire evolution, Israel remains the woman who is unfaithful to her lover. (Jer. 3:20)

Sometimes this historical evolution is described under the image of an unfaithful wife. Ez. 16 is remarkable from this point of view. Verses 1-14 are evidently an allusion to the reign of Solomon (cf. 3 K. 10); verses 15-25 describe the progressive decline (infant sacrifice: cf. 4 K. 16:3: Achaz; 4 K. 21:6: Manasses); verses 26-34 recall the various unfortunate alliances with Egypt (v. 26), with Assyria (v. 28; cf. 4 K. 16:7-18) or with the Neo-Babylonians (v. 29). Verses 35-52 chronicle the ignominious way in which Israel is handed over to foreigners. In verses 44-52 Samaria is compared to Gomorra, which was totally destroyed. Finally, verses 53-63 contrast the shameful past with the promise of a better future. Despite this easily recognizable course of a many sided evolution in the course of Israelite history, the prophets are very much conscious of the profound unity of the sinful nation. This becomes evident when one compares similar figures: for example, that of the poor wretch in whom "from the sole of the foot to the head there is no sound spot" and who is covered with "wound and sweat and a gaping gash, not drained, or bandaged, or eased with salve" (Is. 1:6, 8), or that of the man stalked by an avenging God in the *Book of Lamentations*. (3:1-9)

A third facet of the woman image that symbolizes the unity of Israel is that of motherhood. Under this figure of the "mother" the prophets also allude to infidelity, but especially to the conversion and the reestablishment of the people (especially after the exile).

Isaia castigates the sinners among his people in these words: "But you draw near, you sons of a sorceress, adulterous, wanton race!" (Is. 57:3; cf. 50:1; 51:18-20) More frequently, however, the figure of the mother in the Book of Isaia suggests the return of the exiles. Yahweh exhorts the people as follows: "Look about and see, they are all gathered and coming to you. As I live, says the Lord, you shall be arrayed with them all as with adornments, like a bride you shall fasten them on you." (Is. 49:18); "Raise a glad cry, you barren one, who did not bear, break forth in jubilant song, you who were not in labor, for more numerous are the children of the deserted wife than the children of her who has a husband, says the Lord." (Is. 54:1)

Jerusalem is exalted as the happy mother in this imposing description: "Raise your eyes and look about; they all gather and come to you; your sons come from afar, and your daughters in the arms of their nurses. Then you shall be radiant at what you see, your heart shall throb and overflow." (Is. 60:4-5); "Can a country be brought forth in one day, or a nation be born in a single moment? Yet Sion is scarcely in labor when she gives birth to her children." (Is. 66:8) In a passage of the Prophet Baruch, Sion speaks to her "children": "Fear not, my children; call upon God . . . With mourning and lament I sent you forth, but God will give you back to me with enduring gladness and joy." (Bar. 4:21, 23) Evidence that the figure of the mother is applied to Israel lies in the change from the plural to the singular in the following passage: "My children, bear patiently the anger that has come from God upon *you* (plural), *your* (singular) enemies have persecuted *you* (singular), and *you* (singular) will soon see their destruction and trample upon their necks." (Bar. 4:25)

The prophets sometimes place similar figures side by side. Isaia announces to "the mother of Sion": "Your people shall all be just, they shall always possess the land, they, *the bud of my planting,* my handiwork to show my glory." (Is. 60:21) Such a mixture of figures is particularly observable in the *Book of Lamentations.*

A lonely widow (Lam. 1:1), "a princess . . . made a toiling slave" (Lam. 1:1), Jerusalem "weeps bitterly by night, tears upon her cheeks, with no one to console her." (Lam. 1:2) "Daughter Sion" (Lam. 1:6; 2:1, 4, 8, 13, 18; 4:22), "daughter Juda" (Lam. 1:15; 2:2, 5), "daughter Jerusalem" (Lam. 2:13, 15), or "daughter of my people" (Lam 2:11; 4:6, 10) represents a community which has its priests (Lam. 1:4, 19; 2:6, 20; 4:13), its virgins (Lam. 1:4, 18; 2:10, 21), its princes, (Lam. 1:6), its elders (Lam. 1:19; 2:10), its sanctuary (Lam. 1:10; 2:7, 20), and its prophets. (Lam. 2:9, 14, 20; 4:13) Despite this great diversity of members, Jerusalem constitutes an indissoluble unity: "Jerusalem is defiled; all who esteemed her think her vile now that they see her nakedness; she herself groans and turns away." (Lam. 1:8)

The entire population of the beseiged city speaks as one: "Look, O Lord, upon my distress: all within me is ferment, my heart recoils within me from my monstrous rebellion." (Lam. 1:20 cf. 2:11) "My groans are many, and I am sick at heart." (Lam. 1:22; cf. 5:15, 17: "The joy of our hearts has ceased . . . Over this *our* hearts are sick, at this our eyes grow dim.") The passers-by are astonished and "hiss and wag their heads over daughter Jerusalem: 'Is this the all-beautiful city, the joy of the whole earth?'" (Dam. 2:15) The author of Lamentations urges the stricken city: "Cry out to the Lord: moan, O daughter Sion! Let your tears flow like a torrent day and night; let there be no respite for you, no repose for your eyes." (Lam. 2:18) This striking description of a profound sorrow apparently aims at emphasizing that the entire population has been afflicted and that it forms one single corporate entity.

This corporate characteristic explains the shift from the singular "the virgin of Jerusalem" to the corporate "we": "Let us search and examine *our* ways . . . Let us reach out *our* hearts toward God in heaven! . . . *We* have sinned and rebelled." (Lam. 3: 40-41) The poet speaks of "Sion's precious sons" in the plural (Lam. 4:2) but immediately shifts to the singular: "The punish-

ment of the daughter of my people is greater than the penalty
of Sodom." (Lam. 4:6) Possibly in certain passages an individual
is complaining (as in 3:1: "I am a man who knows affliction from
the rod of his anger"), but the poet shifts almost imperceptibly
from his own personal suffering to the sufferings of the people,
because his own "represents," or better yet, sums up the sufferings of the community.

4. *The Sapiential Books*

Although they are marked by individualism, the sapiential
books reveal the same ideas about the concrete personification of
the people in a single individual. This is particularly discernible
in the "I of the psalms" which we will speak of in the following
chapter. The corporate role of the person who, in the singular,
prays for all the members of the community follows very clearly
from the abrupt shift, frequently repeated, from the singular to
the plural. In verse 6 the author of psalm 43 praises God: "Our
foes through you *we* struck down; through your name we trampled
down *our* adversaries." In the very next verse the "we" is
changed to "I": "For not in *my* bow did *I* trust, nor did *my*
sword save *me.*" The very next verse returns to the plural: "But
you saved *us* from *our foes.*" The singular reappears again in verse
16: "All the day *my* disgrace is before *me,* and shame covers *my*
face." Almost immediately (v. 18) the plural returns: "All this
has come upon *us.*" Manifestly the poet conceives of the community as having the traits of a single person, who is the concrete
symbol of the community's common lot. The one praying the
Psalm feels himself identified with the concrete totality of his
people, or at least completely involved in its common destiny.

Moreover, the psalms borrow certain prophetic images, which
we spoke of before, and which reveal a mode of corporate
thinking. The community is pictured under the figure of the vine
(Ps. 79:9), one and many at the same time, thanks to a single
life; or as the "virgin daughter of Sion."[56] Ps. 9:15; 72: 28

---

56   The term is also applicable to pagan nations; cf. Ps. 136:8: "O
     daughter of Babylon."

LXX) The delicate figure of the infant resting in the arms of its mother symbolizes the confidence of the people in Yahweh: "Nay rather, I have stilled and quieted my soul like a weaned child. O Israel, hope in the Lord." (Ps. 130:2-3). The exiles "by the streams of Babylon" who have no desire to rejoice: "How could we sing a song of the Lord in a foreign land?" (Ps. 136:4) pour out their bitter sorrow in terms of personal lament: "If I forget you, Jerusalem, may *my* right hand be forgotten! May *my* tongue cleave to *my* palate if I remember you not." (Ps. 136:5-7)

Other than in the psalms, the sapiential books have only one or the other example which pictures the community under the traits of an individual person. *Sirach* speaks of the figure of the first born: "Show mercy to the people called by your name: Israel, whom you named your first-born." (Sir. 36:11) The last part of the quotation indicates a profound awareness of the reality of the figure: God "has made" Israel His first-born, that is to say, He treats her as His favorite son.

THE NINTH THEME

The Legal "Thou"

We find an interesting phenomenon in the legal prescriptions, especially in the hortatory style of *Deuteronomy*. Since the laws are addressed to the entire nation we would expect to find the plural pronoun "you." As a matter of fact, there is a continual shifting from the plural to the singular person. (The singular "thou" of the legal texts).

1. *The Laws of the Exodus*

Moses instructs the people concerning the feast of Azymes: "This day of your (plural) departure is in the ninth of Abib. Therefore, it is in this month that you (singular) must celebrate this rite, after the Lord, your God, has brought you (singular) into the land of the Chanaanites." (Ex. 13:4-5) The use of the

singular is sometimes explained by the fact that it is the father
of the family who must in the last analysis observe the law.[57]
(Ex. 13:10) But we must note that the text refers to both father
and son: "On this day you shall explain to your son, this is because of what the Lord did for *me* when I came out of Egypt."
(Ex. 13:8) For "with a strong hand the Lord brought *you* (singular) out of Egypt." (Ex. 13:9) Evidently the "me" and the
"you" refer to the entire community, which in some way is summed
up in the individual Israelite who fulfills the rite in question.

An apparently awkward gloss may throw some light on the
basis of this thought. Regarding the first born it is written: "When
the Lord, your God, has brought you (singular) into the land
of the Chanaanites which [*now the gloss:* he swore to you (singular) and your (plural) fathers] he would give you (singular),
you shall dedicate to the Lord every son that opens the womb;
and all the male firstlings of your animals shall belong to the
Lord." (Ex. 13:11-12) The gloss correctly interprets the singular
"you" of the legal formula as a corporate "you."

The covenant Code is filled with prescriptions which shift
with the greatest ease from the singular to the plural: "Neither
gods of silver nor gods of gold shall you (plural) make for yourselves. An altar of earth you (singular) shall make for me."

---

57 According to H. Cazelles, *Etudes sur le Code de l'Alliance*, Paris,
    1946, 125 n. "the plural formulas" would have a more "theological"
    character than the singular formulas: "The commandments in the
    singular are more cultic than theological." We might point out that in
    cult the individual is more "corporate" than in secular life.—With
    good reason, N. A. Dahl, *Das Volk Gottes. Eine Untersuchung zum
    Kirchenbewusstsein des Urchristentums*, Oslo, 1941, 141, draws at-
    tention to the fact that "every Israelite is a representative of Israel,"
    and he sees therein an "appreciation of the individual as a representa-
    tive of Israel."—Regarding the more or less cultic act of Dt. 26:4-11,
    W. Zimmerli, *Das Alte Testament als Anrede*, 1956, 11 makes the
    the following remarks, which seem very pertinent: "Here the peasant
    of later Israelite times enters the sanctuary with the basket of
    harvest fruits before the altar of his God, and relates in the presence
    of his God the events of the exit and re-entry into the country as his
    very own personal history, and he knows that he is called to answer
    for it."

(Ex. 20:23-24) This shift cannot be explained by a difference of origin or *Sitz im Leben,* for often the change of pronouns takes place in the same law: "You (singular) shall not molest or oppose an alien, for you (plural) were once aliens yourselves in the land of Egypt." (Ex. 22:20; 23:9) "You (plural) shall not wrong any widow or orphan. If ever you (singular) wrong them and they cry out to me, I will surely hear their cry." (Ex. 22:21-22; cf. Ex. 23:25) Sometimes the mention of the plural may be a later addition. Such is probably the case in the law of Ex. 22:24: "If you (singular) lend money to one of your poor neighbors among my people, you (singular) shall not act like an extortioner toward him by demanding interest from him." [For the latter part the French has "You (plural) must not charge him any interest."] In any case the last part of the quotation is an undeniable interpretation of the initial "you" in the collective sense. Contrariwise, the return to a singular "you" seems to imply a more pronounced nuance of personalism: "Give (plural) heed to all that I have told you. Never mention (plural) the name of any other God; it shall not be heard from your (singular) lips." (Ex. 23:13)

2. *Deuteronomy*

In taking up the Deuteronomic legislation we notice a similar phenomenon. In exhortations other than the laws properly so called we frequently find formulas such as the following: "Do (plural) what is right and good in the sight of the Lord, that you may prosper, and may enter in and possess the good land which the Lord promised on oath to your (singular) fathers, thrusting all your (singular) enemies out of your way." (Dt. 6:18-19) "The wrath of the Lord would flare up against you (plural) and quickly destroy you (singular)." (Dt. 7:4) "You are a people sacred to the Lord, your God; he has chosen you (singular) from all the nations on the face of the earth. It was not because you are the largest of all nations that the Lord set his heart on you (plural) and chose you (plural). (Dt. 7:6-7)

There is no good reason to accept the hypothesis proposed by H. Cazelles about the Covenant Code; namely, that the singular "you" refers to ritual practices which one individual can perform. The ritual context, as a matter of fact, is not always present;

and even where it is plainly present, the attention of the sacred
writer is concerned more with the collective aspect of the precept
than with its cultic aspect. The singular pronoun "you" has a
corporate aspect, as its alternation with the obviously collective
plural "you" in the following cultic sentences shows: "But if you
(singular) forget the Lord, your (singular) God, and follow
other gods, serving and worshipping them, I forewarn you (plural)
this day that you (plural) will perish utterly." (Dt. 8:19) "You
(singular) must doom them all—the Hethites, Hevites and Jebu-
sites . . ., lest they teach you (plural) to make any such abominable
offerings as they make to their gods, and you (plural) thus sin
against the Lord, your (plural) God." (Dt. 20:17)

Even when there is no allusion to the fundamental truth:
"You (singular) are a people sacred to the Lord, your (singular)
God" (Dt. 14:2, 21), the author of *Deuteronomy* still incorporates
the entire Chosen People in a singular "you" which expands into
a corporate "you" in the plural. This shift from the singular "you"
to the plural "you" often takes place in the same sentence: "The
land which you (singular) are to enter and occupy is not like
the land of Egypt from which you (plural) have come." (Dt. 11:
10) "On the day you (plural) cross the Jordan into the land
which the Lord, your (singular) God, is giving you (singular)."
(Dt. 27:2) Sometimes even the grammatical construction is
faulty, as in the following: "Teach them to your children, speaking
of them at home and abroad." (The French translation has
"teach" in the plural and the possessive pronoun referring to the
"home" in the singular.) (Dt. 11:19)

We can conclude that in the *Book of Deuteronomy* the singular
pronoun "you" frequently has a collective meaning; it applies
to the entire community of the "children of Israel." Further
evidence is to be found in two typical passages of Chapter 28.

The threats which Moses levels against the people if they are
unfaithful to Yahweh are very clear: "Should there be any
kind of sickness or calamity not mentioned in this Book of the
Law, that too the Lord will bring upon you (singular) until you
(singular)are destroyed. Of you (plural) who were numerous
as the stars in the sky, only a few will be left." (Dt. 28:61-62)
The end of the list of threats is no less formal: "The Lord will
send you (singular) back in galleys to Egypt, to the region

I told you (singular) that you (singular) were never to see again; and there you (plural) will offer yourselves (plural) for sale to your (singular) enemies as male and female slaves." (Dt. 28:68) There can be no doubt: the singular "you" refers to the entire nation, which will be reduced to a restricted number of individuals: "He (the Lord) will establish you (singular) as a people sacred to himself." (Dt. 28:9; 29:12)

In the use of the singular "you" we become vividly aware of the idea of "corporate personality," according to which the nation, while being made up of many individuals, remains nonetheless profoundly one. The divine Covenant has a very definite end in view: "That you (plural) may enter into the covenant of the Lord, your (singular) God . . . so that he may now establish you (singular) as his people and he may be your (singular) God, as he promised to you (singular) and as he swore to your (singular) fathers Abraham, Isaac and Jacob." (Dt. 29:11-12)

3. *The Priestly Code*

The priestly code differs very little from the Covenant Code or the Deuteronomic Code in this regard. In it we also find the sudden shifts in the use of pronouns from the singular "you" to the plural "you."

Regarding the Sabbath law it prescribes: "When you (plural) enter the land that I am giving you (plural), let the land, too, keep a sabbath for the Lord. For six years you (singular) may sow your field, and for six years prune your vineyard, gathering in their produce." (Lv. 25:2-3) We cannot say that here the singular pronoun is explained by the fact that the precept must be fulfilled by the individuals who possess the fields, because the same use of pronouns is employed for liturgical celebrations which are without a doubt collective. For example, here is a regulation regarding the Jubilee Year: "Seven weeks of years shall you (singular) count . . . Then, on the tenth day of the seventh month let (plural)the trumpet resound." (Lv. 25:8-9) Sometimes the individual is rather explicitly designated by the addition of the pronoun "every one:" "In this year of Jubilee, then, *every one of you* shall return to his own property. Therefore, when you (singular) sell any land to your (singular) neighbor or buy any from him, do not deal unfairly." (Lv. 25:13-14)

From all that has been said, we can conclude without a doubt that the idea of "corporate personality," both secondary and primary, both vertical and horizontal, is a part of the very warp and woof of the Old Testament.[58] If anyone takes the trouble to read the Old Testament texts in this corporate frame of reference, where the individual is perceived with his collective overtones, he is morally sure of reading them in a correct perspective.

Without a doubt we can say that the law of contradiction can never be abrogated, and that, in the last analysis, the individual is never identified with the group in a static or unchangeable way. We can assert, at the very least, that the term "corporate personality" can be considered as a concise expression to describe in summary fashion the solidarity which exists between the individual and the community. But truth demands that we add that the idea of "corporate personality" seen in a realistic and concrete perspective, enhances many biblical passages and gives them an undeniable fullness. Having demonstrated this in a general way, it now remains to apply the idea to six particular cases.

58   H. H. Rowley, *The Servant of the Lord*, 1954[2], 38-39 makes this excellent comment: "Wheeler Robinson was not the first scholar to call attention to this, but amongst English-speaking persons his name is most closely associated with it, and he has been the most persistent advocate of this key to much Old Testament thought."

3

Concrete Applications of the Idea of "Corporate Personality"

A. *ADAM*

In Adam, the common father of mankind, we have a typical example of the theme "the ancestor and his descendants." After recalling the general implications of the "theme of the ancestor," we will examine in greater detail the meaning of the expressions "Adam" and "the children of Adam," in order to apply them to the famous pericope of the *Epistle to the Romans* in which "Adam" appears as the "type" of Christ. (Rom. 5:12-21)

1. *The Israelite Conception of the Ancestor*

In Hebrew thought the tribe was the sum total of the descendants of one same ancestor. Very often this common ancestor has the same name as the tribe. Israel is the patriarch but also the people descendant from him,[1] that is to say, the twelve tribes organized as an amphictyony.[2] It is evident from some

---

1 L. Rost, *Israel bei den Propheten* (*BWANT* IV, 19), Stuttgart, 1937, 2. In Gn. 47:27 there is no way of knowing whether the words: "Now Israel dwelt in Egypt" refer to the patriarch or to the people; the plural which follows: "They acquired property there" seems to indicate that it is question of the people, but the people are the patriarch.—Cf. the same assimilation in Bar. 2:15: "Israel and his descendants bear your name."—The mention of "loins" (in the French) (Gn. 35:11; 46:25) does not prove *per se* the physical reality of the posterity.

2 G. Von Rad, in *ThW III*, 357, remarks that "in any case, Israel has been from the very beginning a sacral concept; it signifies the totality

texts that strict consanguinity between the "Israelites" and the Israelite ancestor is not always necessary.[3] To each individual tribe it is clear "that it (strict consanguinity) was a theory," for the tribe consisted in "a temporary confederation of previous social groups."[4] The consanguinity which is claimed "is in many cases no more than theoretic and symbolic. In fact, the relationship is a mystic bond, a community of soul brought about by certain rites of fraternization."[5]

When we examine the conditions demanded by *Deuteronomy* for the aggregation of a non-Israelite into the community of the Chosen People (Dt. 23:2-24:9), we realize immediately that the exclusion of certain foreigners is not based on political or racial motives but on religious and cultic considerations.[6] The feeling

of all those who have been chosen by Yahweh and who are united to carry on the cult of Yahweh."—O. Eissfeldt, *Der Gottesknecht*, p. 22, wishes to explain the formula *'āsāh nebālāh beyisrā'el* (Gn. 34: 7; Dt. 22:21; Jos. 7:15; Jg. 20.6; Jer. 29:23) as "to do evil to the defender of right and of morality, that is say, to the ancestor (Jacob-Israel), who is present and incorporate in each generation."

3   N. A. Dahl, *Das Volk Gottes. Eine Untersuchung zum Kirchenbe-wusstsein des Urchristentums*, Oslo, 1941, 4: Israel is not "the entire bodily posterity of the forefathers; whoever shares in the Israelite character and in the blessing of the patriarchs belongs to Israel ... Even foreign people (can) be accepted into Israel if they join the Israelite character."

4   A. Lods, *Israel des origines au milieu du VIIIe siècle*, 1930, 224: "Artificial brotherhood, ordinarily brought about by the exchange of blood, was considered as genuinely equivalent to natural relationship."

5   A. Causse, *Du groupe ethnique à la communauté religieuse. Le problème sociologique de la religion d'Israël*, Paris, 1937, 23.

6   J. Hempel, *Das Ethos des AT*, l.c., 78. Compare with the statement of 1 Mc. 12:21 which, at first sight, is preplexing: "It is found in writing concerning the Spartans and the Jews, that they are brethren, and that they are of the stock of Abraham." This text proves that a difference of race is not an absolute obstacle against the introduction into the assembly of Yahweh of an individual not born of Abraham.— A. Lods, *Les antécédents de la notion d'Eglise en Israël et dans le*

of belonging which animates "the posterity of Abraham" (Ne. 9:2) and which shines forth from the statements: "We are the children of Abraham" (Jn. 8:33) or "We have Abraham for our father" (Mt. 3:9; cf. Jn. 8:39), is not based on "historical" descent through a chain of successive generations from the patriarch Abraham.[7] For, to be "the son of Abraham" implies first of all to "do the works of Abraham." (Jn. 8:39) The ancestor "according to the flesh" (Rom. 4:1) could have "children" who were not of the flesh but were "children of the promise." (Rom. 8:9) The true "children of Abraham" are those who share in the faith of the patriarch (Gal. 3:7), for "he (Abraham) received the sign of circumcision . . . in order that he may be the father of all who, while uncircumcised, believed, . . . and the father of the circumcised, not of those merely who are circumcised, but also of those who follow in the steps of the faith that was our father Abraham's while yet uncircumcised." (Rom. 4:11-12)

The most important characteristic in the figure of the patriarch is that he bears within himself the "people" which "descends" from him.[8] In the language of the primitives we would say that he is *par excellence* "a reservior and a source of *mana*."[9] According to biblical mentality we would have to say that God, the personal God of the Covenant, deals with the race through the intermediary of the ancestor. To call Abraham is to call the entire race which descends from him. (Gn. 12:2) The holy nation knows itself chosen and predestined in the corporate personality of the ancient patriarch.[10]

judaïsme, 1939, 7-50, p. 41, says that the situation described in Esd. 2:59-63 (cf. Esd. 9:10; Ne. 92) is "in disagreement with all Israelite antiquity."

7   K. Galling, *Die Erwählungstraditionen Israels*, ZAW Bhft 48, Giessen, 1928, 2.

8   As we have already noted, the Hebrew word for "people" (*'am*) designates a group of similar beings (cf. Pr. 30:25: "Ants—a species not strong," or Jl. 2:2: "a people numerous and mighty!" or groups of human beings having a common purpose. (cf. 3 K. 20:15: "he mustered after them the people"). The emphasis is on the identity of spirit or attitude, rather than on a common origin.

9   L. Lévy-Bruhl, *L'âme primitive*, Paris, 1927, 51.

10 T. W. Manson, *The Son of Man*, in *BJRL* 1949-50, 171-193, p. 182

It would certainly be incorrect to interpret the words "your father Abraham" (Jos. 24:2), or "children of the race of Abraham" (Ac. 13:26) or "the offspring of Abraham" (Is. 41:8; cf. Jn. 8:37, 39, 56) as stripped of all historical value in the sense that all corporal descent would be excluded and the words would refer only to "the spiritual unity of the race." What must be noted is that the idea of "descent" includes not only a chain of physical generations but also other groups of human beings having no blood relationship with Abraham but aggregated to him artificially. Similarly Jacob-Israel is certainly the genealogical ancestor in the strict sense of a certain number of "children of Israel," [11] but we must remember that the "children of Israel" include many others who are not physically descended from the patriarch. The formula "children of Israel" is a "traditional simplification," [12] which must be interpreted with great care.[13]

2. *The Meaning of the Terms "Race," "To Beget," and "Child"*

We know that the Hebrew expressions which refer to physical birth ("race," "to beget," "child") admit of many meanings which are sometimes far removed from the idea of physical generation properly so called.

quotes *Berésith rabba* 44, 27a, where Is. 41:8 is explained as follows: "I have chosen you (in Abraham), and I have not rejected you, in Abraham."

11   M. Noth, *Das System der Zwölf Stämme Israels* BWANT IV, 1), Stuttgart, 1930, 91 is of the opinion that "the personification of Israel and the transfer of this title to the individual and distinguished person of Jacob are the fruit of a rather late *saga* which attempts to connect the history of the patriarchs with the history of the Israelite tribes." We might well ask if the genealogical bond between the three patriarchs and the "twelve tribes" is not much more "historical" than M. Noth thinks. In any case, the tradition is long and strong.

12   G. E. Wright, *The Biblical Doctrine of Man in Society*, London, 1954, 49.

13   Compare Est. 9:27: "The Jews took upon themselves and their seed, and upon all that had a mind to be joined to their religion, so that it should be lawful for none to pass these days without solemnity (days of Phurim)." Cf. Est. 9:31: "by themselves and by their seed."

The "seed" (*zèra'*) of the serpent in Gn. 3:15 is certainly not to be interpreted in the physical sense any more than the term "brood of vipers" in Mt. 3:7. Frequently the word *zèra'* has an obviously metaphorical meaning. "Aaron and his sons" (*la "semence d' Aaron"*) (Ex. 28:43; 30:21; Lv. 21:17; 22:3-4; Nm. 17:5) as well as the "line of Sadoc" (Ez. 43:19) refer to priests in general. (Cf. 1 Mc. 7:14) The "descendants of Jacob" (Ps. 21: 24; Is. 45:19; Jer. 33:26; cf. Is. 29:23) are the Chosen People who "fear the Lord." (Ps. 21:24) The people of Israel (*"race d' Israel"*) in Jer. 30:10 are the captives who belong to the Chosen People. The descendants of the suffering man in psalm 21, who will serve the Lord, are certainly not physical descendants— particularly not if we hold the psalm to be directly messianic.[14]

When applied to God the metaphor is most evident. Sinners in Israel make up the "sinful nation, . . . evil race" of Yahweh. (Is. 1:4) In Is. 57:3 LXX the sinful people are called "you sons of a sorceress, adulterous, wanton race!"[15] Similarly when the *Book of Isaia* speaks of the people as "rebellious children, a worthless race" (Is. 57:4: *yildé pèsa'*), there can be no doubt that a metaphor is being used. The figure of the "descendants of Israel" (Is. 43:5: "From the east I will bring back your descendants"; cf. Is. 44:3; 45:25; 48:19; 54:3; Jer. 31:36, 37; 46:27) passes imperceptibly from the patriarch Jacob to the nation personified: "the holy people and blameless race." (Wis. 10:15)

The terms *yālid or hôlîd bén* ("to beget a son") do not necessarily imply the idea of carnal generation. We have spoken before of the prophetic imagery of Sion begetting children (Is. 66:8) or of Jerusalem who "has no one to guide her of all the sons she bore" (Is. 51:18) or of the same city begetting sons to Yahweh (Ez. 16:20) or of Juda (Oholiba) and of Samaria (Ohola) begetting sons and daughters for the same national God. (Ez. 23:34, 37) In the preceding pages we have also alluded to the fact that the genealogies use the term "to beget" for all sorts of relationships, even for commercial relationships: Elam,

---

14 The same thing can be said about the "posterity" of the suffering Servant of Yahweh (Is. 53:10).

15 In the opposite sense, Zacharia speaks of "the seedtime of peace." (Za. 8:12)

Assur, and Aram are begotten by Sem (Gn. 10:21); Mesraim begets Caphthorim (Crete) "from whom the Philistines sprang" (Gn. 10:13; 1 Par. 1:11); Chanaan becomes the father of Sidon (a city). (Gn. 10:15; 1 Par. 1:13) All these expressions are metaphors used to express a more or less close association. The metaphor becomes even more apparent in the following cases: when Jephte is spoken of as being begotten by Galaad (a geographical location) (Jg. 11:1; cf. Nm. 26:29-34) or when Yahweh is said to have begotten the king of psalm 2:7, or when Yahweh is called "the Rock that begot you." (Dt. 32:18)

What is more, even if the word *yālad* (to beget) is used to mean generation, the emphasis is on the transfer of juridical titles rather than on the physical dependence. The word *bén* "son" signifies "heir" rather than a "physical son." The complaint of Abraham: "O Lord God .... I am childless" is paraphrased immediately by: "To me you have given no descendants; the slave born in my house will be my *heir*." (Gn. 15:2-3) The true son is the one who will inherit. Sara, wishing to get rid of Ismael, says to Abraham: "Cast out this slave-girl with her son; for the son of this slave-girl shall not be *heir* with my *son* Isaac." (Gn. 21:10) The connotation of "heir" which the word *bén* takes on is rather evident in this text from *Jeremia*: "Has Israel no sons? Has he no heir?" (Jer. 49:1) In *Proverbs* 17:2 "an intelligent servant" assumes the role of a son in this sense that he "will share the inheritance with the brothers." The "son of Neomi" (Rt. 4:17) really is the son of Ruth (Rt. 4:13), but he is described as belonging to the line of Neomi and as being her heir. The desire to furnish an heir to a man who has died childless is the basis of the levirate law. (Gn. 38:3-10; Dt. 25:5) To die "without children" (that is, without heirs) is considered a divine punishment. (Nm. 3:4; 27:3; 4 K. 1:17) Sterility is a great misfortune for a woman because she is deprived of heirs and defenders. (Jg. 13:2, 5, 7, 24; 1 K. 1:20; 4 K. 4:14) Contrariwise, to have begotten a son is a consolation for a dying mother (1 K. 4:20) because she has an heir.[16] Further evidence for the significance of hereditary succession is found in certain expressions: "The

16 Normally it is the "son" who is the heir, to the exclusion of the daughter. (Cf. Nm. 27:4, 8)

good man leaves an inheritance to his children's children" (Pr. 13:22), "the children of saints" (Tob. 2:18; 8:5), and the Pauline passage in which it is said of the Christians: "if we are sons, we are heirs also."[17] (Rom. 8:17; Gal. 3:29; 4:7)

Regarding the term *bén*, we have already seen that besides the meanings of "physical son," or rather, "successor of heredity" and one who continues another in time (Ex. 10:2; 13:8; Dt. 5: 25; 6:2; 2 K. 18:18; Ps. 73:6-7) there are other shades of meaning, all of which express in some way or other that a particular person or being belongs to a particular group.[18]

The "sons of God" (Gn. 6:2) are beings living familiarly with God, but there is no question at all of physical sonship.[19] Ordinarily the term refers to the celestial beings (Jb. 1:6; 2:1; Ps. 28: 1-2; 88:7; Pr. 30:4; Dn. 3:25) or even to the stars (Jb. 38:7) But it can also refer to the people and to upright men (Dt. 14:1, Sir. 4:10 LXX),[20] or to judges (Ps. 81:1; cf. v. 6: "sons of the Most High"; Sir. 4:11 Vg.)

17 In case of adoption, the individual is treated "as a son," having the right to inherit. (Ex. 2:10) Certain texts speak of God as the adopting father; Yahweh corrects His people "as a man disciplines his son" (Dt. 8:5; cf. Dt. 1:31; Pr. 3:12; Jer. 31:20); He adopts kings: "I will be to him a father, and he shall be to me a son." (2 K. 7:14; 1 Par. 17:13; 22:10; 28:6; Ps. 79:16) Sometimes the word "as" is missing; for example, in Is. 1:2 where Yahweh says: "*Sons* I have raised and reared, but they have disowned me!"; cf. also Is. 30:1; Jer. 3:14,22: "rebellious children"; Is. 30:9: "deceitful children"; Is. 63:8: "children who are not disloyal"; Is. 43:6; 45:11: "*my* children"; Ex. 4:22-23: "Israel is my son, my first-born"; Dt. 32:20: "sons with no loyalty in them"; Ps. 72:15: "the fellowship of your children"; Os. 11:1.
18 Cf. chap. II, par. B.
19 Compare with the Ugaritic texts in which *bn il* means "an individual god" or "gods." Cf. D. H. Gordon, *Ugaritic Literature,* Rome, 1949, 132: *bn il* (in Hebrew: *bené-'ēlim*); or C. H. Gordon, *Ugaritic Handbook,* Rome, 1947, 129: *ab bn il* ("the father of the gods"); 157: *mphrt bn il* ("the assembly of the gods"); 138: *bn ilm mt* ("the god Mot").
20 Cf. A. Schollmeyer, *Sumerisch-babylonische Hymnen und Gebete an Schamasch,* Paderborn, 1912, 52, 1.14: *amelu mar ilišu:* "a man, son of his god." (Text CTXVII, pl. 21, ll. 64-67)

The inhabitants of a region or of a city are habitually grouped under the term "sons of . . .," the ancestor often being fictitious or symbolical. Sometimes simply the geographic name itself is used, which expresses a concrete whole. Thus we have "the children of Bethlehem" (Esd. 2:21; Ne. 7:26; Jer. 6:1), "the children of Jericho" (Esd. 2:34; Ne. 7:37), "the children of Jerusalem" (Ps. 50:18; 53:13; 59:4; Jer. 5:7; Jl. 4:6),[21] "the sons of Sion" (Ps. 146:13; 148:2; Is. 49:22, 25; Jer. 30:20; Jl. 2:3; Za. 9:13), "the children of Samaria."[22] (Ez. 23:10) In other places the idea of the ancestor is more pronounced, as when we speak of "the children of Edom" (Ps. 136:7), "the children of Esau" (Dt. 2:4, 12, 22, 39; Jud. 7:8), "the children of Lot" (Dt. 2:19; Jg. 3:13), "the children of Heth" (Gn. 23:3, 5, 7, 10, 16, 20; 25:10), "the sons of Hemor, the father of Sichem" (Gn. 33:19; 34:2), "the descendants of Seir the Horrite" (Gn. 36:20; 2 Par. 25:11), or "the descendants of Enac" (Nm. 13:33; Jos. 15:14; Jg. 1:20).

Foreigners are called the "sons of travel" (*"fils de la pérégrinité"*) (*bené nékār*) (Gn. 17:12, 27; Ex. 22:43; Lv. 22:25; Ez. 44:7-9; Ps. 17:46; 143:7, 11; Is. 56:3; 60:10; 62:8), in contrast to "sons of the home," (*"fils de la maison"*) that is to say, those belonging to the family (for example, the slaves born in the home: Gn. 15:3; Co. 2:7) or "sons of my people" (that is to say, my countrymen: cf. Gn. 23:11; Lv. 19:18: "the sons

21 Compare with the "daughters of Jerusalem" (Ct. 1:5; 2:7; 3:5,10; 5:8,16; 8:4) the "daughters of Chanaan" (Gn. 28:1,6,8; 36:2), the "daughters of Moab" (Nm. 25:1), or the "daughters of the nations" Ez. 32: 16,18).

22 The subjects of foreign nations are also called "children of this or that region or city." For example, "children of Eden" (4 K. 19:12; Is. 37:12), "children of Egypt" (Ez. 16:21), "children of Greece" (Za. 9:13), "children of Ethiopia" (Amos. 9:7), "children of the East" (Gn. 29:1; Nm. 1:3; 3 K. 5:10; Is. 11:14; Ez. 25:4), "children of Noph" (Jer. 2:16), "children of Assyria" (Ez. 16:28; 23:7), "children of Babylon" (Ez. 23:15), "daughters of Babylon" (Ps. 136:8), "daughters of Tharsis" (Is. 23:10). (In many cases the new C.C.D. translation does not preserve the same idiom as the French translation.)

of your people"; Ex. 3:11; 33:2; 37:18; Jg. 11:5; 14:16, 17; 1 Mac. 6:24, Is. 22:4; Jer. 4:11 etc.).

Besides indicating membership in a geographic or national group, the term *bén* designates a number of other varied relationships. It may indicate a community of life such as in the stereotyped expression "children of aliens" (Lv. 25:45: *bené tôs vebîn*) to designate those who participate in a restricted way in the life of the Israelite people. Those belonging to a clan are called "children of the clan" (Nm. 36:3 Jer. 35:5, 18: the Rechabites); the "sons of the prophets" are members of the groups of professional prophets. (3 K. 20:35; 4 K. 2:3, 5, 7, 15; 4:1, 38; 5:22; 6:1; 9:1; Amos 7:14)

Very often the term *bén* is used in figurative expressions which stress the idea of relationship: a vale is spoken of as "son of oil," that is to say "fertile." (Is. 5:1) Lucifer, the morning star is called "son of the dawn." (Is. 14:12) The "children of the kingdom" (Bar. 5:6; cf. Mt. 8:12) are the heirs of the kingdom. The relationship indicated by the word "son" is sometimes very vague. The rebellious are spoken of as "sons of rebels" (Nm. 17:25); a person who deserves stripes is called "the son of striking" (*"fils du frapper"*) (Dt. 25:2; *bèn makkôt*); scoundrels are called "sons of Belial." (Dt. 13: 13; 1 K. 2:12; 10:27; 25:17; 3 K. 21:10, 13; 2 Par. 13:7) Prisoners are "sons of captivity" (Esd. 4:1), the brave are "sons of power" (Jg. 21:1; 1 K. 18:17; 2 K. 2:7; 3 K. 1:52; 4 K. 2:16; 2 Par. 17:7; 1 Mac. 3:58), evildoers are called the "sons of iniquity" (2 K. 3:34; 7:10; Os. 10:9; Ps. 88: 23; Sir. 16:1), hostages are "sons of pawning" (4 K. 14:14: *ta' arûbôt*), groups of plunderers are called "sons of the troop."[23] (2 Par. 25:13; Mi. 5:1) In the same way the equivalent feminine

23 Examples are numerous. "Children of the threshing-floor" are those who have been trampled on on the threshing-floor (Is. 21:10); "children of your sterility (*šikkûlaik*)" are the individuals thought lost (Is. 49:20); "children whom you cherish" (Mi. 1:16); "the two sons of oil" are those who have received an anointing (Za. 4:14); a "son of the night" is a tree sprung up over night (Jon. 4:10); arrows are "the children of the bow" (Jb. 41:20) or "daughters of the quiver" (Lam. 3:13); those doomed to death are "the children of death" (Ps. 78:11; 101:21).

term "daughter of" is used to express all sorts of meanings: the
satellites of a city-state are simply its "daughters." (Nm. 21:25;
Jos. 15:47; Jg. 1:27; 1 Par. 7:28; 2 Par. 13:19; Ez. 26:6; Jer.
49:2; Ne. 11:25; 1 Mac. 5:8, etc.) The pupil of the eye is "the
daughter of the eye" (Ps. 16:8) as are tears (Lam. 2:18), whereas
songs are "daughters of song." (Co. 12:4)

In all the preceding examples the terms "son" or "daughter"
imply a certain individuation of the species which is concretized
in a special situation. Sometimes one's attention is specifically
drawn to this individuation. A priest, for example, is "a son of
a priest" (Esd. 2:61; 7:7; 8:15; 10:18; Ne. 12:35; 1 Par. 9:30);
a layman is "a son of the people" (2 Par. 35:5, 7; 2,13); a noble
is "a son of a noble" (Co. 10:27); a king is "a son of a king"
(Ps. 71:1); a bull is "a son of a bull." [24] (Gn. 18:1; Lv. 9:2;
Nm. 7:15; 2 Par. 13:9)

In order to understand properly a certain number of common
biblical phrases, it is necessary to harken back to the principles
just enunciated. The "sons of Asaph" (a more or less legendary
figure) as "the sons of Core" are singers. (2 Par. 35:15; Ps. 41:1;
43:1; 45:1; 46:1; 48:1; 83:1; 86:1; 87:1) The title "sons of Aaron" is given to all the priests indiscriminately. (Lv. 1:5; 11; 2:2, 3,
10; 13:2; 21:1; Nm. 10:8) Yahweh is served by the "priests
of the Lord, the sons of Aaron, and the Levites." [25] (2 Par. 13:9;
cf. Sir. 50:16) The "sons of Israel" can very legitimately be interpreted as the members of the sacred league of the twelve tribes,
known simply as *Israel*. The corporate meaning of the term is
evident in several cases; for example, in the history of the Gabaonites. These Gabaonites "were not (originally) of the children

24 In the same way, "the children of the porters" are porters (Esd.
    2:42), "sons of the singing men" are singers (Ne. 12:28), "daughters
    of ostriches" are ostriches (Is. 43:20; Jb. 30:29; 34:13). A wise man
    is called "a child of wisdom" (Sir. 4:11) or "the son of a prudent
    man" (Prv. 28:7), a turtle dove is called "a son of a dove." (Lv.
    1:14; Nm. 6:10) Very frequently the term *bén* indicates age: a "son
    of such or such a number of years" is a man of such an age (Gn.
    5:32; Ex. 7:7; Dt. 6:1, etc.); the same holds for the feminine *bat*
    (Gn. 17:17; Lv. 14:10; Nm. 6:14; etc.).
25 Sometimes they are called "priests, descendants of Levi." (Dt. 21:5)

of Israel (*b*^e*ne-yis'rā'él*) but the remains of the Amorrhites; and
the children of Israel (*b*^e*né-yis'rā'él*) had sworn to them." (2 K.
21:2) When Elias takes "twelve stones according to the number
of the tribes of the sons of Jacob" (3 K. 18:31), he implicitly
recognizes the amphictyonic character of the Israelite confederation. The "sons of Israel" designate the organized community of
Israel (Ex. 12:3, 6; 16:1, 2, 9, 10; 35:1, 4, 20; Nm. 1:2; 27:
20: Jg. 18:1) as a unity (Ex. 35:29; Lv. 17:2, 5, 12, 13; 19:2)[26]
and not at all as the descendants from a common carnal ancestor.

Summing it all up, we can say that the term *bén* (son) has
an extremely large number of meanings in Hebrew. Whenever
there is a rather intimate relationship between two persons, the
Hebrews are apt to use the "father-son" terminology. A typical
example of the use of *bén* is found in the sapiential literature:
"my son" or "my sons" frequently means disciple(s).[27] Somewhat
similarly *bén* frequently signifies a subordinate: Joseph speaking
to his brothers (Gn. 43:29), Samuel in the service of Heli (1 K.
3:6, 16; 4:16), David in his relations with Saul (1 K. 24:17;
26:17, 21, 25), Achimaas in his relations with Joab (2 K. 18:22),
the priests scolded by Exechias (2 Par. 29:11), Achaz submitting
himself to Theglathphalasar. (4 K. 18:7: "I am thy servant, and
thy son.")

It seems that etymologically the word *bén* must be associated
with the root *bānāh* (as the Aramaean *bar* is derived from the

26 The distinction between *'édāh* and *qāhāl* (designating the "communi-
    ty of Israel") is difficult to determine. According to A. Causse, *Du
    groupe ethnique,* Paris, 1937, 220, n. 3 "the term *qāhāl* designates
    the popular assembly brought together to participate in the functions
    of national life, deliberations, feasts, bearing arms; *'édâ* is rather the
    cultic assembly."—W. Eichrodt, *Theologie des Alten Testaments,*
    Leipzig, 1933, 1, 9, paraphrases *'édāh* as "the circle of the human
    members of the Covenant," whereas *qāhāl* is "the unity of this group"
    in virtue of the "divine call." In turn, B. Luther, *Kahal und 'éda als
    Hilfsmittel der Quellenscheidung in P und in der Chronik,* in ZAW
    56 (1938) 44-46, p. 44 thinks that they are synonyms.
27 Cf. Is. 19:11; Ps. 33:12; Prv. 1:8,10; 2:4; 3:1,11; 4:10,20; 5:1; 6:1;
    7:1; 19:27; 23:15; 24:13; Co. 12:12; Sir. 3:17; 4:1; 6:23; 10:28; etc.
    Similarly "my daughter," "my daughters"; cf. Rt. 1:11; 2:2; 3:10;
    Ps. 44:11.

verb *bārā*). In Akkadian the verb *banu I* means "to organize, to create a structured whole."[28] The same fundamental meaning is had in Hebrew. The verb *bānāh* refers to the construction of a home (Gn. 33:17; 2 K. 7:5, 7, 27: the temple; 3 K. 9:3, 10, 24; 16:32: the temple of Baal; 3 K. 22:39: the "house of Ivory"), of a fortification (Dt. 20:20; 3 K. 11:27: the "*millō*"), of an altar (Ex. 20:25; Jg. 6:26; 4 K. 21:4), of a gate (4 K. 15:35), of a city (Dt. 6:10; Hb. 2:12; Ps. 122:3), of a platform (4 K. 16:18), of a mast (Ez. 27:50), of a tower (Is. 5:2; Ca. 4:4).

Sometimes it is question of a *re*construction (Ez. 36:36; 44: 28; 45:13: Is. 58:12; 60:10; 61:4; Dn. 9:25; Ps. 50:20; 101: 17), or of additions. (Lam. 3:5) Frequently the term is understood ina figurative meaning: it has to do with the founding of a family (household) (Gn. 16:2; 1 K. 2:35; 3 K. 11:38; Rt. 4:11), the consolidation of a throne (Amos 9:11; Ps. 88:5), the creation of Eve (Gn. 2:22: God arranges the rib of Adam), or of the heavens. (Amos 9:6) Especially in the *niphal* form the verb *bānāh* has the meaning of "consolidating," of "forming an indestructible whole." (Jer. 12:16; 31:4; Za. 1:16) If it is true that the Hebrew language constantly is aware of the whole meaning of a root in all its derivatives,[29] the noun *bén* must in some way carry the meaning of belonging to a structured whole. Each *bén* is in intimate and structural relationship with a "father," of whom he is a participation of an individual expression.

3. The Meaning of the Terms "Adam" and "Sons of Adam"

The principles which we have just explained can be applied without difficulty, it seems, to the expression "sons of Adam," which is so frequent in the Bible. We know that the term *ādām* has both an individual and a collective aspect.[30] The individual

---

28 C. Bezold, *Babylonisch-assyrisches Glossar*, Heidelburg, 1926, 91 translates "building, creating, forming, producing, *planning*." The relation of *bén* to *bānāh* is evident in the words of Sara, the wife of Abram: "Perhaps I shall get children through her (Agar)" (literally: "I shall be built up from her"-'*ibbānêh mimmênnâh*) (Gn. 16:2; cf. also Gn. 30:3, referring to Rebecca).

29 J. Pedersen, *Israel I-II*, 111.

30 G. E. Wright, *The Biblical Doctrine of Man in Society*, 1954, 49. Cf.

usage is rather rare, whereas the collective meaning is much more frequent.[31] Practically only in the accounts of creation and of the fall is the word *ādām* used to indicate an individual noun. The same meaning is found also in Gn. 4:1: "The man (Adam) knew Eve his wife" and in Gn. 5:3: "When Adam was one hundred and thirty years old, he became the father of a son."[32] The expression "like Adam" (Mt.: *ke'ādām*) of Os. 6:7 is puzzling. [The C.C.D. edition translates it as "in their land."] It might allude to the town Adam (Jos. 3:16), unless one is forced to render it by the collective "like men." In Za. 13:5 the Vulgate translation "Adam exemplum meum ab adolescentia mea" should read "I have owned land (*ādām* for *adāmāh*) since my youth." The *Book of Sirach*, 49:19 speaks of the "splendor of Adam" (*tif'èrèt 'ādām;* cf. cf. Is. 44:11)[33] and in 33:10 of his formation from the earth. The prayer of Tobias refers undoubtedly to Gn. 1-3: "Thou madest Adam from the slime of the earth, and gavest him Eve for a helper." (Tob. 8:8) Perhaps there is an allusion to an individual person in Jb. 15:7: "Are you indeed the firstborn of mankind?" (*rî'šôn ha' ādām*)[There are two other texts (Jb. 31:33 and Ps. 72:5) which in the original may lend themselves to a singular translation, but which are translated in the Confraternity Version in a collective sense.]

Over and beyond these texts, the term *'ādām* or *hā'ādām*

also A. J. Wensinck, *The Idea of the Western Semites Concerning the Navel of the Earth,* in *Verhandelingen der Akademie der Wetenschappen,* Amsterdam, XVII, 1, 1916, 21; C. Lattey, *Vicarious Solidarity in the OT,* in VT I (1951) 267-74, p. 269. According to A. Jones, *Unless Some Man Show Me,* 1951, 83, the Assyrian root *udmu* means "the human race."

31 According to L. Kohler, *Theologie des Alten Testaments,* Tübingen, 1953[2], 114, it is easy to note the cases among the 510 uses of the word *'ādām* where the meaning is not men in general but a particular man.

32 Cf. Gn. 4:1, "The man (*hā'ādām*) knew Eve his wife." The Septuagint translates Gn. 2:4 by *biblos geneseôs anthrôpôn;* and Gn. 6:1 (*hā'ādām*) by *hoi anthrôpoi.*

33 N. Peters, *Der jüngst wiederaufgefundene hebräische Text des Buches Ecclesiasticus,* Freiburg, 1902, 426.

(with the article) has a patently collective sense: "humanity,"
"the human race," or "some men," "any man whatsoever."

In chapters 1-3 of *Genesis* the Vulgate sometimes translates
as *Adam* (Gn. 2:19-23, 25; 3:8, 9, 12, 17, 20-22, 24); other times
more correctly as *homo*. (Gn. 2:7, 8, 15, 16, 18) The concept
"mankind" (*ādām*) of Gn. 1:26 is without a doubt collective,
since the verb of which it is the subject is in the plural ("let
them have dominion"); it refers to human kind, as does (Gn. 9:5.[34]
The same thing is to be said about Gn. 1:27 (*hā'ādām*), where
the author has in mind not a single couple but the entire human
race. The collective meaning of *Adam* in Gn. 6:7 is evident from
its contrast with the collective *bᵉhèmāh,* "beasts." [35] When God
regretted having made man, He was thinking of the entire human
race as it existed at the time of the deluge. (Gn. 6:6, 7; cf. 8:21:
"the inclination of man's heart is evil" refers patently to men
in general.")

The same shade of meaning (mankind in general) is found
in a number of other texts: "You have been told, *O man,* what is
good, and what the Lord requires of you." (Mi. 6:8; cf. Jb. 28:
28) "Man, born of woman ... When a man dies, all vigor leaves
him." (Jb. 14:1, 10) "All flesh would perish together, and man
would return to the dust." (Jb. 34:15) "Man is a breath; his days,
like a passing shadow." (Ps. 143: 3:4) (cf. also Jb. 33:17;[36];
Pr. 20:24; Jer. 10:23)

34 Cf. J. Boehmer, *Wieviel Menschen sind am letzten Tage des Haxa-
    ëmerons geschaffen worden?* in ZAW 34 (1914) 31-35, p. 32. The
    allusions to this text are well known: Is. 45:12: "It was I who made
    the earth and created mankind (literally *'ādām*) upon it"; Sir. 15:14:
    "When God, in the beginning, created man"; Sir. 17:1: "The Lord
    from the earth created man"; Dt. 4:32: "Ever since God created man
    upon the earth"; Jb. 20:4: "Since man was placed upon the earth";
    Za. 12:1: "Thus says the Lord, who spreads out the heavens, lays the
    foundations of the earth, and forms the spirit of man within him";
    2 Mc. 7:23: "The Creator of the world, that formed the nativity of
    man." Cf. also 2 Mc. 7:28.

35 Cf. also Gn. 7:23; Ex. 9:25; 12:12; etc., Lv. 27:28; Nm. 3:13, etc.;
    Jer. 7:20; 50:3, 51:62; Ez. 14:13-17; 28:8; 36:10-12; Za. 2:8; Ps.
    35:7; 134:8; Co. 3:19; Sir. 40:8.

36 This notion of "mankind in general" is found especially in the sa-

Very close to this meaning of mankind in general is the all-inclusive sense of "all men," "everybody." [37] In answer to Isaia's question: "How long, O Lord?" God replies: "Until the cities are desolate . . . until the Lord removes men (*'ādām*) faraway." (Is. 6:12) The divine threat in So. 1:3: "I will sweep away man (*'ādām*) and beast" harkens back to God's plan to destroy all men in the deluge. (Gn. 6:7) Often one comes across the expression *kol hā'ādām* ("all men," "the totality of men"). [38] But even where the prefix *kol* is missing, the all-inclusive sense of the word is evident. Speaking of human liberty, Sirach says: "Before man[39] are life and death, whichever he chooses shall be given to him." (Sir. 15:17) In the three following quotations, the term "men" manifestly refers to all men: "You (O Lord) raise grass for the cattle, and vegetation for men's use." (Ps. 103:14) "Yet like men, you (judges) shall die." (Ps. 81:7) "Beyond intrigue and folly and sin, it is arrogance that men find abominable." (Pr. 24:9) (Cf. 2 K. 23:3). [40]

piential writings. Coheleth, for example, wonders: "Who knows what is good for a man in life?" (Co. 6:12); or "What profit has man from all the labor which he toils at under the sun?" (Co. 1:3); "Both the one and the other God has made, so that man cannot find fault with him in anything" (Co. 7:14; cf. 2:24; 6:1,7). "However much man toils in searching, he does not find it out" (Co. 8:17); "Love from hatred man cannot tell" (Co. 9:1). The following passages also refer to "mankind in general": "Thus man, for all his splendor, does not abide" (Ps. 48:13, 21); "Man may make plans in his heart, but what the tongue utters is from the Lord" (Pr. 16:1); "But man himself begets mischief." (Jb. 5:7)

37 Very often "man" (*hā'ādām*) means simply the indefinite "one"; cf. Co. 3:13, 22; 10:14; 11:18; 12:5; Is. 2:20; Ez. 20:21 (custom which "one" should observe); Pr. 12:14; 28:12,28; Lam. 3:39; Ps. 57:12; Ps. 123:2.

38 Cf. Gn. 7:21; Ex. 9:19; Nm. 12:3, 16:28,32; Lv. 16:17; Jb. 21:32; 36:25; 37:7; Jg. 16:17; Jer. 10:14; 31:30; 51:17; 3 K. 3:38; Co. 7:2; Sir. 13:15; Ps. 115:11; 2 Mac. 2:41; 5:42, etc.

39 N. Peters, *Der jüngst wiederaufgefundene hebräische Text*, l.c., 359: *Lifné 'ādām* (in the singular); the Septuagint translates *enanti anthrôpôn* (in the plural).

40 Cf. Pr. 23:28 *bā'ādām*, that is to say, "in the midst of men." The same expression is found in Gn. 9:6; Jr. 31:20, Ps. 67:19.

When used with a negative (no man), the term has an even more all-inclusive meaning. No man merits absolute confidence: "Cursed is the man who trusts in human beings." (Jer. 17:5; Ps. 117:8) All men are sinners: "For there is no man who sinneth not." (3 K. 8:46; cf. Co. 7:20) Very often the expression "no one" or "nobody" can be substituted for "no man": "Let not any man's (no one's) heart be dismayed." (1 K. 17:32); "There is no man (nobody) who is master of the breath of life." (Co. 8:8; cf. also Is. 38:11)[41]

In order to express the adjective "human," the Hebrews often had recourse to the phrase "of man." In these cases the collective character of the words *'ādām or hā'ādām* cannot be doubted.[42] Thus they speak of "the custom of men" (2 K. 7:19: *tōrat hā'ādām* which the Vulgate translates *"lex Adam";* cf. also Ne. 9:29), "human bone" (Nm. 19:16; Ez. 39:15; 3 K. 13:2; 23: 14, 20), "human cords" (Os. 11:4: in the Vulgate *"in funiculis Adam"*) or of "the thoughts of men."[43] (Ps. 93:11)

41   See the following for the same shade of meaning: Sir. 11:2b: "Despise not a man for his appearance"; Sir. 46:19: "No one dared gainsay him (Samuel); Jb. 32:21: "I would not be partial to anyone"; Ps. 104:14: "He let no man oppress them"; Co. 7:20: "There is no man on earth so just as to do good and never sin"; Jer. 2:6: "A land which no one crosses, where no man dwells"; Is. 6:11: "Until the cities are desolate, without inhabitants, houses, without a man, and the earth is a desolate waste." (cf. Jer. 32:43; 33:10,12)

42   In the case where *'ādām* is used attributively, there is no exception. Cf. Dt. 20:19: "Are the trees of the field men?"; 1 K. 15:29; Jb. 11:12; Is. 31:3,8; Ez. 28:2,9.

43   The adjective "human" can mean "that which belongs to a man" or "that which is weak like a man." In the first meaning the Bible speaks of "the breath of man" (Prv. 20:27); "human intelligence" (Prv. 30:2); "their form was human" (Ez. 1:5,26); "the face of a man" (Ez. 1:10; 10:14; 41:19); "foot of man" (Ez. 29:11; 32:13); "human hands" (Is. 37:19; Ez. 1:8; 10:8; Dt. 4:28; 2 K. 24:14; 4 K. 19:19; 1 Par. 21:13; Ps. 134:15); "men's blood" (Hb. 2:8,17; 1 Par. 17:17); "human excrement." (Ez. 4:12,15) In the second meaning the Bible speaks of "worthless is the help of man" (Ps. 59:13; 107:13); "human pride" (Is. 2:17); "the works of the hands of men" (2 Par. 32:19); and "the eyes of man" (Pv. 27:20).

The term *'ādām* can mean not only mankind in general but also each individual and concrete member of that general concept. This can be expressed by such phrases as "any man" or "any man whatsoever." Sometimes this nuance is expressed explicitly as in Co. 7:28: "One man" (*'ādām'èhad*); more frequently, however, it is indicated by the context. Such is particularly the case in legal prescriptions, where *'ādām* evidently means "anyone," as does *awilu* in the Code of Hammurabi. (cf. Lv. 1:2; 5:3, 4, 22; 7:21; 13:2, 9; 18:5; 24:17; 27:29; Nm. 5:6; 19:13, 14; Jg. 16:7,11) This particularized meaning is likewise obvious in the following passages: "Any man to whom God gives riches and property" (Co. 5:8); "When he distorts men's rights" (Lam. 3:36); "Though a man burdened with human blood." (Pr. 28:17) In the sapiential books virtues and vices are more clearly shown in concrete individuals. The meaning of *'ādām* in the following examples is generally individual: "wicked man" (Jb. 20:29; 27: 13), "a wicked man" (Pr. 11:7), "a scoundrel" (Prv. 6:12), "a fool of a man" (Prv. 15:20; 16:9; 19:3), "a man who has labored with wisdom." (Co. 2:21)[44]

Sometimes *'ādām* means "some men," a certain number of men," "a small group of men," as in the following passages: "Men he devoured" (Ez. 19:3, 6; cf. 36:13, 14); "One man tyrannizes over another" (Co. 8:9); "The arrogance of some men will be abased" (Is. 2:11); "the scorn of men" (Ps. 21:7: (*tèrpat 'ādām*); "Deliver me, O Lord, from evil men." (Ps. 139:2)[45]

---

44 The shade of meaning "one individual man" is evident in such phrases as the following: "Whoever sheds the blood *of man*, by man shall his blood be shed" (Gn. 9:6); or "What can *man* do against me?" (Ps. 55:12; 117: 6); or "If *a man* at anytime shall rise, and persecute thee (David)" (1 K. 25:29); or "*a man* was come, who sought the prosperity of the children of Israel" (Neh. 2:10). The meaning of an "individual" (as opposed to the nation) is found in Jb. 34:29; Pr. 28:2. Sometimes the substantive *nèfèš* is added; the expression *nèfèš 'ādām* designates an individual of the people (Nm. 31:35,40,46; 1 Mc. 2:38; 9:2) or "a prisoner" (I Par. 5:21), "a slave" (Ez. 27:13), or "a corpse" (Nm. 9:6,7; 19:11).

45 The meaning "some men" is probably found in the well known expression "happy is the man" (*'ašré 'ādām*); cf. Ps. 83:6, 13; Prv. 3:13; 8:34; 28:14.

4. *The Meaning of "Bèn-'Adām"*

The analysis of the word *'ādām* has shown that it has a variety of meanings, most of which bear a collective nuance. "Adam" means all humanity when considered quantitively or generically; it means a part of that whole (some one, some) at other times. We should not be surprised, then, to find that the expression *bèn-'ādām* has the meaning of " a member of the human collectivity," but never the meaning of a descendant of Adam as an individual. Two forms of the expression are found: one in the singular (*bèn-'ādām*), the other in the plural (*bᵉné-'ādām*).

The singular is used in the attributive sense, as for example, in Nm. 23:19: "God is not man that he should speak falsely, nor human (son of man), that he should change his mind," or in Ps. 145:3: "Put not your trust in princes, in man (son of man) in whom there is no salvation." Now and then the Hebrew parallelism equates "man" and "son of man": "How much less man, who is but a maggot, the son of man, who is only a worm." (Jb. 25:6) or: "What is man that you should be mindful of him, or the son of man that you should care for him?" (Ps. 8:5)[46] The individual meaning of the expression *bèn-'ādām* is evident in the title found in *Daniel,* "son of man" (Dn. 8:17) and especially in *Ezechiel* (85 times altogether: cf. 2:1, 3; 3:1, 4, 10; 4:16; 8:5, 6, 8; 11:2 etc.; often under this form "but as for you, son of man" *wᵉ'attāh bèn'ādām*: 2:6, 8; 3:25; 4:1; 5:1; 7:2; etc.) Similarly the negative expression *lo' bèn'ādām* means "not a man," "no one" as in Jer. 49: 18, 33; 50:4; 51:43.

The plural form *bᵉné'ādām* seems to be a little less frequent. Its meaning is occasionally individual, but more often collective. The particularized meaning can be seen in the following: "But if the sons of men (stir thee up against me) they are cursed in the sight of the Lord" (1 K. 26:19) or "the stripes of the children of men." (2 K. 7:14) On the other hand, the collective meaning is used much more frequently. The "sons of men" are simply all

---

46 In Is. 51:12 and 56:2 the terms "mortal man" (*ᵉnòš*) and "the son of man" (*bén 'ādām*) are used in parallel fashion. In Ps. 79:18 the expressions "the man of your right hand" and "the son of man whom you yourself made strong" are identified.

those who make up the human race or share the human situation. Divine wisdom finds delight "in the sons of men" (Prv. 8:31); the theocratic or messianic king is "fairer in beauty . . . than the sons of men." (Ps. 44:3; cf. Ps. 57:2)

The collective character of the phrase (*bené'ādām* is sometimes emphasized in the context; for example, by the addition of "all." In the prayer of Solomon there is a passage in which he says to Yahweh: "For thou only knowest the heart of *all* the children of men." (3 K. 8:39; 2 Par. 6:30) The contrast between "man" and "beast" in Jer. 36:29 and Dn. 5:21 indicates the general sense of the term. The parallelism between "men" and "children (or sons) of men" in the two following texts indicates that the latter phrase refers to mankind in general: "To you, O men, I call; my appeal is to the children of men." (Prv. 8:4); "like raindrops on the grass, which wait for no man, nor tarry for the sons of men." (Mi. 5:6) Likewise in the two following texts the translation of the phrase in question presumes its use as referring to all mankind: "So marred was his look beyond that of man, and his appearance beyond that of mortals." (Is. 52:14); "Then something like a man's hand touched my lips." (Dn. 10:16)[47]

Because Yahweh's "eyes are open to all the ways of men" (Jer. 32:19) and because "from heaven the Lord looks down, he sees all mankind" (Ps. 32:13) Yahweh's providence is universal. Frequently the Bible speaks of the "works of God, his tremendous deeds among men (sons of men)." (Ps. 65:5; 106: 8, 15, 21, 31) Yahweh makes known to men (sons of men) His might (Ps. 144:12); Yahweh "looks down from heaven upon the children of men" (Ps. 13:2; 54:3); "How great is the goodness, O Lord, . . . you show in the sight of men." (Ps. 30:20) Whereas "His (God's) searching glance is on mankind (sons of men)" (Ps. 10:4), "the children of men take refuge in the shadow of your wings." (Ps. 35:8)

The sapiential books, which speak of man's earthly life in general, sometimes use the formula *benéhā'ādām. Coheleth* uses it frequently. For example, he speaks of "human luxuries (luxuries of the children of men)" (Co. 2:8), of "the task which God has appointed for men (children of men)" (Co. 3:10), of their con-

---

47 For the meaning of Dn. 7:13, cf. section E.

duct (Co. 3:18), of their subjection to death which they share with the animals (Co. 3:19; verse 21 is translated *"spiritus filiorum Adam"* in the Vulgate), of the evil in their hearts (Co. 9:3; cf. Pr. 15:11), of their subjection to misfortune which overtakes them unexpectedly. (Co. 9:12) All these predictions refer evidently to mankind in general.

By way of conclusion we can say that the words $b^e né(h\bar{a})$ *'ādām* should not be translated "sons of Adam" (as the Vulgate does in Ps. 88:48; 89:3; 114:16), for the expression does not refer to the physical descendants of Adam as such, but rather to mankind in general and to its human condition.

5: *"Adam" in the New Testament*

As we have just seen, the term *'ādām* in the Old Testament seldom refers to the first man, but ordinarily to the totality of men. When we shift from this usage in the Old Testament to its use in the well known passage of St. Paul in *Romans* 5:12-21, we run up against a difficulty. It seems clear that the Apostle sees in Adam "who is a figure of him who is to come" (Rom. 5:14) only a single well characterized individual. Yet our previous analysis has shown that the term Adam has a collective connotation. The best solution to this problem, it seems to us, is to recognize quite frankly that St. Paul looked upon Adam as a "corporate personality."

Already in 1925 H. Wheeler Robinson wrote, although with a bit of exaggeration: "Except for the doctrine of corporate personality, there would have been no doctrine of original sin, the doctrine that Adam's sin condemned the race to death, because he was the corporate representative of the race, and they must share in his condemnation (a very different idea from that of the biological inheritance of tendencies to evil, with which it is sometimes confused)." [48]

Can we use the 'theological import" of the idea of "corporate personality" [49] to elucidate the Pauline idea of original sin? An

---

48   H. Wheeler Robinson, in S. A. Peake, *The People and the Book*, Oxford, 1925, 378.

49   H. Wheeler Robinson, *Redemption and Revelation*, l.c., 259; cf. p.

attentive reading of Rom. 5:12-21 will show that in the mind of St. Paul the sin of Adam affected all mankind in a way that is at least comparable to the redemptive act of Christ. Mankind (*'ādām* in the Old Testament meaning of the word) is considered to be the extension of the first sinner, "his clan." [50] Precisely because of this the sentence of death was pronounced on the "children of Adam," that is on all members of mankind, because of the sin of their representative (Adam), the perpetrator of the first sin. As always, when there is question of a "corporate personality," it is extremely easy to shift from the individual Adam to the collective Adam, since the latter, mankind in general, shares in the status of the "ancestor."

We can speak of the inclusion and anticipation of all mankind in the first sinner: "For just as by the disobedience of the one man the many were constituted sinners, so also by the obedience of the one the many will be constituted just." (Rom. 5:19) We have here two completely unified groups which are contrasted, the one that has sinned (Adam and his descendants), the other which is saved (Christ and His members). [51] Let us note especially the mysterious inclusion of all mankind in Adam who perpetrates the one all-encompassing transgression. (cf. Rom. 5:18) In each of the groups we have the transmission of effects from one individual to the multitude, and that because mankind constitutes one single whole under one leader. As soon as Adam (the leader) sins, the group (the collective Adam) takes on the condition of sin; all the "children of Adam," that is, all those who fall under the term

149: "The doom and suffering which came upon the race because of the sin of Adam."

50 C. H. Dodd, *The Epistle of Paul to the Romans,* in *The Moffatt NT Commentary,* London, 1946[11], 79. Dodd explicitly uses the term "corporate personality."

51 S. Hanson, *The Unity of the Church in the NT,* Uppsala, 1946, 66-67. —Cf. H. Koehnlein, *La notion de l'Eglise chez l'Apôtre Paul,* in *RHPR* 17 (1937) 357-77, p. 368: "Christ died for all men, so that they may no longer be a solidarity of sinners; not the *peccatorum communio,* but the *sanctorum communio.* By the just act of one man, all men have been taken up in the *dikaiôsis zôès.* Because Christ redeemed men for the curse of the Law, the *eulogia tou Abraam* is for them and makes of them the descendants of Abraham."

"man," become sinners when Adam sins. For, whatever happens to the head of the group happens *ipso facto* to the body dependent upon it.[52]

This, then, seems to be St. Paul's line of reasoning. One man sinned (Rom. 5:12); but this man is not alone, for he represents and is the incarnation, as it were, of all mankind. That is why St. Paul states: "All have sinned" (Rom. 5:12) All are guilty of sin since all die, even those who lived at a time when the Law did not punish by death strictly personal sins. In the thought of St. Paul, the individual and the group are identified: Adam represents, that is to say he *is* the human race; the human race, in turn, is present, or rather, takes part, in some way in the act of the first man. Even if they have not committed personal sin, all the "sons of Adam" are truly sinners (Rom. 5:14), for even though sin was born in one human will, it affected the entire human group. From the very first, mankind shares in the lot and the condition of its representative.

We can conclude, then, that St. Paul's extension of culpability from the individual Adam to the collective '*ādām* is based on the biblical category of "corporate personality": "Since we were all[53]

---

52   A. Marmorstein, *Paulus und die Rabbiner,* in ZNW 30 (1931) 271-85, p. 273, quotes a text of *Deuteronomy Rabbah* 9:4: "You (Moses) die through the sin of Adam, who brought sin into the world." Although not culpable of personal sins, not having transgressed any precept, Moses is subject to death solely because of the sin of Adam.—Cf. Lyonnet, *Le péché originel et Rom.* 5:12-14, in RSR 44 (1956) 63-84, p. 81: "In verse 12 Paul stated that because of Adam, sin, and with it death . . . , has engulfed all mankind."—The idea of a "mass of sin" (as opposed to a "mass of grace") seems obvious in Rom. 11:32, where it is stated that "God has shut up all in unbelief, that he may have mercy upon all."

53   The "mystical" interpretation of the words "*in quo omnes peccaverunt*" of Rom. 5:12 is generally known. This exegesis of the Latin fathers (St. Augustine) takes into account only the Vulgate (the words *ef 'hôi* of the original Greek text are a simple conjunction: "since"); this exegesis presupposes a Platonic viewpoint which looks upon Adam as a universal idea of which individual men are the participation. We might well wonder whether the Platonic "idea" is not the philosophical elaboration of the more down-to-earth and less

in Adam, we all sinned voluntarily in him, and rightly share his guilt." [54]

The realistic character of this idea definitely belies those who would interpret the first sinner "Adam" as a device, a kind of substitute to replace the more "real" concept of mankind. [55] Precisely because of the great fluidity of the concept of "corporate personality," we should not consider the "condensation" of the group in the representative individual as a gimmick of style or as a literary device, but rather as a concrete reality. God is dealing wtih the entire human race when he deals with Adam because "in a real sense for ancient thought, he was the race. Because of Adam's sin, God passes sentence of death on the race. That sentence is a just one, because all sinned (in Adam)." [56] The text of St. Paul, if we interpret it in the light of the concept of "corporate personality," presupposes the true reality of the first (as well as the second) Adam, rather than considers them as mythical or fictitious.

This contention is confirmed by the study of rabbinical texts, from which, St. Paul, although he did not take the totality of his doctrine (for he received it through revelation), may have bor-

theoretical idea of "corporate personality"; cf. H. Wheeler Robinson, *The Christian Doctrine,* 1913, 190, n. 1.

54 H. Wheeler Robinson, *The Christian Doctrine of Man,* 1913, 190; also in A. S. Peake, l.c., 378; also *Redemption and Revelation,* l.c., p. 208.

55 This is the idea of C. H. Dodd, *The Epistle of Paul to the Romans,* London, 1946[11], 79 (with reference to 1 Cor. 15:22: "as in Adam all die") or of K. Barth (according to S. Hanson, *The Unity of the Church in the NT,* 68: "a non-historical person.")

56 H. Wheeler Robinson, *The Christian Doctrine of Man,* 121. The author adds (rather unexpectedly): "But Paul has not connected this fact (all have sinned) causally with his conception of the race as (corporately) constituted sinners through Adam's transgression." It seems to us that "the inclusion" of all in Adam brings with it *ipso facto,* a certain influence (a certain "causality") of Adam on these others.—Cf. G. Lafont, O.S.B., *Sur l'interprétation de Romains V,* 15-21, in RSR 55 (1957) 481-513, p. 512: "The first Adam sinned and opened up into humanity the forces of sin and death which lead to the multiplication of sin and which tend to the definitive doom of all men."

rowed the concepts in which he phrased it. In later Jewish thought, sinful humanity is conceived of as present in the loins of Adam (as Levi in those of Melchisedech, Heb. 7:9-10), or at least as forming, in some mystically real way one whole with him. The sin of all mankind is ascribed to the first sin, the common root of all others, in this sense that all mankind played an actual part in that sin.

The following very old conviction is expressed by a rabbi of the fifteenth century, R. Moshe: "With the same sin with which Adam sinned, sinned the whole world, for he was the whole world." [57] In chapter 10 of the *Apocalypse of Moses,* Eve laments: "All sinners of my progeny will come to curse me and will say: Cursed be Eva, for she has not kept the observance of the Lord her God, and because of this we shall all die the death." [58] In the *Apocalypse of Adam* or the *Testament of Adam and Eve,* [59] Adam tells Seth of the future deluge and the extermination of the wicked, which will occur because through "the sin of your mother Eve they have all been made sinners."

The classical texts referring to this matter are in the Syrian *Apocalypse of Baruch* and in the *Fourth Book of Esdras.* The first of these apocryphal works [60] shows the relationship between universal death and the sin of Adam: "Adam brought death to the world, and he shortened the years of his descendants." (Ap. Bar. 17:3) "When Adam sinned and when the sentence of death was pronounced on all those who would descend from him, the number of those to be born was fixed as was the place of sojourn for the living and the dead." (Ap. Bar. 23:4) [61] "Whereas Adam was the

---

57 Quoted by F. R. Tennant, *The Sources of the Doctrines of Fall and Original Sin,* Cambridge, 1903, 167, note.

58 *Ibid.,* p. 198. Cf. chapter 32 of the same apocryphal work (in Armenian): "For sin and transgressions came into existence in the world through me" (cf. the Greek translation: *"Hêmarton, kai pâsa hamartia di 'emou gegone en têi ktisei."*)

59 Edited by E. Renan, in: *Journal Asiatique série V,* t. II, pp. 427 ff.

60 Edited by V. Ryssel, in E. Kautzsch, *Die Apokryphen und Pseudepigraphen des AT,* Tübingen, 1900, II, 418.

61 *Ibid.,* p. 421. Cf. Apoc. Bar. 56, 5-6 (edited by Ryssel, p. 434): "The first transgression committed by Adam, the first man" had as its consequence "the premature appearance of death and suffering."—With

first sinner and brought premature death upon all, his descendants have brought upon themselves future punishment or future glorification." [62] (Ap. Bar. 54:15) Similar to the thought of St. Paul "the wages of sin is death" (Rom. 6:23) is that found in the *Apocalypse of Baruch* in which the author shows the relationship between Adam and the physical and moral corruption of all men: "O Adam, what have you done to your descendants? And what shall we say of Eve who listened to the serpent? For all this multitude is condemned to corruption, and the number of those whom fire will devour is incalculable." [63] (Ap. Bar. 48:42-43)

The *Fourth Book of Esdras* contains the same thought regarding the close bond between death and sin. Addressing himself to God, the author declares: "You imposed a single precept on him (Adam), but he transgressed it. Immediately you condemned him and his descendants to death." [64] (4 Esd. 3:7) In the follow-

good reason W. Bousset, *Die Religion des Judentums in neutesta-mentlichen Zeitalter*, 1913[2], 468, observes that there is question of the doctrine of *hereditary death*, but not yet in an explicit way of hereditary *sin*. We should note, however, that according to the Hebrew mentality, "the wages of sin is death." (Rom. 6:23)

62 D. Kautzsch, *Die Apokryphen*, l.c., 433. At the end of this passage, the author returns to the tenet of individual responsibility: "Adam is, then, the occasion of sin for himself alone; we have become, each for himself, an Adam." (54, 19)—Cf. W. D. Davies, *Paul and Rabbinical Judaism*, London, 1948, 33: "That Adam's sin involved all his posterity, the righteous as well as the wicked, is sound Rabbinical doctrine (cf. Sir. 15:14; 4 Esd. 3:8; Ps. Sal. 9:4) but the Rabbis were always anxious to safeguard human freedom, and so could not regard the relation between Adam's sin and the sinfullness of mankind as directly causal." We might point out that it is not question of an exterior cause which begets a distance as well as a union, but rather of an inevitable juridical condition which exists since the first sin.

63 E. Kautzsch, *Die Apokryphen*, l.c., p. 430. Cf. Apoc. Bar. 18:11: "The multitude ... participated in the darkness of Adam." Individual sin is not overlooked here either; cf. Apoc. Bar. 48:46: "You know the number of those who descend from him (Adam), and to what extent they have sinned before your face."

64 E. Kautzsch, *Die YApokryphen*, ed. H. Gunkel, 353: "*In nationibus eius," kai eis tas geneas autou.*—Cf. in H. L. Strack-P. Billerback, *Kommentar zum NT aus Talmud und Midrasch, III*, 1926, Munich,

ing the contamination of the state of sin—real *spiritual* death—
becomes more explicit: "Because of his evil heart Adam fell into
sin and guilt; the same thing takes place in all those born of him.
Thus the evil becomes more entrenched. The Law was indeed in
the hearts of the people, but the evil seed was also present."[65]
(4 Esd. 3:21) But the most important text relating to this matter
is that of chapter 7:118: "Ah, what have you done, Adam? When
you sinned, your fall affected not only you but us, your descen-
dants.Of what good is it to have received the promise of eternity,
if *we* have done the works of death?"[66] Elsewhere—outside the
Apocalypse of Baruch and the *Fourth Book of Esdras*— we find
the same idea regarding a relationship of causality between the
death of each man and the sin of Adam. We read in *Midrash
Coheleth* 43 (ad. 7:13): "When the angel announced to Moses
'the time is now approaching for you to die' (Dt. 31:14), Moses
said to God, 'Because of what sin?.' And God replied to him,
'Because of the sin of the first Adam.'" *Bereshit Rabba* c. 19
carries this comment of R. Jochanan ben Zakkai regarding Gn.
3:8: "Their eyes were opened when they understood the evil they
had brought upon future generations."[67]

227, the explanation of Dt. 32:32 by R. Jehuda (c. 150): "You are
the children of the first man, who brought death by way of punishment upon you and your descendants who will come after you until
the end of time."

65 E. Kautzsch, *Die Apokryphen*, l.c., p. 354.—We can compare 4 Esd.
3:26: "They (the inhabitants of this town) acted in every way like
Adam and all his descendants; for they had a perverse heart." (cf.
4 Esd. 7:48); or 4 Esd. 4:30-32: "A weed seed was planted at the
beginning in the heart of Adam; what sinful fruit it has produced
since then, and what sinful fruit will it produce until threshing time
comes." The "evil seed" is a technical term for sin. (cf. 4 Esd. 8:53)

66 E. Kautzsch, *Apokryphen*, l.c., p. 377.—According to *Deuteronomy
Rabbah* 9 (ad Dt. 31:14) and according to the treatise *Shabbat* 55a,
since the "catastrophe of the leader of mankind," the children of men
are born in prison, as the children of prisoners (cf. H. L. Strack-P.
Billerbeck, *Kommentar*, III, 227).

67 These texts are quoted by B. Murmelstein, *Adam. Ein Beitrag zur
Messiaslehre*, in *WZKM* 35 (1928) 242-75 and 36 (1929) 51-86,
p. 253.

One suspects the basis for all these Jewish speculations is the traditional rabbinical doctrine of the unity of the human race in Adam. From the very beginning the "body of Adam" contained all humanity, as *Yalkut Shemeoni* teaches: "When God wanted to create the world, he began his creative work with man ... He breathed into him a soul, formed him, and summed up the entire universe in him." [68]

It is possible that the idea of a "primordial man" identical with humanity, comes from Iran and is a characteristic expression of the "Iranian corporate religious sense." [69] But regardless, we must never forget that "as soon as Judaism took note of these concepts about the primordial Man, it transposed them to the figure of Adam, the Jewish primordial man, and modified them according to the essential demands of the Israelite religion.[70] Among these changes we must note one specifically Jewish; namely, that not only the bodies but also the souls of all future men are included in the soul of Adam. (Cf. Ap. Bar. 21:10; 30:2; Esd. 4:35) In the *Fourth Book of Esdras* God expressly states: "When Adam transgressed my precepts, all creation was judged." [71] (4 Esd. 7:11) According to *Exode Rabba* 40:3, the just have their origin in a part of Adam's body; in this thought we have a rather materialistic concretization of the doctrine concerning the corporate soul of Adam.[72]

We find echoes of these Jewish speculations in the altogether singular remark of Tertullian: "Each soul is considered to be in

68 Quoted by G. Quispel, *Der gnostische Anthropos und die jüdische Tradition,* in *EJ* 22 (1953) 195-234, p. 225.

69 So thinks A. Ström, *Vetekornet,* l.c., 239, who thinks that the theme is found in all the Ancient Near East.

70 So, with good reason, points out E. Sjöberg, *Der Menschensohn im aethiopischen Henochbuch,* Lund, 1946, 193.–Cf. A Dupont-Sommer, *Adam "Père du Monde" dans la Sagesse de Salomon,* in *RHR* 119, (1939) 182-203; on pages 185-186 this author connects the title "father of the world" with that of the demiurge (*Timée* 28c) and with that of the *Anthropos,* "the primitive man, creator of the world."

71 E. Kautzsch, *Die Apokryphen,* l.c., p. 369. Cf. B. Murmelstein, op. cit., p. 267.

72 W. Staerk, *Die Erlöserewartung in den östlichen Religionen* (*Soter II*), Stuttgart, 1938, 15, n. 2.

Adam before it is taken up into Christ," [73] or in the more philosophical variant of the Syrian Aphrates: "Adam was conceived in
and remained in the thought of God . . . In him God knew all men
and begot them in this thought." [74]

We can correctly sum up late Jewish thought by saying that it
held that Adam was the sum total of all his descendants; after his
sin he became the sum total of all sinful souls, for in him all his
descendants sinned. [75] St. Paul certainly knew of these rabbinical
doctrines, and he must have looked upon Adam as "an incarnation
of all mankind." [76] The first man transgressed God's precepts; his
fall, which took place once at a given moment in the beginning of
history, explains sin and its consequences in all the sons of Adam.
The primordial transgression is not an event without effects in the
course of history; nor is it a symbolic presentation of general
truths without ties to a determined event; nor the beginning of
a casual chain binding, through physical generation, one atom
(Adam) to other atoms (the human race); but it is concerned
with a profound historical unity which sums up the torrent of
human sin in the malice of the first sinner. The fall of Adam has

---

73   Tert., *De anima* 40: *"Ita omnis anima eousque in Adam censetur esse,
     donec in Christo recenseatur"* (ML 2/719).—Cf. a little ahead (*De
     anima* 20), where Adam is called *"fons et matrix omnium."* According
     to Marius Victorinus (*In ep. ad Gal.* I; ML 8/1155 the Symmachians
     call Christ "Adam and the universal soul" (*dicunt enim   eum ipsum
     Adam esse et esse anima generalem.*)

74   Homily 17 no. 5, quoted by B. Murmelstein, l.c., p. 263.

75   Cf. B. Murmelstein, l.c., p. 85.

76   W. D. Davies, *Paul and Rabbinical Judaism,* London, 1948, 57. On
     page 55 this author reports the Jewish opinion according to which the
     Greek word *Adam* signifies the totality (the four celestial regions), A
     (*natolê*)—d(*usis*)—a(*rktos*)—m(*esêmbria*).—A. Ström, *Vetekornet,* l.c.,
     p. 195, quotes J. Weiss, *Das Urchristentum,* Göttingen, 1917, 330, ac-
     cording to which Adam is "a representative personality . . . , to a certain
     extent the embodiment of humanity." This is also the opinion of A.
     Oepke, *Leib Christi oder Volk Gottes bei Paulus?* in *TLZ* 79 (1954)
     363-368, p. 364: "Adam is the universal personality, both as the tribal
     father of humanity and separately as the representative of Israel.
     These thoughts have had their effects in many ways, in St. Paul as
     well as in later primitive Christianity."

created an historical situation which forthwith places sin in the
heart of every human individual, every "son of Adam." The
concise formula of St. Augustine is true to the thought of the
Apostle without betraying or exaggerating: *"Fuit Adam, et in illo
fuimus omnes; periit Adam, et omnes in illo perierunt."*[77]

In a certain sense we can say that "original sin according to
the first chapters of Genesis (to which St. Paul refers in Rom.
7:11) appears to be the sin of a species, of mankind taken in
the collective sense, of humanity taken as a unity, of a correspon-
sible totality, of humanity in an essential sense."[78] But it is absolutely necessary to reconcile this attitude, which is basically
correct, with Catholic doctrine which says that this sin most certainly is the act of one individual. In order to resolve this impasse
it seems that only one solution is appropriate: the Old Testament
and Jewish notion of Adam as a "corporate personality." At any
rate, this truly biblical category of thought can explain the shift
from the individual to the collectivity, and *vice versa.* The notion
of "corporate personality" includes the necessity of speaking of
these two points of view *at the same time.* Adam is, at one and the
same time, the tip of the cone of humanity and the whole of the
incomplete cone: "When humanity was made up of only a few
individuals, in fact of only two, *'ādām* could mean this primitive
couple. But even as it multiplies, humanity remains always *'ādām*
. . . Adam grows numerically in the course of time; he is not only
an individual but also a species."[79] His sin was not only an isolated

---

77   St. Augustine quotes Ambrose *In Lucam VII,* 25:24; cf. Aug. *Operis
      imperfecti lib. IV,* n. 104 (ML 45/1400). See also *De Civ. Dei XIII,*
      14: *"Omnes enim fuimus in illo uno, quando* OMNES FUIMUS ILLE
      UNUS, *qui per feminam lapsus est in peccatum, quae de illo facta est
      ante peccatum"* (ML 41/586)—For the Greek fathers, cf. Methodius
      (MG 18/69) or Origen (MG 13/337) *en tôi Adam pantes apoth-
      nêskousin.*

78   C. Tresmontant, *Etudes de métaphysique biblique,* Paris, 1955,
      134-135.

79   *Ibid.,* p. 137.—It seems inexact to me to say (cf. p. 138) that "the sin
      of Adam isn't a completed sin" or that "it is still continuing." In a
      certain sense original sin is "completely in the past"; but this past is
      operative today, since "every sin of mankind" is concentrated in the
      sin of our first parents. The past contains in advance the complete

fact which pertains to us only by its consequences as an unfortunate heritage; it was ontologically and identically the sin of
all mankind. That which has been at work in mankind since the
beginning, was already present in essence in the sin of the first
sinner. According to the profound insight of Kierkegaard: "Adam
is both himself and his progeny." [80]

B. *THE KING*

In the first part of his *Psalmenstudien,* Sigmund Mowinckel
makes this comment about Ps. 27:8: "The Lord is the strength of
his people, the saving refuge of his anointed": "It is inexact to
say that parallelism obliges us to interpret 'his anointed' as referring to 'people.' Parallelism does not prove absolutely the
identity between the two. Those who are cognizant with the thought
of the Ancient Orient know that the king and his people are
correlative ideas: the cause of the king is that of his people, and
vice versa. If the king prospers, the people will flourish, or at least,
according to the religious and political theory, should flourish." [81]
All of which means that the king is eminently suited to serve as
proof of our second and third themes: the influence of a given
individual for good or for bad upon the group dependent on
him.

In fact, "in ancient Oriental thought the king is the representative and incorporation of the community to such a degree that
from more than one point of view it is difficult to establish an

unfolding in time (cf. p. 142: "a sin committed formerly does not
cease to be present and actual.")

80   S. Kierkegaard, *Der Begriff der Angst,* 1844, 24: "*Adam ist er und
sein Geschlecht.*"

81   S. Mowinckel, *Psalmenstudien I, Awän und die individuelle Klagepsalmen,* Oslo, 1921, 151, n.1 concerning Ps. 27:8: "The Lord is the
strength of his *people,* the saving refuge of his *anointed.*" The parallelism of the words in italics does not prove their "essential identity"
(the anointed being the same as the people) but "an identity of concept." Cf. Also A. Gentzen, *Det. sakrale Kongedomme,* 1945, 95.

adequate distinction between the king and the people. If the king is godly, divine favor redounds to the people, for in the person of the king they are all godly. If the king is impious, the people are punished, for his culpability extends to the whole people. A favorable oracle for the king contains also a promise for the people, for the community of Yahweh." [82]

We have dealt with the "Savior king" in another place. [83] In Israel, as everywhere in the Fertile Crescent and in "primitive" civilizations, there is an evident correlation between the well-being of the nation and that of the king. In the same way the people is bound up with the king in reprobation and in punishment. In a sense, the king, who is the primary beneficiary of divine blessings or first object of divine anger, may be looked upon as a pipe line through which these blessings and this anger come upon the people. Some have tried to explain this condition by a kind of magical influence, as though the king, as a sorcerer or *shaman,* created the life, the fertility, or the well-being of his people. [84] It seems more correct to say that the king is only the instrument, or, if one

82 S. Mowinckel, *Psalmenstudien II,* 1921, 299; cf. by the same author *Psalmenstudien V, Segen und Fluch im Israels Kult Psalmdichtung,* Oslo, 1925, 36: "Under special circumstances (in cult) the larger I of the people is totally concentrated in the person of the individual. This is especially true of the leader .... Then he is not a representative in the modern sense of the word, but the entire people *is* in him and he *is* the people." See also N. A. Dahl, *Das Volk Gottes,* l.c., p. 21: "Thus the king is a real fact of salvation; his presence is the basis for prosperity and national security .... Through the choosing of the king the people is chosen."—H. Wheeler Robinson, *The Hebrew Conception,* l.c., p. 56 points out that the king is "Yahweh's son" (2 Kgs. 7:14) in imitation of the people. (Os. 11:1)

83 J. De Fraine, S.J., *L'aspect religieux de la royauté israélite. L'institution monarchique dans l'AT et dans les textes mésopotamiens,* Rome, 1954, 370-391.

84 W. C. Graham—H. C. May, *Culture and Conscience,* Chicago, 1936, 170, calls Saul "a local shaman-king."—In turn A. Causse, *Du groupe ethnique,* l.c., 33,1 speaks of "the magical conception of the leader, who sums up in himself all the energies of the social organism." J. Pedersen, *Israel I-II,* l.c., p. 83 exalts the royal "superman" upon whom depend victory, fertility, and the future of the people.

wishes, the point of reception, of the divine blessing (b^{e}rākhāh).[85]
For this blessing comes only from Yahweh; the national God is,
in the last analysis, the fruitful source of the power of the blessing.[86]
That is why the Chosen People thank Yahweh for the blessings
showered on the king: "The Lord has given victory to his anointed
. . . God has blessed you forever." (Ps. 20:4-7; Ps. 44:3)

This personalist view of the "God who acts"[87] does not at all
agree with the picture of the "divine force" stored up in the king
and discharged like a psychic fluid on his subordinates, or dif-
fused like a vital fluid into all the branches of the tree of the
nation.[88] No valid argument for such theories can be drawn from
the poetic imagery of "the tree of life,"[89] such as appears in Ps.

---

85   S. Mowinckel, *Psalmenstudien II*, 114: "Yahweh blesses the people in
     the king: the primitive thought and that of Israel join hands." In this
     very restricted sense the king is "divine," a formula which tends at
     present to be replaced by "sacral king." Cf. G. Widengren, *Sakrales
     Königtum im AT und im Judentum*, Stuttgart, 1955, or J. A. Johnson,
     Sacral Kingship in Early Israel, Cardiff, 1955, and, already in 1945,
     A. Bentzen, *Det Sakrale Kongedomme*.

86   S. Mowinckel, *Psalmenstudien III*, 1924, 93; cf. by the same author
     Studia Theologica (*Lund*) 2 (1948) 81 n. or J. Pedersen, *Israel I-II*,
     l.c., p. 83.

87   Cf. G. E. Wright, *God Who Acts*, London, 1952.

88   S. Mowinckel, *Psalmenstudien III*, 33; J. Pedersen, *Israel* (Danish
     edition 1934) II, 367.

89   G. Widengren, *The King and the Tree of Life in Ancient Near
     Eastern Religion* (*King and Savior IV*), Uppsala, 1951. This Swedish
     author, thanks to some very ingenious comparisons, "discovers"
     everywhere traces of belief in "the tree of life" being associated with
     the king; he points to Ez. 19:10.11, 13-14 where it is said that the
     royal scepters are made of the wood of the vine (p. 37); he recalls
     that "Aaron's staff" really belongs to Moses (Nm. 17:23: p. 39); the
     allusions in Is. 11:1 and 14:19 to a shoot of wood underlines the royal
     character of the figures described in these passages (p. 50); the tree
     of life is hidden in the following phrases: "a righteous shoot" (Jer.
     23:5), "the Shoot" (Za. 3:8; 6:12) (p. 51-52); he draws the same
     theme out of texts such as the following: Is. 53:2 ("He grew up like
     a sapling before him"; p. 53; Ez. 31:2-9 (where Pharao is compared
     to a great cedar; p. 56); Dn. 4:7-9 (Nabuchodonosor's vision of the
     great tree; p. 57). Cf. also I. Engnell, *The 'Ebed Yahweh Songs and*

79:15:16: "O Lord of hosts . . . take care of this vine (cf. Is. 5:7), and protect what your right hand has planted" (cf. v. 18: "May your help be with the man of your right hand"), or in Za. 4:3, 12: (the two olive trees pouring out oil). For in no case can we hold that in the official religion of Yahwehism the king could be identified with the divinity as symbolized by the tree of life.[90] At the most it might be question of the king being assimilated into the divine (cf. 1 K. 29:9; 2 K. 14:17: "an angel God"), not in the sense of a personal assimilation but in the sense of the institution of kingship being given a divine function by Yahweh.[91]

On account of this functional instrumentality of the king, we are lead to conceive of the "kingship ideology" as a "special case of 'corporate personality' ideology."[92] The great importance of the king regarding the lot of his subjects flows from the fact that the king is a "corporate personality," who in some way sums up the individual members of the group, or in whom these members

the Suffering Messiah in "Duetero-Isaiah" in BJRL 31 (1948) 54-93, p. 82 concerning Is. 53:2 kayyōnéq. The imagery is evident in texts such as Os. 14:9: "I am like a verdant cypress tree— because of me you bear fruit!"

90 Cf. J. De Fraine, L'aspect religieux, l.c., pp. 263-284.–I. Engnell, Studies in Divine Kingship in the Ancient Near East, Uppsala, 1945, 175-176 tries to "prove" the identity between the king and the deities by such texts as Gn. 44:16 (Joseph distinguishes himself from "Elohim"; cf. Gn. 45:5), Ps. 8:6 (less than an elohim), Ps. 44:7, Jer. 22:18 (a lamentation in which the dead person is assimilated to Tammuz).

91 H. Von Borch, Das Gottesgnadentum. Historisch-soziologischer Versuch über die religiöse Herrschaftslegitimation, Berlin, 1934, 56: "The institutional type, Oriental in its origin, is founded on the idea that dominion of itself—as an institution—is divine."

92 A Ström, Vetekornet, l.c., p. 128. Cf. R. Aubrey Johnson, in S. Hooke, The Labyrinth, 1935, 73-111, especially p. 74. Also T. Schmidt, Der Leib Christi (sôma Xristou). Eine Untersuchung zur urchristlichen Gemeindegedanken, Leipzig-Erlangen, 1919, 218: "He (the king) is the representative of the people; they are in a certain way embodied in him, and his religious position corresponds to that of the people as a totality."

are united so as to form one single person before God, or before foreigners, or before enemies of the nation.[93]

This is verified first of all in "primitive" communities. The figure of the "leader" dominates the life of the group, since, in a certain sense, it is "the symbolical projection of the community ideal." [94] While remaining distinct from the others, the leader has the gift of directing his subjects in accordance with their own aspirations; in this way he identifies himself with others, while assuming them into his own personality.[95] He is the source of thought and action in behalf of his subjects, for he incarnates the community life. As long as the people or the clan recognize in him the one who accomplishes their desires, his status as leader is secure; for then he conceives and determines the objectives which others see only vaguely, and he succeeds in outlining thoughts which others perceive mistily without being able to formulate them completely. Precisely this continual representation of the people by its leader is the basis for the evident correlation between the two. A purely individualistic view which looks upon the leader as a genius endowed with a prestige and an exceptional mystical power does not satisfactorily explain the office of leader.[96] It is always necessary to take account of a true delegation, even a kind of creation on the part of the group: "In many countries the king descends in a straight line from the old magician or healer; when a special class of magicians was separated from the community and *charged by it* with duties on which depended, as they believed, the public safety and common prosperity, these men, little by little, advanced themselves to material possessions and power; one day the first among them blossomed out as a consecrated king." [97]

93 N. A. Dahl, *Das Volk Gottes*, l.c., 21: "Every Israelite stands before Yahweh as a representative of God's people and bearer of its character; the king does it, however, in a special sense," because he is "the embodiment of the people, who contains all the powers of the people in himself."

94 K. Young, *Social Psychology*, New York, 1946, 249.

95 E. Faris, *The Nature of Human Nature*, New York, 1937[2], 31.

96 *Ibid.*, p. 33.

97 J. G. Frazer, *Les origines magiques de la royauté*, Paris, 1920, 137. Cf. G. Widengren, *Religionens Värld*, Stockholm, 1953[2], 462. Cf. J.

However, while being chosen by the group, the king was not limited to playing a purely passive role; for personal prestige counted much when it was a question of making a king. Even in primitive groups, individuals outstanding for their commanding appearance (cf. 1 K. 10:23) or their prowess in battle (1 K. 8:20) were invested with royal powers. As has been said regarding magicians, the institution of kingship is a "social phenomenon which is produced only by individual effort."[98] We might turn this formula around and say that royalty constitutes a striking example of an individualistic phenomenon which is produced only in a community and for the benefit of that community. The personal prestige of the king can increase indefinitely: he always remains in contact with the social organism which depends upon him and it is this contact which creates the strength of his influence. L. Lévy-Bruhl cites these words of an explorer who was interested in the aborigines of South Africa: "The leader is the earth . . . he is the cock . . ., he is the bull: without him the cows remain sterile. He is the husband: the country without him is like a woman without a husband. He is the man of the village . . . A clan without a leader has lost its reason for existence; it is dead . . . The leader is our great warrior, he is our forest in which we hide."[99]

Frequently primitive peoples exalt the beneficent action of their king. In their eyes he causes "the wind, the harvest, and the rain; he is or believes himself to be the equal of 'God,' the divine being of the Whites."[100] In all these manifestations of royal

G. Frazer, *Le rameau d'or*, (French translation) Paris, 1903-1911, I, 145.

98 H. Hubert and M. Mauss, *Mélanges d'Histoire des Religions*, Paris, 1929[2], 171: "(Among the aborigines of Australia) revelation is often provoked by the individual, who feels himself suited to become a magician, either in conjunction with other magicians, or by predetermined nervous dispositions."

99 L. Lévy-Bruhl, *L'âme primitive*, Paris, 1927, 75. Cf. by the same author, *Les fonctions mentales dans les sociétés inférieures*, Paris, 1928[9], 81: "The well-being of the tribe, its prosperity, and even its existence depend always, in virtue of a mystic participation, on the pick of its leaders, living or dead."

100 L. Lévy-Bruhl, *La mentalité primitive*, Paris, 1925[4], 367.

"power," the trend of thought never passes from one individual (the king) to other individuals, but the latter are thought of as present in the archetype. There is no question of magic, but rather of "mystical concentration": the "great I" of the community, the "collective I," if one wishes,[101] is summed up in the personal "I" of a visible representative. But, in primitive mentality, "to represent something" is to be that something, metaphysically speaking.[102]

To say without further qualification that the Ancient Orient, as a whole, scarcely surpasses the level of primitive or prelogical thought is certainly exaggerated.[103] However we must admit that the idea of a monarchical institution as the realization of the intimate union between the king and his people is not readily explained on the basis of individualistic philosophical categories. On the other hand, the idea becomes perfectly clear if we base it on the notion of "corporate personality," according to which the individual king, without being exalted as an autonomous source of magical influences is rather a powerful summing up of the potentialities of the group subject to him. This is certainly true of the Assyro-Babylonian kings, in whom the peoples of Mesopotamia saw an incarnation of the nation.[104]

Even regarding Egypt where the "divinity" of the Pharao is often emphasized, we must be cautious in our statements: "It is not simply the "I" desirous of self glorification which seeks union with God but the entire people, represented by the divine king. Such an attitude presupposes that the people look upon themselves not as a group of separated individuals but as a truly unified community. The king can only maintain his role as the bearer of the vital forces of the national community rather than as an isolated individual being. Because the nation is identified with the king, it is possible to transfer this relationship in the

---

101 S. Mowinckel, *Psalmenstudien II,* 300 calls this phrase "somewhat distorted."

102 *Ibid.,* We can quote a text of Ignatius of Antioch who applies this principle to the bishop: "Everywhere the bishop is, there the faithful are present." (Smyrn. 8:2)

103 S. Mowinckel, *Psalmenstudien II,* 225; or *Psalmenstudien I,* 97.

104 R. Labat, *Le caractère religieux de la royauté assyro-babylonienne,* Paris, 1939, 323.

hereafter ... (Until the end of the Middle Empire) the people existed only through the king, and the king existed only through the people." [105]

What is true of Egypt is true also, *mutatis mutandis,* in the biblical accounts.

1. *The Pentateuch*

The Pentateuch several times speaks of the effects which the king's act has on all the people, precisely because the two—people and king—form one "corporate personality." Since the Pentateuch does not deal with Israelite kings, its references will be to non-Israelite kings. (Cf. Dt. 17:14-20; 28:36) When Abimelech, king of Gerara reproaches Abraham for the way in which he deserted his wife, he says: "What have you done to *us?* And how have *I* offended you that you should bring down on *me and my kingdom* a great sin? No one should be treated as you have treated me." (Gn. 20:9) Abraham would have been able to call down the wrath of God, and thus the innocent (Gn. 20:4) would have been punished with their king. When the same king Abimelech allies himself to Abraham, he asks him: "Swear to me by God that you will not deal falsely *with me nor with my children nor with my descendants.* As I have treated you with kindness, so must you treat *me and the land* in which you live as a stranger." (Gn. 21:23)

The plagues of Egypt strike not only the hardhearted king but also the entire country. The frogs come "into your (Pharao's) palace and into your bedroom and onto your bed" and also into "the houses of your servants,[106] too, and your subjects." (Ex. 7: 28) Pharao begs Moses to beseech God to remove the frogs from "me and my subjects." (Ex. 8:4-5) The same expression: "upon you (Pharao) and your servants and your subjects" apears several

---

105 W. Wolf, *Individuum und Gemeinschaft in der ägyptischen Kultur,* Glückstadt, 1935, 19-20. In his study of 1936 (ZAW Bhft 66, p. 53) H. Wheeler Robinson refers to this publication and concludes: "It was the people as a whole, represented by the divine king, who had to do with God."

106 In Gn. 45:16 "Pharao and his court" were pleased at the arrival of "Joseph's brothers."

times in the account of the plagues. (Ex. 8:17, 25: flies; Ex. 9:14: jail; Ex. 10:6 locusts; Ex. 12:30: death of the first-born) The common punishment is evidently inflicted because of a common guilt. After the hail Pharao momentarily repents: "I have sinned again! The Lord is just; it is *I and my subjects* who are at fault." [107] (Ex. 9:27) But the monarch soon hardens his heart: "he with his servants." (Ex. 9:34; 10:1) That is why the plagues continue to strike against "Pharao and upon Egypt" (Ex. 11:1), against "Pharao and all his servants and all his land." (Dt. 29:1)

Moses, the opponent of Pharao, is presented as the "leader" of the "children of Israel." The royal servants of Egypt prostrate themselves before him and say: "Leave us, you *and all your followers.*" (Ex. 11:8; cf. Ex. 34:10; 34:27: where God allies himself with you (Moses, and with Israel") [108]

At the time of the passage of the Red Sea, Pharao is identified with his army. (Ex. 14:4) Verse 10 speaks of Pharao approaching, when it is really his army that is pursuing the Israelites. The sacred text in speaking of the obduracy of the Egyptians and Pharao again identifies the two: "But I will make the Egyptians so obstinate that they will go in after them. Then I will receive glory through Pharao and all his army, his chariots and his charioteers." (Ex. 14:17; cf. 14:23) At any rate there is evidence of "the great power that the Lord had shown against the Egyptians." (Ex. 14: 31)

If a king is conquered, he drags down with him his whole country. The Lord says to Moses: "Do not be afraid of him (Og, the king of Basan); for into your hand I will deliver him with *all his people and his land.*" (Nm. 21:34-35) Sehon, king of Hesebon, suffered the same fate: "The Lord, our God, had delivered him to us, we defeated him and his sons and *all* his people."

---

107   In Ex. 7:4 Pharao "will not listen"; and in Ex. 10:17 the king asks pardon for his offense. On both of these occasions the sovereign manifestly represents his subordinates.

108   We might think also of the role of mediator which Aaron (the priest) assumes on the Day of Expiation: "he shall ... then come out and offer his own and the people's holocaust. (Lv. 16:24) Josue also leads his people in the rites of expiation. (Jos. 7:6)

(Dt. 2:33) Cities conquered in battle were subject to massacre with their men, women and children. (Dt. 3:6; 7:2)

The Israelite king of the future will, according to the tenor of the Deuteronomic Law, be subjected to the same punishment, namely exile, as his sinful subjects: "The Lord will bring you, and your king whom you have set over you, to a nation which you and your fathers have not known." (Dt. 28:36)

2. *The Historical Books*

The historical books furnish us with a number of texts illustrating the intimate relationship of the king with his people. In the Books of Josue and Judges a non-Israelite king is frequently swept up in the collective punishment of his "city." Yahweh promises Josue: "I have delivered the king of Hai into your power with his people, city, and land. Do to Hai *and its king* what you did to Jericho and its king." (Jos. 8:1-2) "To strike a city with its king" is a recurring phrase in the Book of Josue. (Jos. 10:28: Maceda; 10:30: Lebna; 10:37: Eglon) It is equivalent to "Josue defeated him (the king of Gazer) *and his people.*"[109] (Jos. 10:33) At the time of the Judges the absence of a king caused general political disorder which was disadvantageous for the people: "In those days there was no king in Israel; everyone did what he thought best." (Jg. 17:6; 18:1; 19:1; 21:25)

The *Books of Kings* and the *Books of Paralipomenon* tell us about the institution of the monarchy in Israel.[110] Everywhere

---

109 Cf. Ne. 9:24: "and gavest them into their hands, with their kings, and the people of the land"; Esd. 9:7: "for our iniquities we and our kings, and our priests have been delivered into the hands of the kings of the lands."

110 Before king Saul there were semi-royal persons such as Gedeon and Jephte. they also are inseparable from their people. The idolatry of Gedeon spells the downfall of his people: "Gedeon made an ephod out of the gold and placed it is his city Ephra. However, all Israel paid idolatrous homage to it there, and it caused the ruin of Gedeon and his family." (Jgs. 8:27) Jephte identifies himself completely with his country. His messengers speak as follows to the king of the Ammonites: "What have you against me that you come to fight with me *in my land?*" (Jg. 11:12; cf. Jg. 11:27: "You wrong me by

the corporate nature of the king is stressed. The motive of the Israelites in asking for a king is stated without equivocation: "There shall be a king over us. And we also will be like all nations." (1 K. 8:19-20) The king is to be anointed, that is to say, invested with the spirit;[111] his possession of the divine *ruah* is a permanent charism which consecrates him to the service of his people.[112] His duty is to "save" (I K. 10:27; cf. Os. 13:10) by the winning military victories and by safeguarding justice. (1 K. 8:20) He will go before his people (1 K. 12:2), forming with them an indissoluble unity, as Samuel remarks in his farewell speech: "If you will fear the Lord, and serve him, and harken to his voice, and not provoke the mouth of the Lord, then shall both you, and the king who reigns over you, be followers of the Lord, your God." (1 K. 12:14; cf. 12:25)

There is a close union between the king and his people both for weal and for woe. Almost spontaneously the sacred writers associate the king with his people. When Abner is shamefully assassinated by Joab, David hastens to say: "*I and my kingdom* are innocent before the Lord forever of the blood of Abner the son of Ner." (2 K. 3:28; cf. 1 Par. 29:14: "Who am I, and what is my people?") King David is convinced that his reign has been blessed by the God of Israel and that because "the Lord had confirmed him king over Israel, and that he had exalted his kingdom over his people Israel." [the French translation has 'because of' instead of 'over'] (2 K. 5:12) What better way to express the idea of the king as the "source of the national well-being." [113]

warring against *me*.") The same formula appears in the reply of the Ammonites: "Israel took away my land." (Jg. 11:13)

111 Cf. J. De Fraine, *L'aspect religieux*, pp. 190-199.

112 E. E. Aubrey, *The Holy Spirit in Relation to the Religious Community*, in JThSt 41 (1940) 1-13 defines "spirit" (*rūah*) as "a miraculous power conferred upon individuals for the welfare of the nation."

113 J. Pederson, *Israel, I-II*, 429: "The king is the nucleus from which the people draw their strength." Compare with the formula of 4 Kgs. 11:17: "And Joiada made a covenant between the Lord, and the king, and the people, that they should be the people of the Lord, and

The union of the people with the king is clearly noted in the liturgical celebrations. The king presides over them, not because he is a "priest" properly so called (that is to say one set aside for special service to God and consecrated specially for the task), but because of his position as "ruler over the people of the Lord in Israel." (2 K. 6:21) It was in his "corporate" role, so to say, that David "danced with all his might before the Lord" (2 K. 6: 14), for it was never David alone but David *"and all the house of Israel* that brought the ark of the covenant of the Lord with joyful shouting." (2 K. 6:15) Similarly the prayer of Solomon is not strictly personal but joined with that of his people: "That thou mayest harken to the supplication of thy servant *and of thy people Israel,* whatsoever they shall pray for in this place." (3 K. 8:30, 36; 2 Par. 6:21) This is more than a mere juxtaposition (the people praying *with* the king); it is one prayer shared in by both. Even the sacrifices are offered in common: "And the king, and all Israel with him, offered victims before the Lord." (3 K. 8:62; 2 Par. 7:4)[114] Obviously the king is considered to be the leader of the holy nation, who "intercedes" for his people (2 Par. 30:18: Ezechias) and around whom his subjects group themselves: "And

between the king and the people." Cf. also 4 K. 23:3 for the covenant of Josias and the people with Yahweh.

114 However, the king is in no way a sacrificing priest in the technical sense of the word. This is explicitly stated in certain texts of *Paralipomenon;* for example, 2 Par. 29:24: "the king *had commanded* that the holocaust and the sin offering should be made for all Israel," and 2 Par. 29:27: "Ezechias commanded that they should offer holocausts." Indeed, as the primary provider of the matter for sacrifice, and as the "leader" of cult, the king represents, in fact "is" his people. Cf. S. Mowinckel, *Psalmenstudien V,* 1924, 35: "The people is in him and he is the people." But as J. Pedersen, *Israel I-II,* 1947², 429 remarks: it is "at the very least difficult to say what the role of the king in the temple cult was, because those who collected the old traditions were not at all interested in his role." On the other hand, we can reverse the argument and say that if the indications of a "sacerdotal" role for the king are rather insignificant in the Old Testament, this condition has a good chance of reflecting an historical reality. If the indications had been considerable, they would have more copiously filtered through the "revision" of traditions.

Solomon made at the same time a solemn feast, *and all Israel with him.*" (3 K. 8:65; 2 Par. 7:8)

Through the intermediary of the king, Yahweh dispenses justice to His people as well as to the king himself. (3 K. 8:59) After the solemn feast of the dedication of the temple by Solomon, the people leave Jerusalem "rejoicing, and glad in heart for all the good things that the Lord has done for David his servant, and for Israel his people." (3 K. 8:66: 2 Par. 7:10 adds "and to Solomon") The great king David is blessed in his people and in his son Solomon, and his people are blessed with him. The intimate relationship of the king (especially as the legitimate successor of David and as depository of the dynastic promise of 2 K. 7) with the numerous people who live under his dominion is expressed very happily by the Queen of Saba before Solomon: "Blessed be the Lord thy God, whom thou hast pleased, and who has set thee upon the throne of Israel, *because the Lord has loved Israel forever,* and has appointed *thee* king, to do judgment and justice." (3 K. 10:9; 2 Par. 9:8) Because Yahweh sees Israel in the (corporate) person of the king (the lamp of Israel),[115] He surrounds the king with His special solicitude. If the king is faithful to the command which Yahweh imposes, doing "judgment and justice to all his people" (2 K. 8:15: David; cf. 2 K. 23:3) it is, in the last analysis, the people of God who profit by it. Basically it is the collective choice which continues uninterruptedly according to the divine promises: "I will dwell in the midst of the children

---

115 These words apply to king David. During his lifetime his men told him: "Thou shalt go no more out with us to battle, lest thou put out the lamp of Israel." (2 K. 21:17; cf. 2 K. 23:4) After the death of David, the same phrase indicates the continuing divine favor for the Davidic dynasty (Ps. 88:30); Yahweh's promise is explicit: "And to his son (Solomon) I will give one tribe, that there may remain a lamp for my servant David before me always in Jerusalem the city which I have chosen, that my name might be there." (3 K. 11:36; cf. 3 K. 15:4; 4 K. 8:19; Ps. 131:17) In 2 Par. 21:7 the theme of the "lamp" is joined to that of the "covenant": "But the Lord would not destroy that house of David, because of the covenant which he had made with him, and because he had promised to give a lamp to him and to his sons forever."

of Israel, and will not forsake my people Israel" (if Solomon remains faithful).[116] (3 K. 6:13)

The *Books of Kings and Paralipomenon* speak frequently of the people's solidarity in the guilt or misfortune of their king. The tragic fate of Saul is a classic example. On the eve of the battle of Gelboe, the ghost of Samuel tells the first king of Israel: "The Lord also will deliver Israel *with thee* into the hands of the Philistines. And tomorrow thou and thy sons shall be with me; and the Lord will also deliver the army of Israel into the hands of the Philistines." (1 K. 28:19) After receiving the news of the death of Saul and Jonathan, "David took hold of his garments and rent them, and likewise all the men that were with him. And they mourned, and wept, and fasted until evening for Saul, and for Jonathan his son, *and for the people of the Lord,* and for the house of Israel, because they (Saul of the Israelite warriors, or both?) were fallen by the sword." (2 K. 1:11-12) The injustice Saul had perpetrated against the Gabaonites followed him even after his death, for the people were punished because of it with three years of famine: "It (famine) is for Saul, *and his bloody house,* because he slew the Gabaonites." (2 K. 21:1) Only after seven of Saul's descendants have expiated the crime by their own crucifixion did "God show mercy again to the land." (2 K. 21:14)

David's ill-starred census of the people (which seems to be entirely authentic, for it in no way flatters the king) was, in the eyes of Yahweh, inspired by pride. What is remarkable about the incident is that not only the king but also all the people are punished: "And the Lord sent a pestilence upon Israel." (2 K. 24:15) As the avenging angel, sent to punish the pride of David in his people, is about to strike Jerusalem, David prays to Yahweh: "It is I; I am he that have sinned, I have done wickedly. These that are my sheep, what have they done?" (2 K. 24:17) We have here the stricken conscience of a king who recognizes that the entire nation is being punished for his personal sin.

The Deuteronomic recension of Israelite history as found in the *Book of Kings* constantly recalls, in dealing with the kings

---

116 In 4 K. 19:34 Yahweh proclaims: "And I will protect this city, and will save it for my own sake, and for David my servant's sake." Cf. also 4 K. 20:16; 1 Par. 22:10.

of the northern kingdom, the fatal chain reaction of sin: "And the Lord shall give up Israel for the *sins of Jeroboam,* who has sinned, and made Israel to sin." (3 K. 14:16) Nadab, the son of Jeroboam, imitates the conduct of his father and "his sons, wherewith he made Israel to sin." (3 K. 15:26) Baasa does the same, and the prophet Jehu tells him in the name of Yahweh: "Thou hast walked in the way of Jeroboam, and hast made my people Israel to sin, to provoke me to anger with their sins." (3 K. 16:2, 13) Zambri, in turn, did "evil before the Lord, and walked in the way of Jeroboam, and in his sin, wherewith he made Israel to sin." (3 K. 16:19) The sins of Jeroboam, the son of Nabat, "wherewith he made Israel to sin" (3 K. 16:26; 4 K. 3:2; 10:29; 13:2, 11; 14:24; 15:9, 18, 24, 28; and especially 4 K. 17:21-22) are a kind of "corporate sin."[117]

Achab, the husband of Jezabel the Sidonian, ranks first among the kings of Samaria noted for their impiety. To his infidelity to Yahweh is attributed the drought that plagued Israel during his reign. (3 K. 17) When the king meets Elias, he says to him: "Art thou he that troublest Israel?"; but Elias retorts: "I have not troubled Israel, but thou and thy father's house, who have forsaken the commandments of the Lord, and have followed Baalim." (3 K. 18:18) Elias looks upon Achab as the scourge of Israel because he has brought Israel to its ruin. When the king refuses to kill a man under the anathema of Yahweh, the prophet tells him: "Thus saith the Lord: Because thou hast let go out of thy hand a man worthy of death, *thy life* shall be for his life, *and thy people for his people.*" (3 K. 20:42)

The southern kingdom of Juda also had its wicked kings. The account of Solomon's accession to the throne of David is colored with the idea that the successive revolts (Absalom, Adonias) were due to the social and sexual abuses of the king rather than to political blunders.[118] As Yahweh tells Solomon: "If you and your

---

117 H. H. Rowley, *The Faith of Israel,* 1956, 108: "an act of corporate sin."

118 J. Hempel, *Das Ethos des AT,* ZAW Bhft 67, Berlin, 1938, 88: "For the narrator of the accessions to the throne, it is the social and sexual abuses of the ruler (not his political ineptitude) which provoke revolts."

children revolting shall turn away from following me, . . . I will take Israel from the face of the land . . ., and Israel shall be a proverb, and a byword among all people." (3 K. 9:6-7) Freqently the *Books of Paralipomenon* stress the connection between the king's plan "to serve false gods" and the inevitable anger of Yahweh against all his subjects. Roboam "forsook the law of the Lord, *and all Israel with him.*" (2 Par. 12:1) Joram received the following threatening message from Elias: "The Lord will strike *thee* with a great plague, *with all thy people,* and thy children and thy wives, and all thy substance." (2 Par. 21:14) Achaz was the cause of his country's decline: "For the Lord had humbled Juda *because of Achaz* the king of Juda, for he had stripped it of help, and had condemned the Lord." (2 Par. 28:19) Even the good king Ezechias "did not render again according to the benefits which he had received (cure from sickness), for his heart was lifted up; and wrath was enkindled against him, and against Juda and Jerusalem." (2 Par. 32:25) Other Judean kings, especially Manasses, the successor of Ezechias, are commonly recognized as the instigators of their people's sins: "The Lord turned not away from the wrath of his great indignation, wherewith his anger was kindled against Juda, because of the provocations wherewith Manasses had provoked him." (4 K. 23:26; cf. 21:21; 24:3)

From the preceding we can conclude unhesitatingly that all the historic tradition of the Jewish people gives evidence of a close union between the king and his subjects. Even at the time of the Machabees, the leader of Israel is intimately united with the nation. (1 Mac. 11:30, 42; 15:1-9: "thee, and thy nation, and the temple") To meddle with the king is to meddle with the people; to humble the king is to humble the people; to honor the king is to give honor to the people.

3. *The Prophetic Books*

We find the same identification in these books. In his last conversation with Sedecia, Jeremia describes the solidarity binding the destiny of Jerusalem with its king: "Thus says the Lord God of Hosts, the God of Israel: If you surrender to the princes of Babylon's king, *you shall save your life; this city* shall not be destroyed with fire, and you and your family shall live. But if you do not surrender to the princes of Babylon's king, *this city* shall fall into the hands of the Chaldeans, who shall destroy it with fire, and *you shall not escape their hands.*" (Jer. 38:17:18)

Sometimes the prophetical books speak of the benefits to be gained by the identification: "I will renew with you the everlasting covenant, the benefits assured to David." (Is. 55:3); or "I will raise up a righteous shoot to David; as king he shall reign and govern wisely, he shall do what is just and right in the land. In his days *Juda will be saved.*" (Jer. 23:5-6); or "The anointed one of the Lord, *our breath of life,* . . . he in whose shadow we thought we could live on among the nations." (Lam. 4:20)

More frequently, however, the prophets concentrate on pointing out the evil influence of the wicked kings. Achaz brings punishment upon Juda because he would not believe the word of Isaia: "The Lord shall bring upon *you and your people* and your father's house days worse than any since Ephraim seceded from Juda." (Is. 7:17) Similarly, the people suffer because of the evil of Manasses (Jer. 15:4), Sedecia (Jer. 24:8; 29:16), and Joakim. (Jer. 36:31)

The neighboring pagan kings, as well as the kings of Israel and Juda, form one single unity with their people in the sight of God. Jeremia is to have "Pharao, king of Egypt, and his servants, his princes, *all the people under him*" drink of the Lord's cup of judgment. (Jer. 25:19) Sedecia must submit himself to Nabuchodonosor and to his people: "Submit your necks to the yoke of the king of Babylon; serve him *and his people.*" (Jer. 27:12) The solidarity that binds together Israel "and their kings" (Ez. 43:7) is portrayed in the threat of Ezechiel: "The prince shall be enveloped in terror, and the hands of the common people [119] shall tremble." [120] (Ez. 7:27) On the other hand, the kings share in the punishment inflicted on a faithless people: "You carried out

---

119   The "common people" (cf. Dn. 9:6) are the citizens of Jerusalem, who enjoy full civil rights. They elect kings Josias (4 Kgs. 21:24, 2 Par. 32:25) and Joachaz (4 K. 23:30, 2 Par. 36:1) and join in cult (Lv. 20:2,4; Ez. 39:13). Cf. E. Gillischewski, *Der Ausdruck 'am hā'ārêc im At,* in ZAW 40, (1922) 137-142.

120   In Ez. 45:22, the "prince" offers "on his own behalf, and on behalf of all the people of the land, a bull as a sin offering."

the threats you spoke against us and against *those who governed us*." (Dn. 9:20)

4. *The Sapiential Books*

These books also have traces of the "corporate" notion of the king. This is particularly true in the "royal" psalms, but also in other sapiential books. According to Jb. 29:25: "I (the king) chose out this way and presided." The *Book of Proverbs* frequently notes the relationship between the status of the king and the welfare of his people; for example: In many subjects lies the glory of the king; but if his people are few, it is the prince's ruin." (Prv. 14:28) The following picturesque similes bring out the same truth: "In the light of the king's countenance is life, and his favor is like a rain cloud in spring." (Prv. 16:15);[121][122] "Like a roaring lion or a ravenous bear is a wicked ruler over a poor people." (Prv. 28:15) Under the imagery of these thoughts lies the same thought as in Wis. 6:24: "a prudent king, (is) the stability of his people."

In the royal psalms the king quite often appears under a "corporate" aspect. The people rejoice over the good fortune of the king, as in psalm 19:6: "May we shout for joy at your victory." The king is made "a blessing forever" (Ps. 20:7), which is to say that he has become an inexhaustible source of good fortune for his people. Psalm 44:4 also brings out this same idea: "Gird your sword upon your thigh, O mighty one! In your splendor and your majesty ride on triumphant in the cause of truth and for the sake of justice." The ideal king "shall govern your people with justice." (Ps. 71:2); "He shall have pity for the lowly and the poor." (v.13); "In him shall all the tribes of the earth be blessed." (v. 17); during his reign "may there be an abundance of grain upon the earth."[123] (v. 16) In psalm 83:10 the psalmist beseeches God: "O

---

121 A. Lods, *Lsraël des origines au milieu de VIIIᵉ siecle*, Paris, 1930, 457.
122 Cf. Ps. 71:6: "He (the son of the ideal king) shall be like rain coming down on the meadow, like showers watering the earth."
123 It is not at all easy to determine whether psalm 71 is directly Messianic or whether it became "Messianic" through a re-reading of the original "royal" meaning. According to S. Mowinckel, *Psalmenstudien II*, 306, its Messianism comes from the fact that the psalm

God, behold our shield, and look upon the face of your anointed."
Psalm 88:39 tells of Yahweh's rejection of his anointed one: "Yet
you have rejected and spurned and been enraged at your anointed."
Whether "your anointed" is the king alone or all the people, the
entire country suffers: "You have broken down all his walls; you
have laid his stronghold in ruins." (Ps. 88:41)

Regarding these royal psalms we may well wonder whether
there are cogent proofs for saying that the Israelite king in his
role as the "servant of Yahweh" was considered to have passed
from death to life, through a vicarious suffering[124] "in favor of
the people whose sins he bore and for whom he was responsible."[125] In any case, we can say that the idea of a "corporate"
representative is inherent in the concept of the Savior-King.

C. THE PROPHETS

No one doubts that the prophets were sent by Yahweh, and
therefore were His representatives. The English author R. Aubrey
Johnson does not hesitate to say that, in a certain sense, the
personality of the great prophets is swallowed up in that of their
divine master,[126] so that sometimes it is impossible to distinguish

> pictures in the future the ideal type of the Davidic king. (Cf. also
> J. Pedersen, *Israel I-II*, 1947², 655) In any case, there is an identity
> of characteristics between the king and the Messias. Like the king, the
> Messias has a following of the faithful. Just as a king without fol-
> lowers makes no sense, so the Messias is inconceivable without his
> "people." Cf. for the New Testament, N. A. Dahl, *Das Volk Gottes*,
> Oslo, 1941, 40: "Just as the king embodies the people, so does the
> Messias embody the Messianic people, the new Israel."

124 I. Engnell, *Studies in Divine Kingship*, 1945, 176, n. 4 enumerates
    psalms 17, 21, 48, 115. Not even the closest inspection of the psalms
    reveals any reference to the king.

125 *Ibid.*, 35. The parallelism with the Hittite kings (pp. 63; 66-67), or
    with the West-Semitic kings of the North (p. 90), or with the kings
    of Ras-shamra (p. 173),—if the interpretation is exact—proves nothing
    regarding Israel.

126 R. A. Johnson, *The One and the Many*, l.c., p. 37; "More than 'repre-

between Yahweh and his agent. The lament of Jeremia over the sins of the people ends with these words: "Violence upon violence, deceit upon deceit: they refuse to recognize *me*, says the Lord." (Jer. 9:5) The addition of "says the Lord" transfers his otherwise ambiguous message to the One whose messenger he is.[127] At the beginning of his prophecy, Aggai states: "And the Lord's messenger, Aggai, proclaimed to the people as the message of the Lord: I am with you, says the Lord." (Ag. 1:13) We have here, in all probability, an example of the messenger so identifying himself with his master that he speaks exactly as He would.

On the other hand H. Wheeler Robinson repeatedly has drawn attention to the fact that the prophet is convinced that he represents, in fact, *is*, in a certain sense, the entire community of the "children of Israel." He is not only "the friend of God" (Wis. 7: 27) but also the intimate associate of his fellow men; he is "an eye turned toward God" (cf. Is. 29:10: "He has shut your eyes [the prophets]") and also "a mouth turned toward Israel"[128] (cf. Jer. 15:19: "You shall be my mouthpiece"; cf. also Ex. 4:16)

The majority of prophetical writings furnish evidence for the contention that "the prophet's own relation to his people is expressed through the ancient category of 'corporate personality.'"[129] (the second general theme) Everywhere there is evident a sincere and sympathetic identification between the divine messen-

---

sentative'; the prophet was Yahweh in person."—Cf. H. H. Rowley, *The Servant of the Lord and Other Essays,* 1954[2], 119-120, quotes the following in confirmation of this thesis: G. Hölscher, *Die Propheten,* 1914, 25 and H. W. Hertzberg, *Prophet Und Gott,* 1923, 12.

127 In Jr. 8:17-18 it is difficult to determine who is speaking: "I will send against you poisonous snakes, against which no charm will work when they bite you, says the Lord. My grief is incurable, my heart within me is faint." The addition of "says the Lord" again proves the close union between Yahweh and His prophet.

128 H. Wheeler Robinson, *The Psychology and Metaphysic of "Thus saith Yahweh",* in ZAW 41 (1923) 1-15, p. 9; or, by the same author, *Redemption and Revelation,* l.c., 149.

129 H. Wheeler Robinson, *The Old Testament, Its Making and Meaning,* London, 1937, 79.

ger and the members of the Chosen People.[130] This might be
explained by the fact that the prophets come from certain Israelite
circles desirous of safeguarding the old community spirit of the
Yahwist or Davidic promises.[131] But it seems certain that the
prophetic charism transcends a narrow provincial piety, it is not
esoteric but truly and genuinely social: "The one who becomes
a prophet is not merely responding to the call of a particular
vocation, but is binding himself to the life of a community, a
true condition of such a vocation." [132] It could hardly be otherwise,
for always "in the Old Testament, religious consciousness and
personal vocation are tied to the destiny of the group; this doctrine
is expressed, embodied, and fulfilled in the great religious personalities." [133] The prophets certainly occupy a place of honor
among the latter. It is easy to see, then, that "the religious experiences which the prophet enjoys never isolates him from the
Israelite community. One cannot exaggerate the union between the
prophet and Israel, nor the consciousness that both the prophet and
Israel have of this union." [134]

130   H. Wheeler Robinson, *Hebrew Psychology*, in S. A. Peake, *The
      People and the Book*, Oxford, 1925, 353-382, p. 375.
131   J. Pedersen, *Israel I-II*, 1947², 566, and 568. Cf. Is. 59:21: "This is
      the covenant with them which I myself have made, says the Lord:
      My spirit which is upon you and my words that I have put into your
      mouth shall never leave your mouth, nor the mouths of your children
      nor the mouths of your children's children from now on and forever,
      says the Lord." Possibly the "you," to whom these words are ad-
      dressed, is the people. But they may be addressed also to a more
      restricted group, such as a group of prophets.
132   A. Neher, *Amos. Contribution à l'étude du prophétisme*, Paris, 1950,
      XV.—In *Studies in Old Testament Prophecy, presented to Prof. Th. H.
      Robinson*, Edinburg, 1950, N. W. Porteous studies "the basis of the
      prophets moral teaching" (pp. 143-56). On page 50 he draws atten-
      tion to Jer. 7:25: "From the day that your fathers left the land of
      Egypt even to this day, I have sent you untiringly all my servants
      the prophets," and notes that there is question here of a true tradi-
      tion. The prophet is never alone; he is one of a succession of prophets
      like himself.
133   Y. Congar, O.P., *Esquisses du Mystère de l'Eglise*, 1941, 14.
134   Michel-Marie de La Croix, in *Elie, le Prophète, II*, 1956, 160.

If we delve deeper into this solidarity of the prophets with Israel, we discover a twofold aspect. The prophet belongs to Israel first of all in the sense that from his union with Israel comes the radical power to be a prophet: "The basis of the prophetic vocation is being one of the prophetic people."[135] The prophet belongs to Israel in an even more intimate way through his experiences: he sums up most forcefully in himself, as a privileged member of the community, Israel's consciousness of being the Chosen People. Basically, the prophet lives the experience spoken of in the *Book of Baruch*: "Blessed are we, O Israel; for what pleases God is known to us!" (Bar. 4:4) Both the non-prophetic and the prophetic writings proclaim and illustrate this position of the prophet in the midst of the Chosen People.

1. Non-Prophetic Writings

The role of the prophets reveals certain characteristic traits which are rather revealing from our point of view. The term *nābî* seems originally to have been associated more or less directly with great power of intercession.[136] The prophet is one who "represents," that is "makes present" his people before God when he prays for them. Abraham is called a "prophet" (Gn. 20:7; 17; cf. 18:22-23), and the text adds explicitly: "he will pray for you (Abimelech) that you may live." Moses, the greatest prophet of Israel (Dt. 34:10; cf. Dt. 18:18; Wis. 11:1; Os. 12:14; Jer. 15:1) is a powerful intercessor according to Pharao. (Ex. 8:4, 8, 26, 27) Time and time again he succeeds in averting the anger

135 *Ibid.*, pp. 160-161. The author speaks of a "prophetic vocation, essential, constitutive of Israel"; "Israel is the people whom God has chosen for Himself to prepare and announce the coming of the Messias; among the nations it is witness to God's designs upon the world." Pertinent here are the words of Moses: "Would that all the people of the Lord were prophets! Would that the Lord might bestow his spirit on them all!" (Nm. 11:29) or Ps. 104:15: "Touch not my anointed, and to my prophets do no harm." or Jl. 3:1: "Your sons and daughters shall prophesy." (Cf. 1 Par. 16:22).

136 N. Johannson, *Parakletoi. Vorstellungen von Fürsprechern für die Menschen vor Gott in der alttestamentlichen Religion, im Spätjudentum und Urchristentum*, Lund, 1940, 4-7: Moses.

of Yahweh. (Ex. 32:11-14; 32:30-33) At Thabera "when the people cried out to Moses, he prayed to the Lord and the fire died out." (Nm. 11:2, 10-15) On the occasion when Yahweh sent serpents to punish the people, "the people came to Moses and said, 'We have sinned in complaining against the Lord and you. Pray the Lord to take the serpents from us.' " (Nm. 21:7) When Yahweh was on the point of exterminating his people, "Moses, his chosen one, withstood him in the breach to turn back his destructive wrath."[137] (Ps. 105:23; Dt. 9:18, 26-29) Not only the people in general (Nm. 14:19-20; Dt. 9:18-20), but also particular individuals, such as his brother Aaron and his sister Mariam (Nm. 12:13) benefitted at times from his intercessory prayer.[138]

Another important figure endowed with the prophetic charism of intercession was Samuel. Faithful prophet of the Lord in Silo (1 K. 3:20; cf. 2 Par. 35:18; Jer. 15:1, Sir. 46:13), Samuel has all Israel gather at Masphath that "I may pray to the Lord for you." (1 K. 7:5) After his farewell address, "all the people said to Samuel: 'Pray for thy servants to the Lord thy God, that we may not die!" (1 K. 12:19) Sirach sums up the prophetic role of Samuel when he says: "He too, called upon God." (Sir. 46:16)

Elias, in turn, intercedes with Yahweh for the son of the widow 3 K. 17:20), and prays for the people assembled at Carmel: "Hear me, O Lord, hear me, that this people may learn that thou are the Lord God."[139] (3 K. 18:37)

Yahweh himself works through the prophets and through his spirit brings about the salvation of the people.[140] The prophets, in turn, thank God for the salvation he has brought the nation.

137   R. Bloch, in: Moïse, l'homme de l'Alliance, Paris, 1955, 127, quotes
      Ass. Mos. XII, 6 (Ed. Clemen 14): "(Dominus) me constituit pro
      eis et pro peccatis eorum."

138   Sometimes Aaron assists Moses in his office of intercessor. (Nm.
      16:22) Later the prophets pray together with the leaders of the
      people (the kings, e.g.): "And Ezechias the king, and Isaias the
      prophet the son of Amos, prayed against this blasphemy, and cried
      out to heaven." (2 Par. 32:20)

139   Cf. the request of Jeroboam I to an anonymous "man of God" in 3 K.
      13:6: "Entreat the face of the Lord thy God, and pray for me, that
      my hand may be restored to me."

140   A. Jepsen, Nabi, Soziologische Studien zur alttestamentlichen Litera-

Mariam, the prophetess, Aaron's sister, answers the rejoicing women with the refrain: "Sing to the Lord, for he is gloriously triumphant; horse and chariot he has cast into the sea." (Ex. 15: 20:21) The prophet is always and everywhere interested in promoting the welfare of the community to which he is attached. When the Lord revealed himself to Samuel, "the word of Samuel came to pass to all Israel." (1 K. 3:21) This word comprised not only prayer for the people but also teaching of the "good and right way." [141] (1 K. 12:23)

Certain prophets enjoyed some influence in the enthronement of kings; for example, the prophet Nathan, who together with Sadoc the priest, anointed Solomon (3 K. 1:34, 35) for the welfare of the people. Several prophets played an important role in the king's court; such were the historiographers in the reign of David: "Samuel the Seer, Nathan the prophet, and Gad the Seer." [142]

Elias, the great prophet of the ninth century, had a very lively awareness that he represented his faithless people: "With zeal have I been zealous for the Lord God of hosts, because the children of Israel have forsaken thy covenant. They have destroyed thy altars, they have slain thy prophets with the sword.[143] (3 K. 19:14) Yahweh answers this prayer: "I will leave me seven thousand men

tur und Religionsgeschichte, Munich, 1934, 30.—Recall to mind Debora, "the prophetess" who meets out justice in the name of God (Jg. 4:4), or Samuel, the "faithful prophet" who annoints Saul (1 K. 10:1), and especially David. (1 K. 16:13)

141 A. Jepsen, Nabi, l.c., p. 107: "Samuel is the Nabi appointed by God, who secretly directs the fate of Israel according to Yahweh's will, who calls and deposes kings, and whose word is absolutely true and must be heard."

142 Cf. for Solomon, "the words of Nathan the prophet, ... the books of Ahias the Silonite, ... the vision of Addo the seer." (2 Par. 9:29) For Roboam, "the books of Semeias the prophet, and of Addo the seer." (2 Par. 12:15) For Abia, "the book of Addo the prophet." (2 Par. 13:22)

143 A. Neher, L'essence du prophétisme, Collection Epiméthée, Paris, 1955, 211, draws attention to the twelve stones of Elias's altar (3 K. 18:31) which symbolize all the people.

in Israel, whose knees have not been bowed before Baal, and every mouth that hath not worshipped him kissing the hands." (3 K. 19:18) The very enigmatic title given to Elias (4 K. 2:12) and later to Eliseus (4 K. 13:14): "My father, my father, the chariot of Israel, and the driver thereof" probably emphasizes the profound significance of the prophet in the life of his people.[144]

The prophets are the public conscience of Israel. Without them "no one of us knows how long." (Ps. 73:9) Like Samuel, the prophet "raised his voice as a prophet, to put an end to wickedness." (Sir. 46:20); like the twelve minor prophets they "reestablish the tribes of Jacob." (Sir. 48:10) Frequently the prophets suffer hardship at the hands of the kings because they dare to proclaim their opinions openly. During the reign of Asa, the seer Hanani was put into prison: "Asa was angry with the seer, and commanded him to be put in prison; for he was greatly enraged because of this thing; and he put to death many of the people at that time." (2 Par. 16:10) Evidently the prophet's message reflected the thoughts of those same people. On the other hand, the good kings willingly recognized the exceptional value of the prophets as representatives of the people. When Josaphat wanted to encourage his people, he cried out: "Believe in the Lord your God, and you shall be secure, believe his prophets, and all things shall succeed well." (2 Par. 20:20) In the course of the Syro-Emphraimite war, Obed, the messenger of Yahweh, touches the consciences of some of the warriors of the northern kingdom who were about to enslave some of their Judean prisoners. Reproached by the prophet: "Moreover you have a mind to keep under the children of Juda and Jerusalem for your bondmen and bondwomen, which ought not to be done, *for you have sinned* in this against the Lord your God." (2 Par. 28:10), the Ephraim leaders confess their guilt: "You shall not bring in the captives hither, *lest we sin against the Lord.*" (2 Par. 28:13)

At the beginning of the reconstruction of the temple, the prophets Aggai and Zacharias helped the people in their work.

---

144   According to A. Neher, *L'essence du prophétisme*, l.c., p. 180, the
        term *avi* ("my father") could be "a technical term which, at one
        time, designated the prophets." Neher compares Dt. 26:5: "My father
        (Abraham) was a wandering Aramean."

(Esd. 5:2; cf. 6:14) This presence of the prophets is to be interpreted as a symbol and assurance of the divine presence, as is indicated in the great prayer of the *Book of Nehemias*: "And thou (Yahweh) didst forbear with them for many years, and didst testify against them by thy spirit by the hand of thy prophets." (Ne. 9:30)

2. *Prophetic Writings*

In these writings there are frequent allusions to a great solidarity between the prophet and those to whom he addresses his message: Isaia expresses the keen awareness he has of the intimate bonds that bind him to the sinful people: "I am a man of unclean lips, living among a people of unclean lips." (Is. 6:5) But just as his sin is burned away by the embers of the Seraphim, so Yahweh will purify the people. He will wash away "the filth of the daughters of Sion" (Is. 4:4); His promise is precise: "I will ... refine your dross in the furnace, removing all your alloy." (Is. 1:25) The same prophet suffers because of the hardheartedness of his people who will not accept the divine message: " 'How long, O Lord?' I asked." (Is. 6:11) Isaia is convinced that he is "signs and portents in Israel." (Is. 8:18) The "us" of Is. 9:5: "A child is born to us, a son given us" expresses the joy of the prophet sharing in the good fortune of his people. (cf. Is. 32:15: "until the spirit from on high is poured out on *us*"; Is. 32:18: "*My people* will live in peaceful country.")

The pressing invitations to repentance betray a profound love and a deep sharing of life: "Return, O children of Israel, to him whom you have utterly deserted." (Is. 31:6; cf. Is. 22:4: "Do not try to comfort me for the ruin of the daugter of my people.") In another context we sense that the prophet makes his own the sentiments of the people, particularly when he inveighs against Sennacherib: "She despises you, laughs you to scorn, the virgin daughter Sion." (Is. 37:22) The name of Isaia's son, Shear-Jashub, contains a consolation for all Israel: "A remnant will return, the remnant of Jacob, to the mighty God." (Is. 10:21) The "prophecy in action" of Is. 20:3 when Isaia went "naked and barefoot for three years as a sign and portent against Egypt and Ethiopia" has the inhabitants saying: "Look at our hope!

We have fled here for help and deliverance from the king of Assyria; where can we flee now?" (Is. 20:6)[145]

Isaia exercises his function as prophet by interceding for king Ezechias. The messengers of the king implore him: "Send up a prayer for the remnant that is here." (Is. 37:4) Isaia's prayer in Is. 33:2 seems to be a thoroughly collective prayer: "O Lord, have pity on *us,* for you we wait. Be our strength every morning, our salvation in time of trouble!" (cf. in the *Apocalypse of Isaia,* 25:9: "Behold our God, to whom we looked to save us!") Similarly the *Psalm of Isaia* (63:7-64:11) seems to fit in with the idea of corporate prayer: "The favor of the Lord *I* will recall, the glorious deeds of the Lord, because of all he has done for *us;* for he is good to the house of Israel, he has favored *us* according to his mercy and his great kindness." (Is. 63:7)

But Jeremia, even to a greater degree than Isaia, shares in the sufferings and hopes of his people: "My breast! My breast! how I suffer! The walls of my heart! My heart beats wildly, I cannot be still, . . . *the whole earth* is laid waste. In an instant my tents are ravaged." (Jer. 4:19-20) There seems little doubt but that the prophet is identifying himself with his people.[146] Yahweh has said: "A tester among my people I have appointed you, to search and test their way." (Jer. 6:27) Little wonder that the prophet grieves for his people and urges them: "Cut off your dedicated hair and throw it away! on the heights intone an elegy; for the Lord has rejected and cast off the generation that draws down his wrath." (Jer. 7:29) Jeremia's deepest suffering, his own Gethsemani[147] lies in this that *"my people* do not know the ordinance of the Lord." (Jer. 8:7) "The injury to the daughter of my people" (Jer. 8:11) overwhelms him: "My grief is incurable, my heart within me is faint. Listen! the cry of the daughter of my people, far and wide in the land! . . . I am broken by the ruin of the daughter of my

145   Compare Mi. 1:8: "For this reason (the crime of Jacob) I lament and wail, I go barefoot and naked."

146   On the other hand, the prophet identifies himself with Yahweh, whose complaint he takes up: "Fools my people are, they know me not; senseless children they are, having no understanding." (Jer. 4:22)

147   The designation of J. Skinner; cf. A. Gelin, *Jérémie,* Collection *"Témoins de Dieu,"* Paris, 1951, 102.

people. I am disconsolate; horror has seized me . . . Oh, that my head were a spring of water, my eyes a fountain of tears, that I might weep day and night over the slain of the daughter of my people." (Jer. 8:18, 21, 23; cf. 14:17; 23:9; 50:6)

The words of Yahweh indicate that Jeremia's intercession is in the form of a substitution: "Do not intercede on behalf of this people, nor utter a plea *for them.* I will not listen when *they* call to me at the time of their misfortune." (Jer. 11:14; cf. 14:11) The prayer of the prophet is certainly "corporate," for according to his own interpretation it is the people who are calling upon Yahweh.[148]

With all his heart Jeremia enters into the confession of guilt: "Even though our crimes bear witness against us, take action, O Lord, for the honor of your name—even though our rebellions are many, though we have sinned against you." (Jer. 14:7) Because of this attitude, he takes his role as intercessor very much to heart: "Heed me, O Lord, . . . Remember that I stood before you to speak in their behalf; to turn away your wrath from them." (Jer. 18:19-20) Frequently the *Book of Jeremia* speaks of the intercession of the prophet: "Tell me, Lord, have I not served you well? Have I not interceded with you for my enemies?" (Jer. 15:11) During the siege of Jerusalem (588) king Sedecias requests Jeremia to "pray to the Lord, our God, for us." (Jer. 37:3) After the catastrophe of 587, the prophet has to make a similar appeal for the people: "Grant our petition; pray for us to the Lord, your God, for all this remnant." (Jer. 42:2) On this occasion "all the people, high and low" (Jer. 42:1) promise the prophet: "Whether it is pleasant or difficult, we will obey the command of the Lord, our God, *to whom we are sending you,* so that it will be well with us for obeying the command of the Lord, our God." (Jer. 42:6; cf. 42:9: "Thus says the Lord, the God of Israel, to whom you sent me to offer your prayer.")

The prophet Ezechiel also realizes his solidarity with his people: "Son of man, I have appointed you a watchman for the house of Israel." (Ez. 3:17; 33:7) He knows that he is respon-

---

148 The Targum, by its reading "when *you* (singular) intercede" (as in Jer. 7:16) instead of "when *they* intercede," destroys the corporate meaning of the prophetic intercession.

sible for the sinner whom he has not warned.[149] (Ex. 3:18, 20)
He carries about with him the sins of Israel, of Juda, and of
Jerusalem.[150] (Ez. 4:4-6; cf. 6:11) In order to symbolize the unclean food the people will have to eat in captivity, he has to eat
barley loaves (Ez. 4:12-13); on another occasion he has to carry
out an act symbolic of Jerusalem. (Ez. 5:5) In all that he does
Yahweh has made him "a sign for the house of Israel." (Ez. 12:
6. 11) When his wife, "the delight of your eyes" (Ez. 24:16) has
died, Ezechiel recalls the divine threat: " I will now desecrate my
sanctuary, the stronghold of your pride, *the delight of your eyes,*
the desire of your soul . . . Ezechiel shall be a sign for you." (Ez.
24:21, 24)

Like all the other prophets Ezechiel intercedes for his people:
"Alas, Lord God! Will you destroy all that is left of Israel when
you pour out your fury on Jerusalem?" (Ez. 9:8; cf. 11:13)[151]
On other occasions he weeps for them: "As for you, son of man,
groan! . . . When it (a report) comes every heart shall fail, every
hand shall fall helpless, every spirit shall be daunted, and every
knee shall run with water." (Ez. 21:11-12) "Cry out and wail,

149 Cf. Os. 9:8; Hb. 2:1; or Ez. 33: 2-3: "Son of man, speak thus to *your*
     (singular) countrymen: When I bring the sword against a country,
     and the people of this country select one of their number to be their
     watchman, and the watchman, seeing the sword coming against the
     country, blows the trumpet to warn the people, anyone hearing but
     not heeding the warning of the trumpet and therefore slain by the
     sword that comes against him, shall be responsible for his own
     death."

150 M. Weber, *Aufrätze zur Religionssoziologie, III. Das Antike Juden-
     tum,* Tübingen, 1921, 381: "In the pain of his pathological paralysis,
     he feels opportunely as fated to expiate the collective guilt of the
     people."

151 The prophet's power of intercession is recognized by Yahweh: "I
     have searched among them (the people of the country) for someone
     who could build a wall or stand in the breach before me to keep me
     from destroying the land, but I found no one." (Ez. 22:30) The ab-
     sence of intercession is perhaps suggested in Ps. 73:9: "Deeds on our
     behalf we do not see; there is no prophet now, and no one of us
     knows how long."

son of man, for it (a sword sharpened and burnished) is destined for my people." (Ez. 21:17)

The *Book of Daniel* gives an account of several prayers, which portray the union of the prophet and his people. Azaria, one of the three "children in the fiery furnace" prays as the representative of his race: "We have sinned and transgressed by departing from you, and we have done every kind of evil...We are...brought low everywhere in the world this day because of our sins...Do not let us be put to shame, but deal with us in your kindness and great mercy." (Dn. 3:29, 37, 42) In the same way the young Daniel prays in the name of all his countrymen: "Ah, Lord, great and awesome God,...we have sinned, been wicked and done evil;...O Lord, we are shamefaced, like our kings, our princes, and our fathers, for having sinned against you... *All Israel* transgressed your law and went astray...O Lord, in keeping with all your just deeds, let your anger and your wrath be turned away from your city Jerusalem, your holy mountain...Hear, therefore, O God, the prayer and petition of *your servant*...When we present *our petition* before you, we rely not on our just deed, but on your great mercy." (Dn. 9:4, 8, 11, 16-18) At the end of the prayer the *Book of Daniel* comments: " I was still occupied with *my prayer,* confessing *my* sins and *the sin of my people Israel,* presenting *my* petition to the Lord, *my* God, on behalf of his holy mountain." (Dn. 9:20)

The marriage of Osee—regardless of whether it is real or allegorical—is presented as the type of all Israel: "Go, take a harlot wife and harlot's children (cf. Os. 5:4: the spirit of harlotry), for *the land* gives itself to harlotry, turning away from the Lord." (Os. 1:2) As Osee continues to love his adulteress wife, so "the Lord loves the people of Israel, though they turn to other gods." (Os. 3:1) Chapters 1 to 3 of *Osee certainly* suggest the intimate union between the prophet and his people. The names of his wife Gomer, his sons Jezrael and Lo-ammi, and his daughter Lo-ruhama are all symbolical. (cf. Os. 1)

The same prophet describes in a very graphic way the repentance of his people, a repentance in which he shares wholeheartedly: "Come, let us return to the Lord, for it is he who has rent, but he will revive us after two days, on the third day he will raise us up, to live in his presence." (Os. 6:1-2) "Return, O Israel, to the Lord, your God; you have collapsed through your guilt ... Return to the Lord; say to him, 'Forgive all iniquity, and receive what is good, that we may render as offerings the bullocks from our stalls.' " (Os. 14:2-3)

Amos, the shepherd of Thecua, carries out his ministry of prophecy ("Go, prophesy to my people Israel." Amos 7:15) by interceding for his listeners and their country. When he sees in vision the swarm of locusts which are to devour all the grass of the country, he exclaims: "Forgive, O Lord God! How can Jacob stand? He is so small!" (Amos 7:1) Acceding to the prayers of the prophet, "the Lord repented of this. 'It shall not be,' said the Lord God." (Amos 7:3) Later on a second prayer springs from the heart of the frightened prophet as he beholds the "judgment by fire." (Amos 7:5)

Michea feels the divine anger which the sins of the house of Israel have provoked: "There is no remedy for the blow she has been struck, rather, it has come even to Juda, it reaches to the gate of my people, even to Jerusalem." (Mi. 1:9) The prophet intercedes for his countrymen and his co-religionists: "Who is there like you, the God who ... will again have compassion on *us,* treading underfoot *our* guilt? You will cast into the depths of the sea *all our sins."* (Mi. 7:19)

The prophet whose message forms the second part of the *Book of Zacharia* must "take the gear of a foolish shepherd," for, says Yahweh: "I will raise up a shepherd *in the land."* (Za. 11:15-16)

Finally, Malachia expresses very plainly the "corporate" aspect when he says: "Have we not all the one Father? Has not the one God created *us*? Why then do we break faith with each other, violating the covenant of our fathers?" (Mal. 2:10)

D. *THE SERVANT OF YAHWEH*

The conflict between the individual interpretation and the collective interpretation of the "servant of Yahweh" in Is. 40-55 is a "seed of discord" and "one of the favorite bones of contention" in exegesis.[152] Many interpreters ask the question: Are we to see in this *Ebed* an individual person *or* the personification of the collectivity? Several exegetes, however, think that the question is out of place; they say that in order to resolve this *crux interpretum* we must fall back again on the idea of "corporate personality." According to them the servant is a chosen individual who influences the group for the good and who, at the same time, represents the group.

All sorts of hypotheses have been dreamed up regarding the meaning of the word *'ĕbĕd*.[153] Basically they all agree in that it indicates some kind of subordinate instrumental activity. But the meaning can vary according to the context. Sometimes the subordination is that of a slave (even in the exaggerated meaning of a term of Oriental politeness). Sometimes the term connotes dependence on a foreign power or on a sovereign king; often it indicates a special mission, frequently one of honor. The "cultic" meaning is not unusual; the brothers of Joseph call themselves "servants of the God of your father." (Gn. 50:17) According to psalm 33:32 "the Lord redeems the lives of his servants"; that is why in psalm 88:51 the community of the adorers of Yahweh pray: "Remember, O Lord, the insults to your servants." The builders of the temple after the exile (520-515) say to the Persian authorities: "We are the servants of the God of heaven and earth." (Esd. 5:11) In the third part of the Book of Isaia we read: "And the foreigners who join themselves to the Lord, ministering to him, loving the name of the Lord, and becoming his servants—all who keep the Sabbath free from profanation and hold to my covenant, them I will bring to my holy mountain and make joyful in my house of prayer; their holocausts and sacrifices will be acceptable on my altar, for my house shall be called a house of prayer for all peoples." (Is. 56:6-7)

152 I. Engnell, *The 'Ebed Yahweh Songs and the Suffering Messiah*, l.c., p. 62, n. 2.–Cf. H. Wheeler Robinson, *The Psalmists*, l.c., 85: "The same vexed question (in Is. 53 as in Ps. 21) as to whether the reference is individual or social."

153 C. Lindhagen, *The Servant Motif in the Old Testament. A Preliminary Study to the 'Ebed Yahweh Problem in Deutero-Isaiah, Uppsula*, 1950.

Very often the term '*ébêd* designates the elect of Yahweh; namely, the entire people: "You, Lord, are our father, our redeemer ... Return for the sake of your servants, the tribes of your heritage." (Is. 63:16-17) The election of the Chosen People is a vocation to cultic service of Yahweh; the entire nation must devote itself to His glory, and each individual is obliged in turn to assure the carrying out of this common duty.

Nonetheless, the term '*ébêd* is frequently reserved for individuals charged with a special and providential duty. In this class we must mention especially those "servants of Yahweh," the patriarchs. The phrase of Dt. 9:27: "Remember your servants, Abraham, Isaac and Jacob" (cf. Ex. 32:13) is so frequent as to be stereotyped. When Isaac receives the divine promise, Yahweh says: "I am the God of your father Abraham; fear not, for I am with you. I will bless you and multiply your descendants for the sake of *my servant Abraham.*" (Gn. 26:24)[154] According to Ez. 28:25 (also 37:25) the land of Palestine has been given to Jacob: "Then they shall live on their land which I gave to my servant Jacob."[155] In Gn. 24:14 and in Dn. 3:35 Isaac is called "your servant."

Not only the patriarchs but also the prophets are called "servants of Yahweh."[156] Amos says so in so many words: "Indeed, the Lord God does nothing without revealing his plan to his servants, the prophets." (Amos 3:7) Yahweh promises to "revenge the blood of my servants the prophets, and the blood of all the servants of the Lord." (4 K. 9:7) He makes known his will through "the hand of my servants the prophets." (4 K. 17:13, 23; 21:10; 24:2; Dt. 9:6-10; Jer. 25:4; 26:5; Ez. 38:17; Esd. 9:11) Jeremia uses the same phrase time and again: "From the day that your fathers left the land of Egypt to this day, I have sent you untiringly all my servants the prophets." (Jer. 7:25; 29:19; 35:

154   According to H. J. Nyberg, *Smärtornas Man*, in SEA 7 (1942) 5-82, p. 77, Abraham would be considered here as the founder of cult.

155   C. Lindhagen, *The Servant Motif*, l.c., p. 285, n. 2, refers to Ps. 104:6: "You descendants of Abraham, his servants." In Gn. 18:3-5 Abraham himself is called "servant of Yahweh"; in Gn. 32:11, Jacob is so called.

156   C. Lindhagen, *The Servant Motif*, l.c., pp. 277-280.

15; 44:4; cf. Za. 1:6) As a matter of fact, the title "servant of Yahweh" is applied to Moses (Nm. 12:7; Ex. 14:31), to Ahias of Silo (3 K. 14:18; 15:29), to Elias (3 K. 18:36; 4 K. 9:36; 10:10), to Isaia (Is. 20:3), and to Jonas. (4 K. 14:25)

Finally, the word *'ébêd* is used to designate kings and rulers.[157] This is especially true of the Israelite leaders, such as David (Is. 37:35; Ps. 17:1: Altogether he is called such some sixty times in the Old Testament),[158] Josue (Jg. 2:8; Jos. 5:14; 24: 29), Caleb (Nm. 14:24), Solomon (3 K. 3:7, 8, 9; 8:28, 29), Ezechias (2 Par. 32:16), or Zorobabel. (Ag. 2:24) But it is used also for some pagan kings, such as Nabuchodonosor (Jer. 25:9; 27:6; 43:10) or Cyrus. (Is. 44:28) The Messias, the king *par excellence,* is also called the "servant of Yahweh." (Ez. 34:23-24; 37:24; Za. 3:8)

When we recall the great variety of meanings which attach to the notion "servant of Yahweh," we begin to see how difficult it is to determine exactly what precise meaning to attach to the "servant of Yahweh" *par excellence* described in the four "poems" of Isaia 40-53. (42: 1-4; 49:1-6; 50: 4-9; 52:13 to 53:12) A certain number of exegetes see in this *Ebed of Deutero-Isaia* "a representative of the people, given the honorary title of 'prophet,' and therefore considered as a prophet whose task and destiny is to work, as the prophets did (cf. Jer.) for the welfare of the people, and to suffer for them." [159] Other interpreters try to prove that the figure of Is. 40:53 is a royal personage.[160]

157 *Ibid.,* pp. 280-88.
158 *Ibid.,* p. 281. Lindhagen believes that the term *'ébêd* applied to David, extols him as the founder of the dynasty (cf. 2 K. 7:19), and as the founder-organizer of the Jerusalem cult. (cf. 2 K. 7:5) Would it not be perhaps more correct to say that David is considered simply in a general way as the divine instrument?
159 O. Eissfeldt, *Einleitung in das AT,* Tübingen, 1934, 382. For the identification of the "servant" with the prophet, cf. S. Mowinckel, *Der Gottesknecht,* l.c., 10.
160 Cf. I. Engnell, *The 'Ebed Yahweh Songs,* l.c., or C. Lindhagen, *The Servant Motif,* l.c., p. 231 and 221, n. 2; or H. S. Nyberg, *Smärtornas Man,* l.c., pp. 75-76; or finally V. de Leeuw, *Le Serviteur de Yahvé, figure royale ou prophétique?* in *L'attente du Messie,* 1954, pp. 51-56. All things considered, we can accept the balanced view of

The question which interests us at the moment is: How must we interpret the four passages cited above which deal with this special "servant of Yahweh"? Among contemporary scholars the analytical concept of Is. 40-55 (as though the text were made up of a number of smaller units) has been replaced by a "more organic view of the construction of these chapters." [161] Perhaps Bernard Duhm was wrong when in his commentary of 1892 on Isaia (*Göttinger Handkommentar Zum A. T.*) he put forth the hypothesis that the four pericopes were to be looked upon as fragments of one single poem independent of the context, or at least as four connected poems whose subject is the same. In any case, a number of problems vanish if we are not held to an identical interpretation of "servant" in the four "songs." [162] The fact that there is a serious doubt about the length (especially the end of the "songs") and the number of the "songs of the servant," seems to prove that the songs do not have an outstandingly distinctive character. It is probably better, then, to explain each pericope (even the "songs of the servant") "in the light of the context in which it has been placed by the writer who planned the work, not in the light of the supposed context for the existence of which there is no real proof ... It is obvious that if one were to select fragments from different parts of a work and piece them together, and then try

C. North, *The Suffering Servant in Deutero-Isaiah*, Oxford, 1956[2], 218: "Though there are undoubtedly kingly features in the Servant, there is nothing in the Songs to indicate that he was to be an anointed king."

161　C. Lindhagen, *The Servant Motif*, l.c., p. 199. Cf. also J. Schildenberger, in *Festschrift Nötscher*, 1950, 200. On the other hand, V. de Leeuw, *De Ebed Jahweh—Profetieën*, Assen, 1956, 285, does not think that Is. 40-55 forms "a closely knit unity"; cf. C. North, *The Suffering Servant*, l.c., p. 160: "It remains that most critics now regard Is. XL-LV (LVI) as a collection of short oracles."

162　J. Pedersen, *Israel III-IV*, 1947, 605 notes very judiciously: "The words of the poems about the Servant fit so naturally into Deutero-Isaiah's view of Israel, that the question as to whether they are from his hand, is only of a purely formal literary interest."—Cf. R. J. Tournay, *Les Chants du Serviteur dans la seconde partie d'Isaïe*, in *RB* 59 (1952) 355-84 and 481-512, p. 359.

to give them a uniform interpretation, this might be something entirely different from that intended by the original writer."[163]

We can conclude from the above considerations that the uses of the word '*êbêd* are not necessarily identical, nor need the word be applied in a univocal sense in the four songs. If we examine the context (chapters 40-56 of *Isaia*) we see that the word '*êbêd* means adorers of Yahweh (Is. 54:17; cf. 56:6; 63:17; 64:8; 66:14), prophets as instruments of Yahweh (Is. 44:26; cf. 66:11), and especially the people whom Yahweh chooses as His mediator to carry the true faith to the nations. The collective meaning of the word '*êbêd*, that is to say, its application to the totality of the people, is frequent in chapters 40-48 of *Isaia*.[164] Most frequently the title '*êbêd* recalls Yahweh's choice of Israel: "But you, Israel, my servant, Jacob, whom I have chosen, offspring of Abraham my friend, . . . you whom I have called my servant, whom I have chosen and will not cast off." (Is. 41:8-9) "Remember this, O Jacob, you, O Israel, who are my servant! I formed you to be a servant to me; O Israel, by me you shall never be forgotten." (Is. 44:21; cf. 44:1: "Hear then, O Jacob, my servant, Israel, whom I have chosen.") Yahweh confirms the word of his servant (Is. 44:26) and assures Cyrus: "For the sake of Jacob, my servant, of Israel my chosen one, I have called you by your name." (Is. 45:4) It is clear that the Chosen People as such is a "servant" of the God of Israel: "*You* are my witnesses, says

---

163 E. J. Kissane, *The Book of Isa. II*, Dublin, 1943, LXV.—H. Cazelles, *Les poèmes du Serviteur*, in *RSR* 43 (1952) 2-54, pp. 16-18 strives to show that the verse which follows a song corresponds with the verse immediately preceding the song in question; but for Is. 48:22 he must resort to a "gloss." Besides, he admits that it is very difficult to determine the end of the "songs." (p. 18) For arguments against the thesis of Duhm, cf. R. J. Tournay, *Les Chants du Serviteur*, l.c., p. 356: "It is impossible to refer them (the songs) consistently and surely either to an individual or to a personified collectivity."

164 C. Lindhagen, *The Servant Motif*, l.c., pp. 152-233. Cf. O. Eissfeldt, *Der Gottesknecht*, l.c., 12.—S. Mowinckel, *Der Knecht Jahwäs* in *NTT* 22 (1921) Bhft 3, directs attention to the plural "servants" (Is. 42:19 LXX; 43:10; 43:20; 54-17) as differing from the singular "servant" (Is. 41:8; 42:19; 44:1; 45:4).

the Lord, my servants whom I have chosen." (Is. 43:10)[165] This
does not at all mean that this same people is not a nation of
sinners: "Who is blind but my servant, or deaf like the messenger
I send?" (Is. 42:19) But Yahweh "redeems" his "servant."
(Is. 48:20; cf. 44:22: "I have brushed away your offenses like
a cloud, your sins like a mist; return to me, for I have redeemed
you")[166]

The use of *'êbêd* to indicate the people is not at all restricted
to chapters 40-48 of *Isaia*. It can be found in many other places.
In the *Book of Deuteronomy* the Canticle of Moses sings: "Surely
the Lord shall do justice for his people; on his servants he shall
have pity." (Dt. 32:36; cf. 32:43: "He avenges the blood of his
servants.") In the prayer of Solomon we find an allusion to the
special consecration of the Chosen People: "Lord God of Israel,
... who keepest covenant and mercy with thy servants that have
walked before thee with all their heart." (3 K. 8:23; 2 Par. 6:14)
Nehemias in turn addresses his prayer to God "for the children of
Israel thy servants." (Ne. 1:6; cf. 1:10, 11 or 2:20: "The God of
heaven he helpeth us, and we are his servants.") The idea of
special election stands out in the prayer Asaph composed at the

165 C. North, *The Suffering Servant*, l.c., p. 179, 181, 184 is of the
     opinion that, if the Servant is Israel in Is. 43:10 and 44:26, we have
     reason to be surprised at the singular "my servant" in Is. 44:26 (in-
     stead of the plural "my servants" as in the LXX and the Targum). It
     is hard to understand, it seems, how Israel can be treated as several
     "witnesses" and at the same time as a single "servant." Thus North
     arrives at the conclusion (pp. 180 and 205) that outside the songs
     the Servant is always (?) explicitly identified with Israel. From this
     he concludes that the Servant of the songs, never being called Israel
     (except in Is. 49:3!) differs from it. If one combines the anonymity
     and the highly individualized character of the Servant of the songs,
     North thinks that the Servant must necessarily differ from the Ebed-
     Israel (p. 286). No one doubts this (cf. 206 par. c), but the distinc-
     tion takes into account only one aspect of "corporate personality."
     (Under another aspect, the Servant and Israel are in some way
     identified.)
166 Compare 2 Par. 6:27 (the prayer of Solomon): "Hear thou from
     heaven, O Lord, and forgive the sins of thy servants and of thy
     people Israel."

instigation of David: "O ye seed of Israel his servants: ye children
of Jacob his chosen" (1 Par. 16:13: cf. Ps. 104:6) and in the
profession of faith in the *Book of Baruch*: "Such is our God; . . .
He has traced out all the ways of understanding, and has given
her to Jacob, his servant, to Israel, his beloved son." (Bar. 3:
36-37) The idea of redemption is evident in *Jeremia*: "But you,
my servant Jacob, fear not, says the Lord, be not dismayed, O
Israel! Behold, I will deliver you." (Jer. 30:10; cf. 46:27)

"My servant Jacob" (Ez. 28:25)is identical with "the descendants of his (Yahweh's) servants." (Ps. 68:37) The plural
(servants—people; cf. Ps. 104:25 or 134: 14 is rather frequent.
We read "the corpses of your servants" (Ps. 78:2), "the shedding
of your servant's blood" (Ps. 78:10), "the sons of your servants"
[in the C.C.D. "his future creatures"]. (Ps. 101:19) In psalm 89
we pray: "Have pity on your servants" (v. 13) and "let your
work be seen by your servants." (v. 16) The singular, on the other
hand, is less frequent. The Messianic psalm 88 speaks to Yahweh
as follows: "Remember, O Lord, the insults to your servants
(singular in the French): I bear in my bosom all the accusations
of the nations." (Ps. 88:51) The "historical" psalm 135 com-
memorates the conquest of the Holy Land in these words: "And
made their land (of the Chanaanite kings) a heritage, for his
mercy endures forever; the heritage of Israel his servant, for his
mercy endures forever." (Ps. 135:22)

It is clear that the meaning of the genitive "servant *of Yahweh*"
varies from expressing simple possession, (the servant belongs to
Yahweh) to expressing a true mission (the servant is sent by
Yahweh), to expressing service (the servant serves Yahweh). It
is equally clear that for our present problem (to find out the
relative values of the individual and the collectivity in the expression) there is no apodictic and exclusive solution.[167]

The best way of reducing the antinomy—in the opinion of a
growing number of recent exegetes—is to apply the idea of
"corporate personality." The purely collective interpretation takes
the "servant" of the poems to be a group or a community, whether

---

167   Already in 1929 G. Gloege, *Reich Gottes und Kirche im N.T.*, Güter-
       sloh (NTliche Forschungen 4) p. 44, focused attention on "a deliber-
       ate shift between an individual and a collectivistic interpretation."

that be historical Israel (the Targum of Is. 49:2; the Septuagint; the older Protestants; Wellhausen; Budde; König) or spiritual Israel (the remnant purified and faithful), or ideal Israel (the "Israelite genius": Davidson; S. Driver, Cheyne), or a special group within Israel made up of prophets (Gesenius) or of doctors (Bertholet).[168] This first solution is not to be rejected out of hand. We must see whether the context will permit such an interpretation. Nonetheless, we must give equal consideration to a solution of the problem based on an individual interpretation.[169] Some have seen in the "servant of Yahweh" either an historical person or an eschatological or ideal person. Among the great historical figures of the Jewish people who have been suggested are the following: Moses (Sellin), Osias (Augusti), Ezechias (Bahrdt), Josias (Staerk), Joachim (Sellin), Cyrus (Vogels), Deutero-Isaias (Mowinckel), Jeremia (Duhm), Zorobabel (Sellin), Eleazar (Bertholet); cf. 2 Mac. 6:18:31; Mosollam (Palacke; cf. 1 Par. 3:19), Isaia (Grotius-Calvin), or an unknown martyr of an unknown age. A rather recent theory identifies the "servant" with the king, or at least with the Messianic king. Other authors think of an eschatological person (Kittel; Rudolph) or an ideal individual person (Gunkel).

The "mixed" solution which holds that the "servant" represents Israel at the same time as being one definite historical person is wonderfully enhanced by the idea of "corporate personality." [170] Already in 1879 Fr. Delitzsch compared the "servant" to a pyramid which at its base is the collectivity of Israel, at its midpoint is the idealized "remnant" of the nation, and at its tip is Christ.[171]

168   Cf. V. de Leeuw, *De Ebed-Jahweh-Profetieën*, l.c., pp. 61-72 and 279-288.

169   *Ibid.*, pp. 72-100.

170   H. H. Rowley, *The Servant of the Lord*, l.c., p. 49: "I think the 'corporate personality' view holds the promise of a reasonable and intelligible interpretation of the whole problem."

171   V. de Leeuw, *De Ebed-Jahweh-Profetieën*, l.c., pp. 66-67 and 100. The author adds the opinion of North who sees in Christ the beginning of a new pyramid, the Church.—Cf. the same thought in G. E. Wright, *The Biblical Doctrine of Man*, l.c., p. 131: "As in the NT, where Christ can be represented both as the Body and as the Head

This somewhat mathematical representation has much in common with the idea which was dear to the Jewish doctors of the Middle Ages: "When we speak of the people, we imply the Messias king; when we speak of the Messias king we imply the people." [172] But we must go a bit further in the direction of the "primitive" and biblical notion of "corporate personality," according to which the mystic identity of a "corporate person" with the group he represents implies a continual shifting from the individual to the collective point of view.[173]

It seems at least inexact to pretend that the idea of "corporate personality" is a creation of the French sociological school.[174] The present study has endeavored to show that this idea is solidly based on the Hebraic thought pattern of the bible. In the songs of the "servant of Yahweh" the entire nation is represented by a figure who resembles a prophet, a king, and the Davidic Messias. As always when there is question of a "corporate personality," there is a continual fluctuation between the collective and the individual aspect of the idea. Putting the idea in other words we can say that: "The Servant of the Songs is thought of as an individual . . . but he symbolizes allegorically a community, namely Israel."[175] Rather than contrast "mathematically" the two solu-

of the Body, so the Servant is Israel and also the representative who in himself embodies Israel."

172 V. de Leeuw, *De Ebed-Jahweh-Profetieën*, l.c., p. 101, n. quotes S. R. Driver—A. Neubauer, *The Fifty-Third Chapter of Isaiah According to the Jewish Interpreters, I-II*, Oxford-London, 1876-1877, II, 129 (Salomon Astruc).

173 *Ibid.*, p. 102, de Leeuw quotes J. Loeb, *La Littérature des pauvres dans la Bible*, Paris, 1892, pp. 191-196, who already used the term "fluid." Cf. also the more recent H. H. Rowley, *The Faith of Israel*, 1956, 121: "Unless we adopt a fluid view of the identification of the Servant, we can find no satisfactory answer to the problem."

174 V. de Leeuw, *De Ebed-Jahweh-Profetieën*, l.c., 103. H. H. Rowley, *The Servant of the Lord*, l.c., 1954[2], 38, insists on "the relevance to O.T. evidence." Similarly G. E. Wright, *The Biblical Doctrine of Man*, l.c., 131: "The figure of the Servant of the Lord is a fluid conception, which, in a manner *typically biblical*, holds within itself both community and individual."

175 J. Lindblom, *The Servant Songs in Deutero-Isaiah*, Lund, 1951, 103.

tions, the individual and the collective, we must make use of both explanations *at the same time*.[176] At the most we must point out that the emphasis on one or the other may vary with the context in which the sons have been placed.

There is no doubt that in the general context of the first two songs the term *'ébêd* is applied to the nation.[177] That is why, as long as there are no decisive reasons for supposing another meaning

This author, it seems, attaches a little too much importance to the symbolical character of the servant, to the "allegorical picture" (p. 102), which has nothing in common with the "realistic" views of H. Wheeler Robinson on "corporate personality" (p. 103).

176   O. Eissfeldt, *Der Gottesknecht*, l.c., pp. 12-13: "In Hebraic thought the unit stands 'before' the individual, or *both are at least simultaneous*." Such was already the opinion of H. Wheeler Robinson in 1925; cf. *The Psalmists*, l.c., p. 85: *"Our distinction and contrast does not hold, and therefore the issue cannot be settled in our terms."* Cf. also *Hebrew Psychology* (in S. A. Peake, *The People and the Book*) l.c., p. 378: "We must not attempt to decide whether the figure drawn in Is. 53 is individual or national." Among modern authors we can quote H. S. Nyberg, *Smärtornas Man*, l.c., p. 75: "The current question as to whether the Ebed is collective or individual is false." Cf. also H. H. Rowley, *The Servant of the Lord*, l.c., p. 39: "(There is) not an antithesis between the individual and the group, but an identification of the individual with the group which he represents."

177   It is inadmissible to avoid mentioning Is. 49:3: "You are my servant, he said to me, *Israel*," which is found in all the versions and in the overwhelming majority of Hebrew manuscripts. Only an *a priori* viewpoint can be responsible for such an exclusion, as H. Johannson remarks in *Parakletoi*, l.c., p. 60: "It is hardly possible to find any other reason to delete the word *yisrä'el* here except that it might stand in the way of an individual meaning." C. R. North, *The Suffering Servant*, l.c., p. 118-19, while declaring that there is no way of suppressing "the evidence of the manuscripts with a good conscience," believes nonetheless that Is. 49:3 is a gloss imitating Is. 44:21, but omitting the necessary parallelism with "Jacob." We can agree with him that the reasons alleged for doing away with an absolutely sure reading are, to say the least, inconclusive. In any case, the interpretation of the Targum of Is. 49:1 also identifies the servant with the people. (Cf. P. Seidelin, *Der 'Ebed Jahwe und die Messiasgestalt im Jesajatargum*, in ZNW 35 (1936) 194-231.

in the mind of the inspired author, the term must be interpreted as designating Israel.[178] This principle cannot be denied by the proponents of the individual meaning; but in their opinion the decisive reasons just mentioned actually exist.[179]

In the first place the "servant" is the exact counterpart of the people; in the second place, the "servant" has a mission to fulfill for Israel, which seems to indicate that he is distinguished from it.

The first objection is based on a long series of contrasts between Israel and the servant. Israel is sinful: "You burdened me with your sins, and wearied me with your crimes ... Your first father sinned; your spokesman rebelled against me till I repudiated the holy gates, put Jacob under the ban, and exposed Israel to scorn." (Is. 43:24, 27, 28; cf. 40:2) "I know that you are stubborn and that your neck is an iron sinew and your forehead bronze ... I know that you are utterly treacherous, a rebel you were called from birth." (Is. 48:4, 8) The sinful people is (spiritually) blind and deaf. (Is. 42:18; cf. 43:8; 48:8) That is why it is subject to just divine anger and to punishment of deportation: "Who was it that gave Jacob to be plundered, Israel to the despoilers? Was it not the Lord, against whom we have sinned? In his ways they refused to walk, his law they disobeyed. So he poured out wrath upon them, his anger, and the fury of battle." (Is. 42:24-25; cf. 50:1: "It was for your sins that you were sold.") Israel's history has been one of continual infidelities; to this faithless people Yahweh addresses a continuing series of invitations to repentance. (cf. Is. 46:8)

The servant, however, is faithful, he carries out his task "until he establishes justice on the earth." (Is. 42:4) He frees prisoners. (Is. 42:7: "To bring out prisoners from confinement"; cf. 49:9) He enlightens the pagans. (Is. 42:6: "a light for the nations"; cf. 49:6) He is full of courage and confidence. (Is. 49:5: "My God is now my strength.")

178   A. Lods, *Les prophètes d'Israël et les débuts du judaïsme,* Paris, 1935, 275: "Israel has a divine mission to accomplish in the world. It is the witness of the true God before other peoples; it is the Servant of Yahweh."

179   E. J. Kissane, *The Book of Isaiah, II,* l.c., p. LX.

Against this objection one can counter by saying that the Servant is to be identified with the "faithful remnant," the true Israel. "Refined ... like silver, tested ... in the furnace of affliction" (Is. 48:10), the purified nation, that is to say, the eventual "servant," cannot be really distinguished from the sinful nation, for the "remnant" continues to be the same nation chosen forever by Yahweh. The identity of the "servant" with the nation becomes very probable when one compares the identical poetical imagery used both for the servant (in the songs) and for the nation (in the immediate context of the songs). The servant as well as the people are thought to be "formed by Yahweh" (42:6; 49:5; and 43:1, 7, 21; 44:2, 21, 24: 45:9), "called by Yahweh" (42:6; 49:1 and 41:9; 43:1; 48:12), "invested with the Spirit" (42:1; and 44:3), "called from birth, from my mother's womb" (49:1, 5; and 44:2, 24; 46:3; 48:8), "the chosen of Yahweh" (42:1; 49: 7; and 41:8, 9; 43:10, 20; 44:1, 2; 45:4), "grasped by the hand of Yahweh" (42:6; and 41:10, 13), "upheld by Yahweh" (42:1; and 41:10). These similarities offer ample evidence for the thesis of the Septuagint (Is. 42:1; and 49:1) that the servant is to be identified with the people.[180] The objection based on the opposition between unfaithful Israel and the innocent servant rests primarily on the innocence of the servant so forcefully expressed in the fourth song. But we must note that in the first two songs with which we are concerned here[181] this innocence is not explicitly stated. In fact, the whole history of Israel shows that Yahweh loves His people always, even when they have been faithless. (cf. *Osee*) Besides, the infidelity of the people does not establish a necessary

180 C. R. North, *The Suffering Servant*, l.c., p. 181.—H. H. Rowley, *The Servant of the Lord*, l.c., p. 51 thinks that for the first song of the servant, the thought of the author is "dominantly collective." As for the Septuagint, cf. K. F. Euler, *Die Verkündigung vom leidenden Gottesknecht aus Jes. 53 in der griechischen Bibel* (*BWANT IV*, 14), Stuttgart, 1934, 125.

181 E. J. Kissane, *The Book of Isaiah*, l.c., p. LXVII. This characteristic comes from the fourth song, and it is not at all proved that the idea of the servant is exactly the same throughout, or that it has the same shade of meaning in all four songs. The context must determine the interpretation.

obstacle to the role of servant, for the *pars potior* of the people, the "true Israel," could assume this role.

The second objection against the identification of the "servant" with the people emphasizes the "prophetic" vocation [182] the former carries out for the people. Authors stress the passivity of Israel: "You grew weary of me, O Israel" (Is. 43:22) Under those circumstances it does not seem probable to them that the nation received a real mission.[183] We can answer, first of all, by saying that the mission of the servant relative to the nation is only a part—and the least part at that—of his charge: "It is too little, he says, for you to be my servant, to raise up the tribes of Jacob, and restore the survivors of Israel." (Is. 49:6) The most important part of the servant's mission is his role as "light to the nations": "I will make you a light to the nations, that my salvation may reach to the ends of the earth." (Is. 49:6b; cf. 42:6) There is no doubt that Israel has assumed this second part of the duty: "Salvation (of the pagan) is from the Jews." (Jn. 4:22; Rom. 9:4-5) Does the first duty of the servant to be "a covenant of the people" (Is. 42:6; cf. 49:8), to "reinstate the tribes of Jacob," [184] and "to bring back the survivors of Israel" make an identification between the servant and the people incompatible? [185]

182 Cf. the mention of "spirit" in Is. 42:1 or of the sharp-edged sword, a figure of the mouth, in Is. 49:2.

183 The objection is formulated by C. R. North, *The Suffering Servant*, l.c., p. 183, following M. Schian (1895) and L. Laue (1898). It is possible that in the "songs" there clearly appears what the epithet "servant" has always implied; namely, the duty regarding the pagans. Cf. Is. 44:23: "The Lord . . . shows his glory through Israel."

184 O. Eissfeldt, *The Ebed-Yahweh in Isa. XL-LV in the Light of the Israelite Conceptions of the Community and the Individual, The Ideal and the Real*, in ET 44 (1932/33) 261-268, p. 267 notes that the mission of the Ebed (a corporate figure in the singular) is addressed to "the tribes of Jacob" (persons in the plural).

185 E. J. Kissane, *The Book of Isaiah*, l.c., LXVIII et 127-128 eliminates very simply the first task in Is. 49:5 by reading instead of "that I may bring back" (*lešôbéb*) the wish "May He (Yahweh) be able to bring back" (*lû šôbéb*). Similarly *lô' yé 'āséf* is changed into *lu yé 'āséf*, may Israel be able to be gathered together." In verse 6 *nāqél* is not translated by "it is too little" but by "it would indeed be too little."

It seems not, provided we remember that the Servant can represent the people who have been purified, the faithful "remnant." Perhaps this remnant may have to be reduced to the circle of the prophet and his disciples,[186] but regardless of how small the remnant becomes, it will always be the heir of all the promises made to the nation as such. For all time this remnant will be able to be conceived as the efficient cause (if the action of restoration in *Isaia* 49:5 is attributed to the servant) or better, the instrumental cause (through the intermediary of whom Yahweh will bring about the restoration) of the post-exilic restoration. The Hebrew verbs *lᵉhâqîm* and *lᵉhâšîb* are ambiguous in Is. 49:6.

Moreover it is certain that several times in the context *Deutero-Isaia* distinguishes between two aspects of the Israelite nation: there is an unfaithful Israel (before the exile) and "servants whom I have chosen." (Is. 43:10) These latter will reconstitute (materially and spiritually) the true people of God. Sometimes an almost imperceptible shifting from one aspect of the Chosen People to the other is evident: "Who was it that gave Jacob to be plundered, Israel to the despoilers? Was it not the Lord, against whom *we* have sinned? . . . So he poured out wrath upon them . . . But now, thus says the Lord, who created you, O Jacob, and formed you, O Israel: Fear not, for I have redeemed you; I have called you by name; you are mine . . . For I am the Lord, your God, the Holy One of Israel, your savior . . . Fear not, for I am with you, from the east I will bring back *your descendants* (your race), from the west I will gather *you* (singular) (cf. 49: 6a) . . . Lead out the people who are blind though they have eyes, who are deaf though they have ears . . . *You* (*plural*) are my witnesses, says the Lord, my servants whom I have chosen." (Is. 42:24, 25; 43:1, 3, 5, 8, 10)

> This interpretation may seem "hazardous" and may seem "to ignore thirty years of study" (C. R. North, *The Suffering Servant*, l.c., p. 159); but it answers, without violating the Massoretic text, the objection of North that the phrase "to bring back the tribes of Jacob" "implies a political meaning and therefore an individual person who would lead the repatriated exiles" (C. R. North, *The Suffering Servant*, l.c., pp. 110-145); for if we admit the simple and clarifying corrections of Kissane, it is Yahweh who brings back and not any political "leader."

186   H. Wheeler Robinson, *The Cross of the Servant*, London, 1926, 37.

The course of events is plainly perceptible: divine punishment follows swiftly upon sin, but (*we'attāh* can mean "nonetheless") Yahweh remembers the eternal choice of Israel; he wishes to save his people and to use them as his witnesses before the pagans.[187]

Throughout the course of their history, the people, though appearing under different aspects, remain essentially identical. In a certain sense we might conceive of the purified Israel as at least an instrumental cause (under the principal action of Yahweh) in bringing back "sinners" to Yahweh.[188] We say "in a certain sense," because it is precisely here that the idea of "corporate personality" can shed some light. The individual traits which are discernible in the first two songs [189] seem to us to demonstrate that the "servant" who speaks here is only the *hypostasis* of the people, an *hypostasis* which includes the "chosen" and in which is realized most completely the divine plan for his people, and through his people for all humanity.[190] This personified *potior pars* turns up elsewhere in the *Book of Isaia*. We are thinking especially of the figure of Sion, desolate because Yahweh seems to have abandoned her (Is. 49:14), whom the Lord, less forgetful than a mother

187 Compare the same thought pattern in Is. 43:28-44:3. (I) put Jacob under the ban, and exposed Israel to scorn. Hear then, O Jacob, my servant, Israel, whom I have chosen .... Fear not, O Jacob, my servant, the darling whom I have chosen ... I will pour out my spirit upon your offspring, and my blessing upon your descendants."

188 O. Eissfeldt, *Einleitung in das AT*, Tübingen, 1934, 382 comments very well: "He (the servant) is identical with it (the community), and at the same time stands as a kind of ideal greatness, a goal and fulfillment before its being, and thereby has claims against it: he can demand something from it, he has an order placed with it."

189 O. Eissfeldt, *Der Gottesknecht*, l.c., p. 12 thinks that the Ebed shows quantitatively more individual characteristics in the songs than outside them. Evidently, if we take into consideration the third, and especially the fourth, songs, he is perfectly correct. But would it not be better to analyze each text separately and in its own context?

190 H. H. Rowley, *The Faith of Israel*, l.c., p. 181: "The election of Israel, and of the Servant, in whom her mission is concentrated, is for universal ends, and for the carrying of the light of the faith of Israel to the ends of the earth."

(Is. 49:15) consoles and strengthens: "Look about and see, they are all (the scattered captives) gathered and coming to you. As I live, says the Lord, you shall be arrayed with them all as with adornments, like a bride you shall fasten them on you ... The children whom you had lost shall yet say to you: 'This place is too small for me, make room for me to live in' " [191] (Is. 49: 18, 20) When the children scattered by the exile return to Sion, it is as though the nation were returning and reestablishing Sion. In this sense the "servant of Yahweh" (Israel after the exile) is exercising a mission in favor of Israel.

To be sure, an interpretation purely and simply collective will not succeed in explaining the first two songs of the "Servant of Yahweh." It is necessary also to consider the individual aspect, if we dare say so, of the "corporate personality." The "servant" is Israel, but an hypostatized Israel, who leads to mother Sion her dispersed children, or who receives the sinners of the Chosen People in his bosom, and in this sense carries out an instrumental role in restoring them. This latter role best interprets the enigmatic *berît-'ām* of Is. 42:6 (first song) or of Is. 49:8. Instead of translating "set you as a covenant of the people," we might translate "the establishment of the people on a new base (alliance)." [192] (cf. Is. 54:10; 55:3; 59:21; 61:8)

In the third song of "the servant of Yahweh" (Is. 50:4-9), the designation "servant" is missing. Only after the citation (if such it is) do we find the following exhortation in the form of a gloss (Marti; Volz) or a redactor's link (Duhm; Fischer): "Who among you fears the Lord, heeds his servant's voice." (Is. 50:10) There is no internal indication to prove Is. 50:4-9 to be a separate song of the servant; for this reason several critics refuse to call this passage a song of the servant (Lane; J. Ley; P. Volz). The

---

191 The same idea is found in Is. 60:4: "Raise your eyes (O Jerusalem) and look about; they all gather and come to you: your sons come from afar, and your daughters in the arms of their nurses." (Cf. Is. 60:9 the verb *lehābi'*, "in order to have return," which recalls Is. 49:6), or in Bar. 5:5: "Up, Jerusalem! stand upon the heights; look to the east and see your children gathered from the east and the west at the word of the Holy One, rejoicing that they are remembered by God."

192 E. J. Kissane, *The Book of Isaiah*, l.c., pp. 37-38.

content of the passage suggests only a "wise man" who endures
persecution but feels sure of the triumph of his cause. (cf. the
didactic exhortation of Is. 51:1: "Listen to me, you who pursue
justice, who seek the Lord.") The identification of this "wise
man"[193] with the Servant is based primarily on the description
of the abuses he endured: "I gave my back to those who beat me,
my cheeks to those who plucked my beard; my face I did not
shield from buffets and spitting." (Is. 50:6) This description,
which recalls the humiliation of the Babylonian king on the
feast of the New Year[194] is (perhaps) unconsciously associated
with that of the fourth song. (cf. Is. 53:3: "He was spurned and
avoided by men, a man of suffering.") We might well question the
basis of the identification: "Does a vague similarity between the
sufferings of the persecuted "wise man" of Is. 50:6 and those
of the "suffering Servant" of Is. 53:11 warrant an identification
between the two? Rather than speak of the passage as a "song of
the servant" would it not be better to consider it (Is. 50:4-9)
simply as a "psalm of personal lament?" (Begrich-Mowinckel)

The fourth song (Is. 52:13-53:12) presents a special problem. There are serious reasons to suppose that the author applies
the term "servant" to a figure who is clearly an individual, but who
at the same time always represents the entire nation,[195] namely

---

193 Compare the words of Jeremia: "But, you, O Lord of hosts, O just
 Judge . . . let me witness the vengeance you take on them, for to you
 I have entrusted my cause!" (Jer. 11:20; cf. 15:15) The allusion to
 Deutero-Isaia seems evident in Is. 51:16: "I have put my words into
 your mouth."

194 J. De Fraine, *L'aspect religieux*, l.c., pp. 303-306. Cf. H. Gressmann,
 Der Ursprung der israelitisch-jüdischen Eschatologie, 1905, 301, who
 desires to derive the figure of the Servant from Tammuz-Adonis.

195 O. Michel, *Prophet und Märtyrer*, BFChrTh 37, 2, Gütersloh, 1932, 18
 believes that the figure of the martyred people, persecuted for its faith,
 brought about the application of Is. 53 to the people. He compares
 Ps. 43; 73; 82. But it must be noted that the representation of the
 people is not only on the level of suffering but also on the levels of
 expiation of sins (Is. 53:6,8,10,12) and of intercession (Is. 53:12
 yafgia'). Concerning this latter point of view cf. N. Johannson, *Parakletoi*, l.c., p. 57. H. Wheeler Robinson, *The Psalmists*, l.c., 85 points
 out also the viewpoint of future restoration.

the Davidic Messias. The only norm of decision is the context.
To abandon the context is to run into certain chaos. But the poem
tells the mysterious story of an innocent person, who, despite his
personal innocence, is striken by God. (Is. 53:4) and spurned
by his fellow men. (Is. 53:9; cf. Ps. 21:7-8) A "revelation"
announces that this innocent person through his sufferings and
death expiates the sins of men, and that in doing so he accomplishes
the plan of God and obtains the reward of a long life and of
royal dignity. The ultimate identity of the Servant remains vague,
but the context into which the poem (probably pre-existing)
was inserted points to him as the king of the new Sion.[196]

Such a figure is most certainly distinguished from the collectivity of the people. Nonetheless, we can conceive of this one
figure[197] as encompassing, in a certain sense, all Israel.[198] In any
case he is evidently its representative: "Yet it was *our* infirmities
that he bore, *our* sufferings that he endured ... He was pierced
for *our* offenses, crushed for *our* sins ... The Lord laid upon
him the guilt *of us all* ... He gives his life as an offering for sin ...
Through his suffering, my servant shall justify many, and their
guilt he shall bear ... (He) was counted among the wicked; and
he shall take away *the sins of many,* and win pardon for their
offenses." (Is. 53:4, 5, 6, 10, 11, 12)

While being individual, the Servant of the fourth song, in

196   E. J. Kissane, *The Book of Isaiah,* l.c., p. LXVIII.
197   It is not at all necessary to suppose, as does C. R. North, *The Suffer-
      ing Servant,* l.c., p. 206, that all the details of Is. 53 are to be al-
      legorized in light of the exile. If Is. 53:7: "like a lamb led to the
      slaughter" recalls Jr. 11:19: "Yet I, like a trusting lamb led to
      slaughter," we can just as well compare: "Yet for your sake we are
      being slain all the day; we are looked upon as sheep to be
      slaughtered." (Ps. 43:23)
198   G. Gloege, *Reich Gottes und Kirche im NT,* l.c., p. 217 speaks of an
      "inclusive relationship" between the servant and the nation. From
      the idea of an individual who represents the people, one passes un-
      knowingly to that of the people themselves. Cf. the resumé of H.
      Cazelles, *Les poèmes du Serviteur,* l.c., p. 8: "The person of the
      leader and the group which he directs are not to be separated; their
      fates and their roles are joined together."

virtue of the oscillation so characteristic of Hebrew thought,[199] "perfectly represents Israel and carries its mission to a unique degree in himself." [200] Possibly the author of the song or the compiler who inserted it in the context of Is. 40-55 had in mind an historical person (Jeremia for example, or Josias); but if such is the case, the life and destiny of the latter served to describe by way of type the nature of the true Israel, such as it should appear to the eyes of the nations.[201]

In summary, then, we can say that neither a purely collective explanation nor a purely individual exegesis gives a satisfactory solution. The Servant is an individual, but an individual who sums up the people.[202] We have here a slow development. The "servant" Israel is evolving toward an individual, a servant *par excellence*. At the same time we must never forget that the original "servant" is the entire nation. Whereas the fourth song evidences an undeniably individual characteristic, the mission of the Servant is not separate from that of Israel but rather identical with it. In

199 H. Wheeler Robinson, *The Cross of the Servant*, London, 1926, 36 compares the movements of the human heart (systolic and diastolic) or of the sea (the flood tide and ebb tide).

200 H. H. Rowley, *The Unity of the Bible*, 1953, 60. The author refers to Lv. 16 where the high priest expiates for ("in the place of" and therefore "in favor of") the entire community. Cf. also H. H. Rowley, *The Faith of Israel*, l.c., 121; or J. Pedersen, *Israel III-IV*, l.c., p. 604: "It is Israel embodied in a person who endures the fate of Israel" (concerning Is. 50:6).

201 J. Pedersen, *Israel III-IV*, l.c., p. 604.—H. H. Rowley, *The Servant of the Lord*, l.c., p. 39: "An actual individual . . . is . . . in his (the author's mind." Cf. S. Mowinckel, *Der Knecht Jahwäs*, l.c., p. 71: "an individual . . . actual person."

202 N. A. Dahl, *Das Volk Gottes*, l.c., p. 42. Cf. W. F. Albright, *From the Stone Age to Christianity*, 1946², 255: "The Servant is the people of Israel, which suffers poignantly in exile and affliction; he is also the pious individual who atones for the sins of the many by his uncomplaining agony; he is finally the coming Saviour of Israel." In the same vein, cf. Catholics J. B. Le Frois, *Semitic Totality Thinking*, in *CBQ* 17 (1955) 315-23, p. 319: "The Messiah . . . one with his people"; R. J. Tournay, in *RB* 59 (1952) 509: L. Bouyer, *Le Mystère Pascal*, Paris, 1947, 309.

a certain measure, Israel is always called upon to manifest herself in the individual Servant, whereas the Servant is always aware
of being the representative of Israel. Precisely this fluctuation in
the thought of the author warrants us to speak of a "corporate
personality." [203]

In the application of these songs of the Servant to Christ,
we can observe the same fluidity as was observable in the Old
Testament thought. While Our Lord Jesus Christ is the "suffering
Servant" *par excellence,* He encompasses in his person the entire
Church, the heiress of Israel. This new Israel accomplishes the
mission of the old Israel by associating herself with the sufferings
and death of her Lord. (Ph. 3:10) He "represents" and gives
value to all the works of the Church, which "suffers with him that
it may also be glorified with him." (Rom. 8:17) [204]

E. *THE "SON OF MAN"*

Our attention has often been drawn to the text in *Daniel* 7:13
where the "Son of Man" appears to be a collective term, a symbol

203   H. H. Rowley, *The Servant of the Lord,* l.c., p. 54; on p. 56 Rowley
      says: "I would stress far more than most interpreters do, the collec-
      tive element in the fulfillment." It is for this reason that C. R. North
      puts Rowley among the group of "collectivists" (cf. *ET* 52, 1940/41,
      220). The thought of H. H. Rowley is equally clear in *The Growth of
      the OT,* London, 1950, 97. By way of summary we might use the
      solution sanctioned by A. Causse, *Israël et la vision de l'humanité,*
      Paris, 1924, 59: "At the beginning the Servant represents the exiled
      people, then the Yahwist community, the minority of *anawim;* at the
      end he is a personal hero, the mysterious liberator, a hero comparable
      to the Messias. For A. Bentzen, *Introduction to the OT, III,* 1948,
      113, the Servant is at one and the same time the Messias, the second
      Isaia, and his circle of disciples.

204   H. H. Rowley, *The Servant of the Lord,* l.c., p. 55. Cf. L. M. von
      Pakody, *Deuterojesajanische Studien II. Der Ebed in der Theologie
      Deuterojesajas,* 1942, 241: "An individual Messianic explanation of
      the relationship of the Ebed-Yahweh songs to Jesus is possible only

for the "holy ones of the Most High."[205] (Dn. 7:18, 22, 27)
There is no doubt that the elect are considered to be intimately
joined in a spiritual community with the person who is hidden
under the puzzling term "Son of Man."[206] Need we go as far
as H. Wheeler Robinson and say that the unity between the Son
of Man and the "holy ones of the Most High" "is so realistically
conceived that it can be concentrated into (cf. our second general
theme) a single representative figure?"[207]

Certain authors have tried to explain the identification between
the "holy ones of the Most High" and the "Son of Man" on the
basis of a royal ideology.[208] In Dn. 7:13-14 the "Son of Man"

when we accept the biblical view about community and the individual, and see what was expected by the people fulfilled in Jesus, its
representative peak or summit." Cf. R. J. Tournay, *Les Chants du
Serviteur*, l.c., p. 509: "Just as the Servant cannot be separated from
the Chosen People, of which he is the prominent representative, so
the Redeemer is united with his Mystical Body."

205 N. Johannson, *Parakletoi*, l.c., p. 183. Cf. M. Noth, *Zur Komposition
des Buches Daniel*, in *ThStKr* 98/99, pp. 143-163, p. 149: "In the
current text of *Daniel* the son of man is a *symbol* of the kingdom of
God." In the same vein, cf. N. A. Dahl, *Das Volk Gottes*, l.c., p. 90;
T. W. Manson, *The Son of Man*, in *BJRL* 1949-50, 171-193, p. 174:
"a symbol as the preceding monsters were." The idea of M. Black,
The Son of Man in the Old Biblical Literature, in *ET* 60 (1948-49)
11-15, p. 11 is slightly different: "The Son of Man is the glorified
Israel in the coming eschatological kingdom."

206 N. Johannson, *Parakletoi*, l.c., p. 107.

207 Cf. *ZAW* Bhft 66, l.c., p. 52.

208 A rather special explanation of the "holy ones of the Most High"
appeared in a study of M. Noth, *Die Heiligen des Höchsten* (Festschrift, S. Mowinckel, 1955), in: *Gesammelte Studien zum AT*,
Munich, 1957, 274-290. Noth claims that the term means the celestial
beings, the angels (following O. Procksch, *Theologie des AT*, 1950,
537). But, on p. 275, n. 7, Noth begins by eliminating "the textually
uncertain passage Dn. 8:24"; on p. 278, n. 12 he minimizes Is. 4:3; the
important verses of Dn. 7:21-22 he says are: "literarily secondary"
(p. 287). On the other hand, he bases his position on the parallel
texts de Ps. 88:6,8; Jb. 15:15; 5:1; Za. 14:5; Sir. 42:17; Tob. 8:15.
Other Scriptural passages mentioned by Noth are rather to be ex-

seems to be enthroned as a king: "When he (the human figure advancing toward God) reached the Ancient One and was presented before him, he received dominion (*šoltân*), glory, and kingship (*malkû*); nations and peoples of every language serve him. His dominion is an everlasting dominion that shall not be taken away, his kingship shall not be destroyed." It is perfectly legitimate to see in the "holy ones of the Most High," who "shall receive the kingship" (Dn. 7:18) and who shall "possess it forever and ever" (cf. Dn. 7:22: "the holy ones possessed the kingdom") the subjects of the king described in verses 13 and 14. A few verses later these same holy ones of the Most High" are called "the holy people of the Most High," (Dn. 7:27) or "the holy people."[209] (cf. Ex. 196: "a holy nation"; also Nm. 16:3; Dt. 7:6; 14:2, 21; 26:19) It is not at all rash, then, to envisage a "corporate" identification of the Messias-King with his people somewhat similar to that described in chapter 2 of *Daniel*: "You, O King, are the king of kings; to you the God of heaven has given dominion and strength, power and glory; men, wild beasts, and birds of the air, wherever they may dwell, he has handed over to you, making you ruler over them all; you are the head of gold."[210] (Dn. 2:37:38; cf. also the phrase of Dn. 2:44: "a kingdom that shall never be destroyed").

The context furnishes a solid argument for interpreting Dn. 7:13-14 as a royal investiture. As the four beasts of Dn. 7:1-8 symbolize undoubtedly four anti-God empires, so the "Son of Man" stands for the eschatological empire of the Chosen People, the reign of God on the earth.[211] Moreover, there is a strict paral-

plained in the meaning of the "the just ones" (Dt. 33:3) or in the meaning of the divinity (Pr. 9:10; 30:3).

209   Cf. Ps. 33:10: "Fear the Lord, you his holy ones." (Cf. Wis. 18:9) or Is. 4:3: "He who remains in Sion and he that is left in Jerusalem will be called holy."

210   A. Ström, *Vetekornet*, l.c., p. 136 speaks of a "rite of enthroning." Cf. E. H. Kraeling, *Babylonian and Iranian Mythology in Daniel ch. 7*, in *Oriental Studies in Honour of C.E. Pavry*, Oxford, 1933, 228-31, p. 230 (Babylonian king).

211   M. Noth, *Die Heiligen des Höchsten*, l.c., p. 283, finds here an indication of an eschatological reign in the heavens.

lelism in the *Book of Daniel* between the terms "king" and "kingdom"; the author employs them interchangeably. According to Dn. 7:23 the fourth beast is a "kingdom"; contrariwise, in verse 17 the four beasts are called "kings." [C.C.D. has "kingdoms"; cf. also Dn. 8:20] Whereas Dn. 8:21 speaks of a "king," the following verse makes mention of "four kingdoms that will issue from his nation, but without his strength." (Dn. 8:22) He who overcomes the four "kings" (Dn. 7:17) must be a king in his own right.[212]

The individual sense of the "Son of Man" in *Daniel* becomes very probable when one consults two apocrypha of the Old Testament which speak of the figure of the "Son of Man"; namely, the *Fourth Book of Esdras* and the *Book of Henoch*. These two writings are formally opposed to a purely collective or allegorical interpretation of the "Son of Man."[213] It is not at all impossible that the figure of the Son of Man, before becoming in *Daniel* the Messianic king of the eschatological kingdom, was originally a divine or semi-divine person. In any case the expression "the semblance of a son of man" [C.C.D. translates "something like a man's hand"] (Dn. 10:16) is very mysterious.[214] Emil H.

212   M. J. Lagrange, *Le judaisme avant J. C.*, Paris, 1931², 66-67: "The ancients would not have conceived of empires (the 'holy ones of the Most High') without their leaders. The 'holy ones' compose the new empire; they will then necessarily have a king to inaugurate it and to rule it, such as Nabuchodonosor, Cyrus, Alexander, Antiochus Epiphanes, but a king who comes from the heavens." H. Gressmann, *Der Messias, Göttingen*, 1929, 345, notes that the symbolism of the phanes, but a king who comes from the heavens." H. Gressmann, *Der* "Both are far removed from each other." Cf. Ap. 17:9-10 where the kingdoms and the kings are put on exactly the same footing.

213   A. Feuillet, *Le Fils de l'homme de Daniel et la tradition biblique*, in *RB* 60 (1953) 197 defends the equivalence of the two phrases "with the clouds" and "on the clouds." H. Gressmann, *Der Messias*, l.c., p. 345 translates '*im ᶜanané sᵉmayyā*' by "flying along the clouds"; T. W. Manson, *The Son of Man*, l.c., p. 174, however, thinks that there is question of a movement "from earth to heaven."

214   C. H. Kraeling, *Anthropos and the Son of Man*, New York, 1927, 128 ff. Cf. W. Staerk, *Soter II. Die Erlöserewartung in den östlichen Religionen*, 1938, 421-38 recalls that the same theory was already defended by von Gall.

Kraeling thought (after Bousset and Gressmann) of the Iranian figure of Gayomart who was joined with the Babylonian god Marduk. However, all things considered, it seems more probable to hold that the expression *bar'enās* (like the Hebrew (*bèn'-ādâm*) is originally a Jewish appellation.[215]

In the *Apocalypse of Fourth Esdras,* chapter 13, which certainly depends on Dn. 7, "something like a man" rises from a rough sea. (cf. Dn. 7:3) This mysterious being takes flight "on the clouds of heaven" (Dn. 7:13) and destroys an anti-God army with the burning breath of its mouth. We notice that the activity of the "Son of Man" is more intense in this context than in the *Book of Daniel.* In Chapter 13, verse 26 of *Fourth Esdras* he is called the "Savior of the world"[216] at least in an instrumental sense. A little farther on we are told explicitly that the Most High frees "those who are on the earth."[217] In verse 52 of chapter 13 the Messias (*filius meus — pais*) is accompanied by those "who are with him," that is to say the celestial court of the angels and the Elect.[218]

In the section of Parables in the *Ethiopian Book of Henoch* (cc. 37-71) the title *bar'enāš* plays a no less important role, and an all the more interesting role in that these "parables" are truly a kind of *midrash* on Dn. 7:13.[219] In chapter 46 the apocalyptic visionary sees a man (*ho huios tou anthrôpou,* in the original of

215   E. H. Kraeling, *Babylonian and Iranian Mythology,* l.c., p. 230. E. Sjöberg, *Der Menschensohn im aethiopischen Henochbuch,* 1946, 193 notes that the Son of man in Dn. is no way thought to be a "primitive man"; he doesn't play any role in creation, doesn't appear as the prototype of humanity, doesn't fight with the forces of chaos, and doesn't perish in such a fight as does Gayomart of Bundahisa.

216   The Latin text of 4 Esd. 13:26 reads: *"quem conservat Altissimus multis temporibus, qui per semetipsum liberabit creaturam suam."*

217   Cf. the Latin text: *"Ecce dies venient quando incipiet Altissimus liberare eos qui super terram sunt."* Cf. W. Staerk, *Soter I. Die biblische Erlösererwartung,* Gütersloh, 1933, 76-77.

218   N. A. Dahl, *Das Volk Gottes,* l.c., p. 91 sees in 4 Esd. 13:5 a "combination of Dn. 7 and Is. 53."

219   It is perhaps exaggerated to see in Henoch's passage about the Son of man Christian interpolations, as J. M. Lagrange suggests, *Le Judaïsme avant J. C.,* l.c., pp. 422-424.

the Ethiopian translator) whose face is filled with beauty like that of one of the holy angels, who possesses justice, in whom justice resides, who reveals all the hidden treasures. For the Lord of spirits has chosen him, and his destiny has surpassed all before the Lord of the spirits in justice forever. (Hen. 46:3) This individual figure—the author seems to say that judging by his looks one would call him a man—will execute judgment just as the "Son of Man" in Dn. 7: "In those days I saw the Ancient seated on the throne of his splendor, the books of the living were open before him, and his entire heavenly army stood before him. The hearts of the holy ones were filled with joy, for the time of justice was near, and because the prayer of the just had been heard and because the blood of the just had been avenged before the Lord of the spirits." (Hen. 47:3-4) The *bar'enāš* of the Book *of Henoch* is pre-existing; [220] he exists "before the sun and before the zodiac" (48:3), or "before the world was created." (48:6) His reign is eternal (48:6); he is a "suport for the just (cf. Is. 42:6; 50:4; 61:1-2) and the holy ones" (48:4), and the "avenger of their lives" (48:7); finally, he is the Messias (48:10; 52:4), the "just one *par excellence*" (38:2), and the "Chosen one." (39:6; 53:6) The title "Chosen one" has been compared with the Servant's titles in Is. 42:1, and the term "just one" harkens back to Za. 9:9-10. [221]

It is moreover very striking that along side the individual "Chosen One"—the Davidic Messias under a new designation—the *Book of Henoch* mentions also "the chosen ones." (39:6; 45:3-6; 49:1; 40:5: "The Chosen One and the Chosen ones") Even more striking is the occasional abrupt shift from the singular to the plural (e.g. Hen. 51:3 is singular; 51:5 has both the singular and the plural). A Norwegian scholar has attempted to explain

---

220 T. W. Manson, *The Son of God*, l.c., 181 ff. argues against the idea of preexistence and prefers to speak of "pre-mundane election" (p. 184), or of an "idea in the mind of God" (p. 188); this last "Son-of-Man-Idea" (p. 188) would be present as much in the person of Henoch as in the Messias. Manson refers to Hen. 71:14 and to Hen. (Slav.) 22:8; 56:2; 63:5.

221 *Ibid.*, p. 75. recalls the expression *'anani*, "man of the clouds" which the Rabbis used to designate the Messias.

this situation by stating that the author of the *Book of Henoch* "was not thinking so much of the biblical figure of the Son of Man as of the people prefigured by it. For him the shift from the 'Chosen One' to the 'chosen ones' would be quite natural." [222] Wouldn't it be better to explain the usage by the well known phenomenon of "the shifting between the individual and the collectivity?" [223] The chosen ones, as a matter of fact, are thought to be closely bound—although they always remain distinct [224]— to the person of the Son of Man.[225] Together with the latter they make up the celestial society of the "holy ones" as shown in Hen. 70:4, where near the Son of Man are "the first fathers and the just of the very early time," [226] or in Hen. 61:12, where "All the chosen ones live in the garden of life."

It seems to be inescapable that in the *Book of Daniel* as well as in 4 *Esdras* and in *Henoch* the "Son of Man" must be conceived as a "corporate" individual, a "corporate personality." [227] It is certain that the Aramaic title "Son of Man" in Dn. 7:13 ($k^e bar'^e n\bar{a}\check{s}$) recalls the Hebrew *bèn'ādām* of Dn. 8:17 where Daniel is characterized in the same way as the prophet Ezechiel;

---

222 N. Messel, *Der Menschensohn in den Bilderreden des Henoch*, in ZAW Bhft 35, Giessen, 1922, 69, recognizes only a few verses (46:2-4; 48:2) as authentic passages (unencumbered with Christian interpolations). Cf. E. Sjöberg, *Der Menschensohn*, l.c., p. 35.

223 T. W. Manson, *The Son of Man*, l.c., p. 188. According to the same author the Messianic terms "the just One" and "the Anointed" are also collective. Cf. T. W. Manson, *The Teaching of Jesus*, 1931, 228.

224 M. Noth, *Zur Komposition des Buches Daniel*, l.c., p. 151 n. quotes very clear texts: "The wisdom of the Lord of Spirits revealed him (the elect) to the saints and the just." (Hen. 48:7)

225 N. Johannson, *Parakletoi*, l.c., p. 107.

226 W. Staerk, *Soter II*, l.c., p. 516, notes that the imaginary design of Henoch is broken, since there couldn't be question of just ancestors having entered heaven before the ministry of Henoch.

227 Cf. M. Black, in *ET* 1948-49, p. 14: "According to the late Dr. Wheeler Robinson's conception of corporate personality." Cf. also T. W. Manson, *The Son of Man*, l.c., p. 190: "another characteristically Hebrew and Semitic idea, that of corporate personality"; or N. A. Dahl, *Das Volk Gottes*, l.c., p. 90, regarding Dn. 7 and Hen.: "It is an individual, and at the same time a collectivity."

it refers therefore to a definite individual.[228] However, this individual being—the first incarnation of a divine design—is also actualized in the people of "the holy ones of the Most High" of the Machabean epoch, and will be even more perfectly fulfilled in the person of the eschatological Messias. We find in chapter 7 of *Daniel* a characteristic view of life and of history: the "Son of Man" is a figure who represents Israel or the people of God, but who will gradually be more and more individualized.[229]

In the New Testament the term "Son of Man" as applied to Christ extols on various occasions his relationships with "the holy ones of the Most High": "The Son of Man is the type of a new people, consecrated to God ... the Church is not a separate function: the destiny of the Son of Man is the destiny of his people." [230] The society founded by Christ is a corporate community endowed with such a strict unity that it is incarnated first of all in Jesus himself. The disciples and the Master together form "the Son of Man" (cf. Ac. 9:5: Christ persecuted in his followers); the disciples can be thought of as "extensions" of the personality of the Master.[231]

228   This is also proved by Dn. 10:16, where the angelic visitor is, in turn, certainly individual (*kid^{e}mût bèn 'ādām*).

229   F. Nötscher, *Daniel*, in: *Echter-Bibel*, Würzburg, 1948, 39: "Through him (the son of man) is the dominion embodied, i.e., exercised, the dominion that is granted to the people of the saints."

230   F. Kattenbusch, *Der Quellort der Kirchenidee*, in *Festgabe für A. Harnack*, 1921, 143-172; cf. W. G. Kümmel, *Kirchenbegriff und Geschichtsbewusstein, in der Urgemeinde und bei Jesus*, in *Symb. bibl. Uppsalenses I*, 1943, 33: "Thus F. Kattenbusch (already in ZNW 12, 1911, 270-286, p. 286) maintained that Jesus in reference to Dn. 7 must have felt himself to be the 'Son of Man' and the representative of the 'People of the Saints,' and must have considered it his task to form this people of the saints among mankind." Cf. the same conviction in C. H. Dodd, in *According to the Scriptures*, 1952, 117.

231   T. W. Manson, *The Son of Man*, l.c., p. 191. This author exaggerates when, referring to Mk. 2:10, 28, he interprets the "Son of Man" as the community acting through Jesus, who represents it and sums it up. In any case, from certain points of view, Jesus transcends the disciples without identifying himself with them purely and simply. T.

Jesus in His person realized the synthesis of the three types of messianism. The words which He pronounced before the Sanhedrin: "You shall see the Son of Man sitting at the right hand of the Power and coming with the clouds of heaven" (Mk. 14:62) prove that He identifies Himself with the "Son of Man" in *Daniel*. But this seems to indicate also His identification with the "holy ones of the Most High," all the more so in that these are to "receive the kingdom" which emphasizes the Davidic hope of the royal messianism.[232] Although at first Jesus rejected the title "son of David," [233] He did accept it on the eve of His passion. Lastly Jesus stressed the ties which bind the "Son of Man" to the "Suffering Servant" of *Deutero-Isaia,* who reveals characteristics which are more "corporate" as well as those which are individual. By way of summary we can say that Jesus represents simultaneously in His person the following three realities: a) the individual person of Christ, the Davidic and "suffering Servant of Yahweh"; b) the collectivity of the new Israel, like the Old Israel, the "servant of Yahweh"; c) the concrete union of the individual Jesus Christ with the members of His Church.[234]

Although the distinction between the individual "Son of Man" and the eschatological "people" of the "holy ones of the Most High" is always preserved in the New Testament, it is sometimes difficult to say whether the Gospel is speaking of the individual coming of Christ or of the consummation of the kingdom of God in His elect. That is the case in Mt. 16:28, for example: "Amen I say to you, there are some of those standing here who will not taste death, till they have seen the Son of Man *in his kingdom."* The coming of Christ "in his kingdom" means that Christians will share fully in the glory of their Lord: "Amen I say to you that

W. Manson takes up his idea again in the *Coniectanea Neotestamentica* (Anton Friedrichsen Festschrift), Lund, 1947, 138-146.

232 Compare the identification of the Son of Man and the Messias in the book of Henoch.

233 J. Jeremias, *Jesus als Weltvollender, BFCT* 33,4, Gütersloh, 1930, 56, believes that Jesus rejected the title "son of David" because he considered it too redolent of purely political hopes.

234 B. J. Le Frois, *The Woman Clothed with the Sun, (Ap.* 12) *Individual or Collective?* Rome, 1954, 236: "The identical symbol represents simultaneously the individual, the collective and the totality."

you who have followed me, in the regeneration when the Son of Man shall sit on the throne of his glory, shall also sit on twelve thrones, judging the twelve tribes of Israel." (Mt. 19:28; Lk. 22: 30) At any rate, the individual interpretation, messianic if one wishes, of the "Son of Man," must always go hand in hand with a clear consciousness of the "corporate" content of the concept. For in Hebrew thought the Messias and the community are so intimately united as to be almost interchangeable. In virtue of the Semitic fluidity with which the shift from the individual to the collectivity takes place, and *vice versa*, the term "Son of Man" (in *Daniel* and perhaps also in the New Testament) sometimes symbolizes the kingdom, sometimes its individual representative.[235]

Ultimately "for the understanding of his (Jesus') use of the term Son of Man we should remember that concept of corporate personality . . . He could think of himself as concentrating in himself the kingdom, whose representative he was."[236] All the redemptive work of Christ can be summarized in the words of St. John: "Jesus was to die . . . that he might gather into one the children of God who were scattered abroad." (Jn. 11:52) At the Last Judgment "when the Son of Man shall come in his majesty and all the angels with him," He shall solemnly affirm the mystic identity between His individual royal person and "the least of my brethren": "Then the king will say to those on his right hand, 'Come, blessed of my Father, take possession of the kingdom prepared for you from the foundation of the world; for I was hungry and you gave me to eat . . . As long as you did it for one of these, the least of my brethren, you did it for *me.'* " (Mt. 25: 31, 34-35, 40) This supreme confirmation of the identity of Jesus with His own (cf. Ac. 9:4) is already enunciated in the Christian's life of union and prayer: "Whatever you ask *in my name,* that I will do, in order that the Father may be glorified in the Son" (Jn. 14:13), that is to say in "the Son of Man": "Now is the Son of Man glorified, and God is glorified in him." (Jn. 13:31)

235 H. H. Rowley, *The Biblical Doctrine of Election,* 1950, 157. Cf. in the same meaning, S. Hanson, *The Unity of the Church in the N.T.,* l.c., p. 11.

236 H. H. Rowley, *The Faith of Israel,* l.c., p. 196.

F. THE "I" OF THE PSALMS

The Book of Psalms contains about 80 psalms in which we
find the word "I." Much discussion has taken place regarding the
meaning of this word, as to whether it refers to the collectivity or
to an individual. For a long time two theories have contended with
each other. Rudolf Smend has given the classical defense of the
"collectivistic" theory in an article about ::The I of the Psalms."[237]
whereas Emile Balla has presented very well the case for the
"individualistic" opinion.[238] Having read these two explanations,
one might well agree with H. Wheeler Robinson when he says:
"This is why the discussion about the 'I' of the Psalms is so inconclusive, and why the interpretation tends to swing from one
side to the other."[239] It is much better to fall back upon the idea
of "corporate personality" (our eighth theme) to give a true
reason for the constant switching from the collective to the individual.

1. The First Thesis

The first thesis, namely that of Smend, begins with the undeniable fact that the cult of the sacred temple for which the
psalms served as the *liber textus* was most certainly collective.[240]
Even if some of the psalms are originally more or less individualistic, for example, those in which the leader speaks (Ps. 4; 61; 72;
121), we must be aware of a "socialization of the individual
experience."[241] The psalms "of the sick" (Ps. 6; 21; 29; 37; 40;

237   R. Smend, *Ueber das Ich der Psalmen*, in ZAW 8 (1888) 49-147
      (quoted henceforth simply as Smend).
238   E. Balla, *Das Ich der Psalmen*, BRLANT 16, Göttingen, 1912 (quoted
      henceforth simply as Balla).
239   H. Wheeler Robinson, in *The Psalmists*, l.c., 83.
240   Smend, pp. 50-51. On page 145 the author refers to Jon. 2; Sir.
      51:1-12; Jud. 16:2-17, which are really collective prayers put in the
      mouth of a single individual.
241   The phrase is H. Wheeler Robinson's, *The Psalmists*, l.c., p. 84. Cf.
      A. Bertholet, *Histoire de la civilisation d'Israël* (French translation of
      J. Marty), Paris, 1929, 327: "In the poetry of the psalms ... it often
      happens that selections which were originally individual were recast

68; 87; 101) have found their places in the psalter because sickness symbolizes any and all weaknesses.[242] In general, anything that seems to be individual has been transformed by its use in the temple into a collective song.[243] Sometimes this transformation is betrayed by the use of the plural "we" in the course of a psalm which began with the singular "I."[244] Another indication is found in the Targum commentary which applies compositions which are apparently individual to the community.(Ps. 22; 37; 55; 68; 87)[245]

Moreover the community feeling was so strong in Israel that it spontaneously expressed itself in a personification (a man or a woman). As we have explained above, we are dealing here with something more profound than a simple artificial "rhetorical figure." Rather we are concerned with a unity so great that in the sight of God the group appears as a single individual. We can add to the many examples already given in the preceding pages some others which show the wide use of the device. An entire tribe is designated by the term "I"; the sons of Joseph speak to Josue in these words: "Why have you given us only one lot and one share as our heritage? Our people are too many, because of the extent to which the Lord has blessed us." [The French version has "Why have you given men . . ."] (Jos. 17:14) The inhabitants of a certain village, says the prophet Zacharia, "shall approach those of another, and say, 'Come! let us go to implore the favor of the Lord'; and, 'I will go to seek the Lord.'" (Za. 8:21) The Israelite nation constitutes a single body closely united, even an

in view of liturgical usage and thus became collective." Sometimes one ascertains the presence of "collectivizing" additions; cf. Ps. 24:22; 27:8; 33:23; 50:20-21; 129:7-8; 130:3). S. Mowinckel, *Psalmenstudien II*, l.c., p. 175 mentions also Ps. 80:15; 128:5; 131:18.

242 Smend, p. 53.

243 *Ibid.*

244 Smend, p. 53 n. 3 mentions the following psalms (the singular passage is in parentheses) 8:2,10 (4); 19:6, 8-10 (7); 59:3, 12-14 (11); 64:4 (5); 65:6, 8-12 (13,20); 67:20,21,29 (25); 73:9 (12); 74:2 (10); 77:3-5 (1-2); 88:18-19 (2-3); 102:10 (1); 105:6,7,47 (4); 117:19 (26-27); 121:2 (1); 122:2-4 (1).

245 Similarly, the Septuagint in the title of Ps. 55 refers the psalm to the nation.

individual person. The people is blessed by the priests with these words: "The Lord bless *you* (singular)" (Nm. 6:22); the people can say: "The Lord takes in hand his banner" [French text has "Yahweh is my banner"] (Ex. 17:15); in the *Book of Zacharia* the people ask "the priests of the house of the Lord of hosts, and the prophets, 'Must *I* mourn and abstain in the fifth month as I have been doing these many years?' " (Za. 7:3) In general the prophets speak to the people in the singular "I" or "you." [246] The decalogue is cast in the singular although it is addressed to the people in general. (Ex. 20 and 34) The same is true of the *Book. of the Covenant* (Ex. 21-23) and of *Deuteronomy.*[247]

As for the psalter, although it is necessary from time to time to take into consideration a truly personal, and therefore exclusively individual experience, in a very great number of cases the "I" seems to indicate the community. Smend admits the existence of

---

246   Smend, p. 61, points to the following passages in the Book of Isaia: Is. 12:1-2 ("On that day, you will say: *I* give you thanks."); Is. 26:9 (*"My soul* yearns for you."); Is. 26:11 ("Let them be shamed when they see your zeal for your people."); Is. 40:27 ("Why, O Jacob, do *you* (singular) say"); Is. 48:5 ("That *you* (singular) might not say, *'My* idol did them.'"); Is. 49:14 ("But Sion said, 'The Lord has forgotten me.'"). In the Book of Jeremia, Smend refers to the following passages: Jer. 3:4 ("But because *you* (singular) have a harlot's brow."); Jer. 4:31 ("Ah, woe is *me!* I sink exhausted before the slayers."); Jer. 10:19 ("Woe is *me!* I am undone."); Jr. 10:20 (*"My* sons have left me."); Jr. 31:18 ("I hear Ephraim pleading: You chastised *me.*"). Together with these passages from Isaia and Jeremia, Smend draws attention to the following: Ez. 37:11 ("These bones are the whole house of Israel."); Os. 2:7,9,14,19 (the unfaithful spouse); Os. 11:3-4 (the "child"); Mi. 7:1 ("Alas! *I* am as when the fruit is gathered."); Mi. 7:7 (But as for *me,* I will look to the Lord."); Ha. 3:16 ("I hear, and *my* body trembles; ... upon the people who attack *us.*").

247   Smend, pp. 61 and 63, argues also from the collective interpretation of the Servant of Yahweh, who nonetheless is expressed in the first person singular (Is. 49:1-5; 50:4-10; 53:7 in the "songs"; Is. 61:1, 10,12; 62:1; 63:7,15 outside the "songs"). On pages 67 Smend draws attention to the "regrettable lack of precision" in texts such as Is. 46:4: "Even when your hair is gray I will bear you; it is I who have done this, I who will continue, and I who will carry you to safety."

some strictly individual passages; for example, Ps. 36:2: "Trust in the Lord and do good" (cf. v. 7: "Be not vexed at the successful path of the man who does malicious deeds."); or Ps. 90:7: "Though a thousand fall at your side, ten thousand at your right side, near you it shall not come"); or Ps. 127:3: "Your wife shall be like a fruitful vine in the recesses of your home; your children like olive plants around your table." The same is true in the following passages: "Neither in my youth, nor now that I am old, have I seen a just man forsaken" (Ps. 36:25); "My heart overflows with a goodly theme" (Ps. 44:2); "The Lord said to *my* Lord" (Ps. 109:1); "I will give thanks to the Lord with all my heart in the company and *assembly of the just*" (Ps. 110:1); "If I forget you, Jerusalem, may my right hand be forgotten! May my tongue cleave to my palate if I remember you not. (Ps.136: 5-6)

Sometimes a personal note breaks forth in a composition that is plainly collective in nature. We can cite Ps. 19:7: "Now I know that the Lord has given victory to his anointed" (cf. v. 6: *"We* shout for joy" or v. 8 "We are strong in the name of the Lord"); Ps. 31:3: "As long as I would not speak, my bones waste away" (cf. v. 11: "Be glad in the Lord and rejoice, you (pl.) just"); Ps. 43:7: "Not in my bow did I trust, nor did my sword save me" (cf. v. 10: "Now you have cast *us* off"; v. 13: "You sold your people"); Ps. 59:11: "Who will bring me into the fortified city?" (cf. v. 12: "Have not you, O God, rejected *us?"*); Ps. 74:10: "But as for me, I will exult forever" (cf. v. 2: "We give you thanks"); Ps. 105:4: "Remember *me,* O Lord, as you favor your people" (cf. v. 6: *"We* have sinned"; v. 47: "Save *us"*); Ps. 134:5: "For I know that the Lord is great" (cf. v. 2: "Praise, you servants of the Lord."[248]

Frequently, however, from the very beginning of the psalms the "I" designates the community. Psalm 128:1: "Much have they oppressed me from my youth, let Israel say" refers without a doubt to Sion. (cf. v. 5) Similarly in the Septuagint version, psalm 73:

---

248 Smend, p. 142, admits that psalms 61 and 72 reflect, at the very least, a personal experience. Concerning Ps. 72, however, he is of the opinion "that nonetheless it was composed for community worship." (p. 124)

12: "Yet, O God, my king (*basileus hêmôn*) from of old." The large number of sacrifices in psalm 65:13-15 reveals the communal character of the psalm. Several times a "we" is followed by an "I" which does not really change the communal character of the psalm but rather underlines the unity of the group. Psalm 35:10 has "we": "In your light *we* see light," but a few verses further on the psalmist switches to the singular: "Let not the foot of the proud overtake *me* nor the hand of the wicked disquiet *me*." (Ps. 35:12) Psalm 49 is quite evidently addressed to the people: "Hear, my people, and I will speak," but throughout the psalm the people are addressed in the singular "you." (cf. v. 7b and 15: "I will rescue you and you shall glorify me."[249] The singular of psalm 84:9: "I will hear what God proclaims" is surrounded on every side by "we" (cf. 84:5-8, 10, 13) and represents undoubtedly the group. Although psalm 136:6: "May my tongue cleave to my palate if I remember you not" was originally individual in tone, the communal context of the psalm in verses 1-4 and 8 has completely absorbed the individual characteristics.[250]

In order to explain this shifting back and forth between the singular and plural. Smend falls back upon the oft suggested solution of a single speaker who makes himself the spokesman of the group. Very often it is the leader or the king. According to Smend psalm 3:6: "When I lie down in my sleep, I wake again for the Lord sustains me" may be the personification of the people; in the same vein psalm 4 is applied to a "popular leader."[251] The advice of psalm 10:1: "Flee to the mountain like a bird" indicates, according to Smend, that the psalm is addressed to an individual (the leader of the holy ones).[252] Although he is willing to recognize

---

249 The identity between "my" and "our" (the people) is very clear in Ps. 61:8-9: "With God is *my* safety and *my* glory, he is the rock of *my* strength; *my* refuge is in God. Trust in him at all times, O my *people!* Pour out *your* hearts before him; God is *our* refuge!"

250 Compare verses 8 and 9 of Is. 26: "For your judgments, O Lord, *we* look to you; your name and your title are the desire of *our* souls. *My* soul yearns for you in the night, yes, *my* spirit within me keeps vigil for you."

251 Smend, p. 88, "Head of the people."

252 Smend, p. 91.

in psalm 26:1-6 the words of a "prince," Smend concludes that verses 4 and 5: "One thing I ask of the Lord ... to dwell in the house of the Lord all the days of my life" prove the communal aspect of the psalm.[253] Despite its affinity with the "confessions of Jeremia," psalm 30 must be interpreted in a communal perspective.[254]

In a considerable number of cases Smend forcefully introduces the collective meaning, when he should at least have left the matter in doubt. Basically the reason for this is that he is guided by some fundamental presuppositions. According to him the "subject" of Old Testament religion is the totality of the nation or the community.[255] He is convinced that "the community had an entirely different attitude toward God and the world than the individual had. It had considerably more duties and sufferings, but also more elevated claims and aspirations." On the other hand "the religious consciousness of the individual Israelite depended on the community consciousness; the individual had first of all to remember his dependence on the community before taking cognizance of his dependence on God."[256]

Relying on these presuppositions, Smend rejects out of hand an "individualistic" explanation of all those psalms in which the individual seems to arrogate to himself religious privileges which, as a matter of fact, belong only to the community. He demands very strong positive proofs for any individualistic interpretation, whereas the communal interpretation has an *a priori* advantage. That is why Smend will not admit that the "evildoers"

253 Smend, p. 98.
254 Smend, p. 101: cf. Ps. 30:14-Jer. 20:10; v. 11-Jer. 20:18; v. 13-Jer. 22:28; 48:38; v. 18-Jer. 17:18.
255 Smend, p. 146. Cf. p. 81: "Yahweh's honor adhered to the people; His sole divinity had to be revealed in the fate of Israel, but not in the fortunes of the individuals." The passages which Smend relies upon certainly speak about the Holy Nation, but do not formally exclude individuals: 1 K. 12:22 ("The Lord will not forsake his people."); Jer. 14:21 ("Remember your covenant with us, and break it not."); Ex. 9:13 ("Let my people go.")
256 Smend, p. 54. Regarding Ps. 129:5 Smend says on page 137: "the prophetic promise of the Messianic future which first of all belongs to the community alone ..."

of psalm 6:9-11 are in any way individual enemies, despite the
description of verses 7-8: "I am wearied with sighing . . . I drench
my couch with my tears. My eyes are dimmed with sorrow; they
have aged because of all my foes." For Smend the "sickness"
described in this psalm is only a figure of the persecution which
Israel suffers.[257] Only in virtue of the *a priori* principle that
"individual piety is necessarily modeled on community piety" and
that "the contrary is absurd and unacceptable," [258] can Smend
write that the formula: "Have pity on me, O Lord, for I am
languishing; heal me, O Lord, for my body is in terror" (Ps. 6:3)
cannot be applied "allegorically" to an individual.[259]

The cry of psalm 7:12 to God, the just judge, cannot refer to
a personal cause, for the individual disappears completely in the
universal judgment with which "the Lord judges the nations."
(v. 9)[260] Smend calls upon the words of Saint Jerome: *"Iste
psalmus totus in persona Ecclesiae per prophetam de Antichristo
cantatur"* to uphold his purely collectivistic explanation of psalm
9. As a matter of fact, it deals with another universal judgment,
which for Smend is enough to exclude any trace of an individual
interpretation.[261]

The certitude of salvation expressed in psalm 12:6: "Let my
heart rejoice in your salvation" and the "lack of precision in the
description of misery" lead Smend to conclude that the psalm is in
no way individualistic but that it flows from the "community consciousness." [262] Complete preservation from death in psalm 15:

257   Smend, pp. 68-72, refers to Is. 1:5-6; 17:11; 33:24; 53:3; Os. 5:13;
      Lam. 1:13.

258   Smend, p. 143.

259   Smend, p. 76.

260   Smend, p. 90. Similarly the phrase of Ps. 56:6, 12: "Be exalted above
      the heavens, O God." could not refer to an individual to be saved
      (p. 118); Ps. 61:12 "One thing God said" is "hardly a personal revela-
      tion" (p. 120); The "exploits of Yahweh" in Ps. 91:2-3 "save only
      the community." (p. 127)

261   Smend, p. 84. It is clear that St. Jerome is not interpreting *ex mente
      auctoris*, but that he is introducing a "Christian interpretation" of the
      psalm.

262   Smend, p. 92. Even psalm 21 is, in the eyes of Smend, a purely col-
      lective composition (pp. 76-79); he refers to verses 23-24 and 27-30

9-11 scarcely applies to an individual, but refers solely to the community.[263] The apparent solicitude of Yahweh for an individual, whom He would refer to as "the apple of his eye" (Ps. 16: 8), seems impossible; that is why Smend is of the opinion that the "I" of this psalm symbolizes "the community persecuted by the wicked."[264] The "servant" of psalm 18:12, 14 is the community;[265] the one protected by the "shepherd" of psalm 22 is Israel;[266] verses 4 and 5 of the same psalm do not at all refer to the nourishment of an individual but to the collective blessing of the harvest (as in Ps. 35:9; 64:5);[267] the "sins of my youth" of psalm 24:7 are the "past sins of Israel."[268] The words "though my father and mother forsake me, yet will the Lord receive me" (Ps. 26:10) do not, Smend assures us, refer to an individual but are a proverb (?) applied to the community.[269] The cry of joy of psalm 31:11: "Be glad in the Lord and rejoice, you just; exult,

to show that it is concerned with the sufferings and the salvation of Israel.

263 Smend, p. 93. The same holds for Ps. 48:16: "But God will redeem me from the power of the nether world." (p. 112); or Ps. 85:13: "You have rescued me from the depths of the nether world." (p. 126); or Ps. 87:7: "You have plunged me into the bottom of the pit." (p. 126)

264 Smend, p. 94.

265 Smend, p. 96.

266 Smend, p. 80, with reference to Gn. 48:15 ("Jacob-Israel was not simply an individual, and furthermore, he is the people *in nuce.*"); Jr. 31:10; Ez. 34:14; Ps. 79:2 ("O shepherd of Israel, hearken"); 28:9.

267 Smend, p. 82.

268 Smend, p. 97, referring to Ps. 128:1-2. While reading the alphabetical psalm 24, one gets the impression of a completely individualistic psalm; however, the end of the psalm, which departs from the alphabetical arrangement and may be a later addition, reveals the ancient interpretation of "I" as referring to the entire nation: "Let integrity and uprightness preserve me, because I wait for you, O Lord. Redeem Israel, O God, from all its distress!" (Ps. 24:21)

269 Smend, p. 98. The objection against the "collective" explanation of texts such as Ps. 26:14 ("Wait for the Lord with courage") is plainly

all you upright of heart" demonstrates, according to Smend, the community character of this psalm which deals with the liberating acknowledgment of sin.[270] Although psalm 33:4: "Glorify the Lord with me" distinguishes the psalmist from his companions, Smend attributes it nonetheless to "the God-fearing in general" probably because of verse 8: "The angel of the Lord encamps around those who fear him, and delivers them."[271] Psalm 34, which in verses 5 and 6 speaks of the "angel of the Lord" cannot be individual, for "such action on the part of Yahweh is incompatible with His way of dealing with a purely personal and individual affair."[272] The apparently individual exhortation of psalm 36:3: "Trust in the Lord and do good" (cf. v. 7: "Leave it to the Lord, and wait for him.") is addressed, in the opinion of Smend, "much less to individual God-fearing individuals than to the community.[273]

"The man" corrected by Yahewh (Ps. 38:12) is the community.[274] The words of psalm 41:10: "Why must I go about in mourning, with the enemy oppressing me?" are "the figurative expression of a collectivity."[275] Not even psalm 50, the *Miserere,* is interpreted in an individual sense by Smend. Verse 13: "Cast me not out from your presence" refers to the humiliation of the nation;

dispelled by the phrase *"Selbstanrede."* Smend refers to Ps. 31:8; 54:23; 119:3; 120:3-5; 129:8; 130:3.

270   Smend, p. 103. The singular of Ps. 31:7 ("You are *my* shelter") is considered misleading; it is not necessarily question of a single individual, for the end of the psalm widens the vision: "Be glad in the Lord and rejoice, you just; exult, all you upright of heart." (Ps. 31:11)

271   Smend, p. 103.

272   Smend, p. 104. Verses 13-14 ("But I . . . afflicted myself with fasting") are said to be "metaphorical" (*"bildlich"* p. 105).

273   The reason given is that the "ownership of the land" of which Ps. 36:34 speaks cannot be but collective. But Smend forgets that the expression can have a figurative meaning, as in the Beatitudes. (Mt. 5:4)

274   Smend, p. 106. Cf. also p. 128 concerning the "man" of Ps. 93:12; or p. 140 regarding Ps. 143:3-4; or p. 141, concerning Ps. 145:10 (Sion).

275   Smend, p. 111.

verse 15: "I will teach transgressors your ways" designates the apostolic mission of the Chosen People.[276]

The profession of faith: "But I, like a green olive tree in the house of God, trust in the kindness of God forever and ever" (Ps. 51:10) "belongs only in the mouth of the community."[277] The prayer of psalm 53:4: "O God, hear my prayer; harken to the words of my mouth" is thought to be "so dull" that it "could only come from the community as such."[278] The cry of confidence of psalm 62:9: "My soul clings fast to you; your right hand upholds me" is said to be "collective." Yahweh upholds the community; there can be no question of this referring to a purely personal affair; rather it is a matter which refers to the totality.[279]

The mention of Israel in the psalmist's meditation on sacred history (Ps. 76:6) proves that "the one who speaks is the community."[280] The proximity of the sanctuary in psalm 90:1 indicates that verses 7 and 13-16 "make better sense" if they are interpreted as referring to the collectivity.[281]

The detailed description of psalm 101:2-13 is considered to be "completely metaphorical"; the same is also true for details as concrete as those of verse 5: "Withered and dried up like grass is my heart; I forget to eat my bread" or verse 10: "I eat ashes like bread and mingle my drink with tears."[282] Verse 16 of psalm 115: "O Lord, I am your servant; I am your servant, the son of

276 Smend, pp. 113:114. For the application of Ps. 50:13 to the nation, cf. 4 K. 13:23; 17:20; 24:20; Jr. 52:8; 2 Par. 7:20.

277 Smend, p. 115. Smend refers to Jr. 11:16: "A spreading olive tree, goodly to behold" (Israel); or to Ps. 91:13-14, the just "planted in the house of the Lord." One might object against Smend's view that this last expression refers to each of the just in particular.

278 Smend, p. 116.

279 Smend, p. 121. It is difficult to admit that Ps. 103:34: "Pleasing to him be my theme; I will be glad in the Lord," "does not refer in any way to an individual" (p. 131).

280 Smend, p. 125. The same attitude regarding Ps. 142:5: "I meditate on all your doings" (p. 140) is criticized by E. Balla, *Das Ich der Psalmen*, l.c., 8: "There is a difference when the poet speaks of the people and when the people or community speaks of itself."

281 Smend, p. 87.

282 Smend, p. 129. The same is true on p. 133 of Ps. 108:21-26.

your handmaid; you have loosed my bonds" is thought to be
"unbecoming in the mouth of an individual" because "only the
community honors Yahweh."[283] Although the great sapiential
psalm 118 contains expressions dealing with an individual experience (verses 53, 115, 136, 139, 158), and although the "I" is
from time to time obviously personal (verses 63, 79, 99, 100),
there cannot be any doubt, says Smend, about the communal
character of the whole.[284]

The argument becomes a bit simplistic when psalm 119 is
said to be "communal" because "the individual God-fearing man
undoubtedly has companions of the same spirit as himself,"[285]
or when Smend says regarding verse 5 of psalm 134: "I know that
the Lord is great" that such an attitude toward the national God
"cannot be the viewpoint of an individual but must come only
from the nation."[286] The dialogue form of psalm 120 goes counter
to an individualistic explanation because "never in *public* cult
is there a dialogue between two individuals."[287]

Psalm 137 cannot be individual, says Smend, for "no individual, not even a king, could attribute to his prayer such a
significance, nor could he conceive the cause of the people and
of Yahweh to be his personal cause."[288] Similarly, according to
Smend, the wish of psalm 138:19: "If only you would destroy
the wicked, O God" cannot possibly be the personal wish of a
single individual; it refers to the destruction of the ungodly among
the community.[289] Because there is more than one enemy in
psalm 139, there is conflict between groups according to Smend.
Consequently verses such as psalm 139:7: "I say to the Lord,

---

283   Smend, p. 133. The term *'ēbēd*, as we have seen, designates Israel,
      but not solely; it probably refers to Israel in Ps. 135:22, but in Ne.
      2:20 "servants" of "the God of heaven" is rather "cultic"; (cf. Esd.
      5:11).
284   Smend, p. 135.
285   Smend, p. 136.
286   Smend, p. 138. The *'ani* is called "emphatic."
287   Smend, p. 137.
288   Smend, p. 139.
289   Smend, p. 139.

you are my God; harken, O Lord, to my voice in supplication" are to be interpreted in a thoroughly collective way.[290]

While recognizing that verse 5 of psalm 140: "Let the just man strike me . . . let him reprove me" can scarcely be applied communally, Smend draws attention to the collective flavor of verse 7: "So their bones are strewn by the edge of the nether world."[291] Despite the distinction in psalm 141:8 between the one who speaks in the first person singular and "the just (who) shall gather around me," Smend holds that it is a community prayer.[292]

One cannot escape the impression that Smend proves nothing in his attempt to prove too much. Fascinated by a too simplistic view of the preponderant, not to say, exclusive role of the post-exilic community,[293] he rejects without sufficient proof a certain number of undeniably individual elements in the psalms. It is a well known law of religious poetry sung during public cult that very personal sentiments very easily insinuate themselves into such a community framework.[294] It is this thought that Emile Balla, the proponent of the sacred theory regarding the "I of the psalms," has so well expressed in his analysis.

2. The Second Thesis

Balla begins with the principle enunciated with so much force and clarity by Gunkel-Begrich's commentary on the psalms: "The collective explanation of the 'I' of the psalms" is "one of the

290 Smend, p. 139.
291 Smend, p. 140.
292 Smend, p. 140.
293 The individual always remains the son of the nation, its only concrete representation; when Yahweh lavishes His solicitude upon the people, as Ps. 21:4-6; 76:12 teaches, He extends it, in the final analysis, to all individuals, past, present, and future. "The apple of his eye (Yahweh's)" is the nation in Dt. 32:10; Za. 2:12; but it is probably an individual person in Ps. 16:8.
294 M. Lohr, *Sozialismus und Individualismus im AT*, ZAW Bhft 10, Giessen, 1906, 34: "The 'I' of so many of the psalms is naturally to be understood of the author, whose religious experiences and moods, because of their typical character, can be appreciated by the community."

worst errors that exegesis of the psalms can be guilty of."[295]
Although Smend has his defenders such as Cheyne,[296] Ehrlich,[297] and Stade,[298] the majority of commentators are agreed that
there are a certain number of psalms which cannot be interpreted
in a collective sense. Such is the opinion of Kautzsch,[299] Baethgen,[300] and Briggs,[301] among others. Among the most bitter anta-
gonists of Smend are Karl Budde, Ernst Sellin, Edward Koenig,
and Herman Gunkel.

The existence of psalms with an individual tone outside the
psalter is, according to the view of Balla, a forceful proof for
the possibility of parallel compositions in the canonical book.
Balla is referring to the lamentations, certainly individual in character, of Jeremia.[302] As examples of "individual lyricism" he mentions the epithalamium of psalm 44 in which the "I" is "a singer
of the court"; the "poetic legends" of psalms 77 and 105 in which
the "I" is a "popular chanter" or a "leader" (cf. Ps. 105:4); the
"oracle" of psalm 109 in which the "I" is "a privileged person
especially favored"; the "song of the pilgrim" of Ps. 121 (cf. verse
8: "because of my relatives and friends"); or the "psalm of
execration" of psalm 136.[303]

In the second place Balla bases his contention on certain

---

295 H. Gunkel and E. Begrich, *Einleitung in die Psalmen,* 1933, 173. Cf.
     H. Gunkel, *Ausgewählte Psalmen,* Göttingen, 1911, pp. IX, 90 and
     253.

296 J. Cheyne, *The Book of Psalms,* 1904, pp. I and LXIV.

297 A. B. Ehrlich, *Die Psalmen,* Berlin, 1905, 6.

298 B. Stade, *Biblische Theologie des AT,* 1905, 329.

299 E. Kautzsch, *Die Poesie und die poetischen Bücher,* Tübingen,
     1902, 49.

300 F. Baethgen, *Die Psalmen,* Göttingen, 1904, XXII.

301 C. A. Briggs, *Critical and Exegetical Commentary on the Book of
     Psalms,* Edinburgh, 1907.

302 E. Balla, *Das Ich der Psalmen,* (henceforth simply Balla) cf. Jer.
     11:18-23, Ps. 82:4; Jer. 15:15-21; Ps. 68:8; Jer. 17:12-18; Ps. 72:4-7;
     Jr. 18:18-23; Ps. 34:12; Jer. 20:10; Ps. 30:14. Cf. also Jb. 3:24; Ps.
     41:4; Jb. 6:4; Ps. 87:7; Jb. 7:7; Ps. 77:39; Jb. 10:10; Ps. 138:13;
     Jb. 19:13; Ps. 37:12; 68:9; 87:9,19; Jb. 23:8; Ps. 138:1-6; Jb.
     30:9-10; Ps. 68:13.

303 Balla, pp. 44-47.

internal characteristics of the texts; for example, the title of psalm 101: "the prayer of an afflicted one when he is faint and pours out his anguish before the Lord," or on formulas in which the "I" of the psalms speaks to other members of the community. Among the latter Balla cites psalm 21:23: "I will proclaim your name to my brethren; in the midst of the assembly I will praise you";[304] also psalm 65:16: "Hear now, all you who fear God, while I declare what he has done for me";[305] and finally psalm 33:4: "Glorify the Lord *with me*, let us *together* extol his name."[306]

Besides, Balla draws attention to one or the other event which seems to refer to an individual rather than to a community. Thus the "I" of some psalms recalls his "birth" (Ps. 138:14; 21:10; 50:7: "my mother"; 70:6; 85:16; 115:16). Strictly speaking one can show that the psalter also speaks of the "birth" of the people, but we must admit that this explanation scarcely applies to all the "births" just mentioned. The allusions to "my father and mother" (Ps. 26:10), to the "shame (which) covers my face" (Ps. 68:8), to an attack directed against "a man" (Ps. 61:4), to a slighted benefactor (Ps. 7:5), to old age (Ps. 36:25; 70:18; cf. however, Os. 7:9 where it refers to the people), to death (Ps.

304 Balla, p. 6. Cf. other mentions of "assembly" in Ps. 21:26: "So by your gift will I utter praise in the vast assembly."; Ps. 25:12: In the assemblies I will bless the Lord."; Ps. 34:18: "I will give you thanks in the vast assembly."; Ps. 41:5: "with the multitude keeping festival"; Ps. 54:15: "You, whose comradeship I enjoyed; at whose side I walked in procession in the house of God!"; Ps. 105:5: "glory with your inheritance"; Ps. 108:30: "I will speak my thanks earnestly to the Lord, and in the midst of the throng I will praise him."; Ps. 110:1: "in the company and assembly of the just"; Ps. 115:14,28: "My vows to the Lord I will pay in the presence of all his people."; Ps. 141:8: "The just shall gather round me."

305 Balla, p. 8, refers to Ps. 77:1: "Hearken, my people, to my teaching" or Ps. 118:63: "I am the companion of all who fear you and keep your precepts."

306 Balla, p. 8, mentions Ps. 27:8: "All who see me scoff at me."; Ps. 30:12: "They who see me abroad flee from me."; Ps. 68:8: "I have become an outcast to my brothers, a stranger to my mother's sons."; Ps. 87:19: "Companion and neighbor you have taken away from me."

38:14: "Ere I depart and be no more"; 12:4; 15:10; 29:10; 40:6), can be explained much better undoubtedly in an individual -oriented framework. Perhaps the same is true for the "illnesses" and the "enemies," although in these cases the imagery can be adapted very plausibly to the community.[307] Verse 4 of psalm 37: "There is no health in my flesh because of your indignation; there is no wholeness in my bones because of my sin" recalls very strikingly the image applied to the collectivity in Is. 1:6: "From the sole of the foot to the head there is no sound spot." Anyone who counters with the passage in *Osee* 6:1 in which Yahweh promises to "bind the wounds" of the people, must not fail to recall likewise the similar imagery in Jeremia which is indisputably individual-oriented: "Why is my pain continuous, my wound incurable?" (Jer. 15:18)

In other places also the individualism of the psalms is obvious: "My throat is dried up like baked clay, my tongue cleaves to my jaws" (Ps. 21:16); "With sorrow my eye is consumed; my soul also, and my body" (Ps. 30:10); "Fear and trembling come upon me, and horror overwhelms me." (Ps. 54:6)[308]

Finally, Balla recalls the existence of individual-oriented psalms among the Babylonians and the Egyptians and a number of biblical lamentations outside the psalter[309] in which illness refers very obviously to a personal deficiency.

Regarding the "enemies," we must concede that the expressions are often emphatic and that sometimes they rather seem to apply to other than purely individual situations.[310] Such is perhaps the

307 Balla, p. 27, is right in pointing out that these phrases indicate a stereotyped style, a recurring, even monotonous, literary type.

308 Balla, pp. 26 and 126 protests against the statement of Smend, as though the maladies were not described graphically enough. He refers to Ps. 37:6: "Noisome and festering are my sores because of my folly."

309 Balla, p. 18. On p. 48 Balla mentions the individual hymns of Jb. 5:8-16; 9:2-12; 12:13-25; 26:5-14; 34:18-29; 36:26 to 37:13; or Dn. 2:20-30; or Sir. 42:15 to 43:33. He also draws attention to the sapiential compositions of Jb. 4:7 to 5:7; 8:11-19; 15:17-35; 18:5-21; 20:5-29; 27:11-23; or Sir. 51:13-20.

310 If "the enemy" is in the singular, there is more chance that the "I" of the psalm refers to an individual person. Cf. Ps. 12:3-5 (but v. 5

case with the imagery of psalm 21:13-14: "Many bullocks surround me; the strong bulls of Basan encircle me. They open their
mouths against me like ravening and roaring lions" or with the
cry of sorrow in psalm 85:14: "O God, the haughty have risen
up against me, and the company of fierce men seeks my life."
(cf. 53:5) We must take into consideration the Oriental style [311]
which exaggerates pathos: "Rise up, O Lord, in your anger; rise
against the fury of my foes; wake to the judgment you have de-
creed. Let the assembly of the peoples surround you" (Ps. 7:7-8).
Besides, these hyperbolic words do not prove *ipso facto* that the
psalm from which they come is collective. It may be that the
afflicted person who is here speaking seeks in his prayer to God
some kind of anticipation of the final judgment against the
wicked.[312] In fact, "enemies" are always considered in the light
of their opposition against God: "Punish them, O God; let them
fall by their own devices." (Ps. 5:11) The psalmist is concerned
about the injury they do against God in persecuting him: "It
crushes my bones that my foes mock me, as they say to me day
after day, 'Where is your God?'" (Ps. 41:11); "He relied on the
Lord; let him deliver him, let him rescue him, if he loves him."
(Ps. 21:9)

also has "my foes"); 16:13: "the wicked" (but v. 14 has "mortal
men"); 40:12: "my enemy" (but in v. 3 "his enemies" and in v. 8
"my foes"); 54:3: "the enemy, the wicked" (but v. 19 has "those
who war against me" and v. 24 "men blood"); 139:2-3: "Deliver me,
O Lord, from evil men; preserve me from violent men, from those
who devise evil in their hearts."; 142:3: "the enemy" (but in v. 9
"my enemies" and in v. 11 "distress").

311 Balla, p. 21, "In his feverish phantasies it appears to the poor sick
man as though the entire world has conspired against him in order to
utterly destroy him." Balla quotes Ps. 56:5: "I lie prostrate in the
midst of lions which devour men."; Ps. 16:9,12: "My ravenous
enemies beset me; ... like lions hungry for prey"; Ps. 63:3: "Shelter
me against the council of malefactors, against the tumult of evildoers"; Ps. 55:8: "In your wrath bring down *the peoples,* O God."
312 *Balla,* p. 43 refers to Jb. 16:9-11: "All my company has closed in on me
.... I am the prey his wrath assails, he gnashes his teeth against me.
My enemies lord it over me; their tongues are agape to bite me."

Although he is opposed to the exaggerated solution of Smend, Balla does admit the existence of a certain number of collective psalms.[313] There are, first of all, the certainly communal lamentations, such as verse 8 of psalm 11: "You, O Lord, will keep *us*"; or the "national complaint" of psalm 78 verse 4: "We have become the reproach of our neighbors"; or the "prayer for the restoration of Israel" of psalm 79 verse 5: "O Lord of hosts, how long will you burn with anger while your people pray?"; or finally psalm 89 verse 1: "O Lord, you have been *our refuge* through all generations."[314] Secondly there are collective hymns of thanksgiving in the psalter, such as "the collective prayer after the annual harvest" of psalm 66, the "prayer against the enemies of Sion" of psalm 128, or the hymn in honor of the Savior of Israel in psalm 123.[315] Besides, it is impossible to deny the collective character of several poems dealing with the liturgical cult. Psalm 20, a "thanksgiving for the king" is a psalm whose communal character is proved, for example, by verse 14: "Be extolled, O Lord, in your strength! We will sing, chant the praise of your might."[316] Psalm 59 is a thoroughly national prayer after defeat (cf. v. 5: "your people" and v. 6: "those who fear you").[317] Psalm 65 can be called "a public thanksgiving,"[318] and psalm

Despite the great number of enemies, Ps. 16:9-12 seems to refer just as much to an individual as the passage of Jb. just quoted.

313   These collective psalms are not, for all that, devoid of all personal feeling. Balla, p. 122, denies the identity of the ideas "community cult" and "non-individual cult," "choral hymn" and "non-individual hymn."

314   Balla, p. 65, referring to Is. 59:9-15; 63:15 to 64:11; Jr. 3:22-25; 9:18-21; 14:2-9; 14:19-22 (the covenant); Os. 6:1-3; 14:4; Jl. 2:17; Mi. 7:14-20; Lam. 5; Dn. 3:21-45 LXX; Sir 33:1 to 36:22.

315   Balla, p. 66 refers to Is. 12:3-6; 25:9.

316   Balla, p. 99: Verses 2-6 of ps. 19 are "sung by a choir of the temple"; verse 7 by "one of the assistants, a chanter or a priest" (p. 100).

317   Balla, p. 97: "a thanksgiving service." On page 98 Balla refers to Ps. 21:24: "You who fear the Lord, praise him." or to Ps. 29:5: "Sing praise to the Lord, you his faithful ones."

318   Balla, p. 98: the choir sings Ps. 65:1-12; verses 13-20 are recited by one of the faithful.

84 a "prayer for peace" (cf. verses 3, 7, 9: "your people"). Sometimes the title of the psalm indicates its use in the liturgy and therefore its communal form. For example, psalm 80: "For the feast of tabernacles" or psalm 117: "Liturgy for the feast of tabernacles" (cf. v. 24: "This is the day the Lord has made; let us be glad and rejoice in it").[319] Similarly, even when the one praying the psalm is indicated as "I," it is sometimes necessary because of the contents to conclude to the collective nature of the composition. Among these Balla includes the "national lament" of psalm 43,[320] the "lament after the sack of the temple" of psalm 73,[321] or the "prayer against the enemies of Israel" of psalm 82.[322]

3. *An Evaluation of the Two Theories*

This summary analysis of the psalter reveals—according to Smend and Balla—that the pronoun "I" is interpreted in two ways; Smend contends that it should be interpreted almost always in a collective sense; Balla holds that while some compositions are undoubtedly collective, there is still room for a large measure of personal lyricism. One wonders, however, whether it is necessary to maintain such a definite distinction between the "collective" and the "personal" in the "I psalms."

For Smend, as H. Gunkel has pointed out, the collective viewpoint is "a last remnant of the allegorical interpretation of Sacred Scripture, which was at one time so general."[323] Whenever anyone is taken up with the idea of allegory, he is inevitably drawn to look upon every use of the first person singular as an allegorization of the community feelings. The position of Balla, on the contrary, seems more balanced. Even when a psalm must be interpreted in a collective sense, it is not at all impossible that an individual

---

319 Balla, p. 101: "a thanksgiving service," with a "leader" (a king, a general), and several choirs.

320 Balla, p. 106: "public lamentation"; cf. v. 10: "You have cast *us* off," despite the singular "my bow … my sword" (v. 7), or in v. 16: "All the day *my* disgrace is before *me,* and shame covers *my* face."

321 Balla, p. 107; cf. Ps. 73:12: "O God *my king.*"

322 Balla, p. 107; cf. Ps. 82:14: "*My* God."

323 H. Gunkel, *Einleitung in die Psalmen,* l.c., 175.

person, a qualified and delegated "prayer," particularly an outstanding person,[324] is expressing the ideas and reactions of his
group.

The procedure by which an individual member represents the
group is the normal pattern of the Old Testament, as our study has
amply demonstrated. Very often words which are attributed to a
group must have been spoken by one person in the name of
the group. By way of examples we have the "Hethites" (Gn. 23:
6), the brothers of Joseph (Gn. 42:10; 43:20; 44:7-9), the
Egyptians before Joseph (Gn. 47:18, 25), the Gadites and Ruben-
ites before Moses (Nm. 32:25-27), the heads of the ancestral
houses in the clan of descendants of Galaad (Nm. 36:2), the
Hevites before Josue (Jos. 9:7), the "house of Joseph" before
Josue (Jos. 17:14), the Ephraimites before Gedeon (Jg. 8:1),
the Israelites before Gedeon (Jg. 8:22), the murderers of Isboseth
before David (2 K. 4:8), the officers of king David (2 K. 15:15),
the servants of David (3 K. 1:2), and "the men of the city" before Eliseus. (4 K. 2:19)[325]

If, then, it is customary for a single individual to express the
feelings of a group, we have the right to assert that in some
passages at least we are not dealing with a personification pure
and simple of the community,[326] but with a "corporate personality,"
who is truly an individual and at the same time the representative
of the group. Outside the psalter we have such a case in Moses as

324 Balla, p. 107, refers to Gn. 44:16, 18-34 (Juda speaking for his
     brothers); Ex. 34:9 (Moses speaking for his countrymen); Dt.
     2:27-29 (Moses, in the name of the people); 1 Mc. 10:70-73
     (Jonathas—the people); Esd. 9:6-15; Ne. 1:5-11; Dan. 9:4-19.

325 Balla, p. 108. On p. 118, n. 2 Balla gives a list of places where an "I"
     or a "you" (singular) evidently refers to more than one. Cf. e.g., Dt.
     2:18 (Moses—the people leaving Ar, the country of Moab); Dt.
     26:5-10 (an individual pronouncing the Israelite "credo").

326 This possibility is never to be excluded. Balla, pp. 116-118, gives
     examples, among others Is. 48:5,7 ("that you (singular) might not
     say"); Is. 49:21 ("You (singular) shall ask yourself."); Jer. 2:20
     "Long ago you (singular) broke your yoke."); Jer. 13:22 ("If you
     ask in your heart"); Jer. 31:18 ("I hear Ephraim pleading"); cf. also
     Bar. 4:9-29; Ez. 35:10; Os. 12:9; Dt. 7:17; 8:17; 9:4; 12:20; 17:14;
     18:16; 31:17.

he sings the victory song after the crossing of the Red Sea: "Then Moses *and the Israelites* sang this song to the Lord: *'I* will sing to the Lord," (Ex. 15:1) In the same way the *Canticle of Debora* (Jg. 5:1) was sung either by the poetess herself (verse 12 notwithstanding) or by one of the Israelite nobles or leaders. Nonetheless, the speaker speaks in the name of the people: "My heart is with the leaders of Israel." (Jg. 5:9) *Isaia* 25 begins with a prayer of thanksgiving: "O Lord, you are *my* God, *I* will extol you and praise your name" that is reminiscent of Ex. 15:1. The prophet is conscious of representing "a strong people (who) will honor you." (Is. 25:3; cf. Is. 63:7)

Anytime that we have an "I" that shifts without any definite reason to the collective "we," there is good probability that the "I" may be an individual who, in some way or other, through the "we" expresses his union with the others of his group.[327] There is no reason to allegorize or to speak of this corporate "I" as a "type of the true Israel." [328] Rather he is a definite individual, a prophet-singer, a leader or notable, a king.[329] But this person—especially if it is the king—represents all the people. Whence we may well think that in those psalms which are patently "national," the "I" which stands side by side with the "we" is precisely the king or the leader of the people.[330] Psalm 43 certainly deals

327 Balla, p. 134.

328 Smend, p. 145, regarding the "Song of Anna" (1 K. 2:1-10): "The 'I' of the community." Similarly, the last verse of the "Song of Ezechias" would prove that there was question of the "I" of the community."

329 Balla, p. 101, refers to the "royal psalms": Ps. 17:44 ("You made me head over nations"); Ps. 17:48 ("O God, who granted me vengeance, who made peoples subject to me"); Ps. 20:13 ("You shall aim your shafts against them"); Ps. 44:6 ("Peoples are subject to you"); Ps. 71:8 "May he rule from sea to sea"); Ps. 109:6 ("He will do judgment on the nations").

330 S. Mowinckel, *Psalmenstudien I,* 1921, 97, presupposes the existence of a "corporate I" who recites the psalm, even in cases where there is no mention of an "I," as in psalms 73; 78; 79; 82 (except the liturgical cry "my God" in verse 14); 89; Lam. 5; Jer. 14:2-9. Cf. H. Birkeland, *Die Feinde des Individuums in der israelitischen Psalmenliteratur,* Oslo, 1933, 124: "And when we have an individual 'I'

with "the people" (cf. verse 13: "You sold your people for no great price"), but verse 16: "All the day *my* disgrace is before *me*, and shame covers *my* face" betrays a single speaker who identifies himself with his people. Similarly psalm 59 contains, in the midst of a series of collective "we's," a single verse which suggests a single representative: "Who will bring *me* into the fortified city? Who will lead *me* into Edom?" (Ps. 59:11)

When we bear in mind the notion of "corporate personality," we can understand without much trouble how the "I" of the psalms seems to contain within itself incompatible qualities. While referring in some cases (not always) to the community, the "I" nonetheless represents an outstanding person who sums up in himself the entire group. This explains the quick shift from the individual to the collective and *vice versa*.[331] At that very moment when he is speaking, the individual who represents in some way or other the community *is* really this community. Therefore he can use the first person singular to speak in the name of this community.[332]

In order to fully understand the exact import of the "I of the psalms" it is important always to keep in mind that each individual Israelite is a member of the people of God and that he is fully convinced of the social repercussions of his conduct.[333] In a certain sense the "I of the psalms" is an Israelite who encompasses all Israel.[334] Depending upon the context, the language of the

before us in the psalms..., then this 'I' has to be *a leader* of the people, at least a king, high priest, military leader, etc."

331   H. H. Rowley, *The Faith of Israel*, l.c., 144. Cf. A. Bertholet, *Histoire de la civilisation d'Israël*, l.c., 367: "As a matter of fact, the boundary between the individual I and the collective I sometimes fluctuates when the author of the psalm occupies a leading, or at least an important, place in the collectivity; in that case his cause can readily be that of the group, and *vice versa*."

332   H. H. Rowley, *The Faith of Israel*, l.c., p. 118-Cf. S. Mowinckel, *Psalmenstudien V, Segen und Fluch in Israels Kult und Psalmendichtung*, 1923, 36: "The chosen representative... expresses the feelings and thoughts of the community and acts in such a way that the entire community acts in him and is bound up with him."

333   C. G. Montefiore, *The Old Testament and After*, 1895, 282-83.

334   S. Mowinckel, *Psalmenstudien V*, l.c., p. 36: "The soul of Israel

psalmist reflects either this one individual or the concrete totality of the nation, without, however, either of these possibilities being absent from the consciousness of the psalmist. Contrariwise, the more general group (the God-fearing, Israel, humanity) is always present to the memory of the individual psalmist. The situation is somewhat similar to the pedal notes of an organ which are always ready to lend body and substance to any melody.[335]

Because it dulls the sharpness of the antithesis between the individual and the collective viewpoints,[336] the notion of "corporate personality" succeeds perhaps best in solving the vexing problem of the identity of the "I of the psalms." The "I" seems to be neither an individual pure and simple nor the personification of the group, nor the "great I" of the collectivity, but all three at once and the same time, one single living voice "which expands or contrasts the scope of his reference from verse to verse."[337]

makes its appearance in the individual Israelite .... In him does Israel exist and live, and in certain cases and under special circumstances the greater I of the people is entirely concentrated in the person of this individual."

335 H. Wheeler Robinson, Inspiration and Revelation in the OT, 1946, 264-65. Cf. H. Birkeland, Die Feinde des Individuums, l.c., p. 341: "The collective character of the individual psalms (is) strong throughout, yes, the individual psalms are even collective."

336 H. Wheeler Robinson, The Hebrew Conception of Corporate Personality, l.c., 57.

337 H. Wheeler Robinson, The OT. Its Making and Meaning, l.c., p. 137. Cf. S. Mowinckel, Psalmenstudien V, l.c., p. 36: "The 'representative' speaks and says 'I'; he does not mean thereby: 'I', the king, the priest, etc., but 'I, Israel.' "

4

The Idea of "Corporate Personality" in the New Testament

Christ came to fulfill the Old Testament, consequently the broad outlines of New Testament teaching come from the Old Testament. We have already had occasion to show this in the Adam-Christ parallel and for the title "Son of Man."

It would not be difficult to multiply examples pointing out the constant use of the idea of "corporate personality" in the New Testament. We would see not only that this concept explains the Pauline thought regarding the unity of the human race and the appellation "Son of Man" but also that this concept is to be found in many other texts.

The Christian message is summed up in the salvific will of the Father who sends His Son that He might establish and strengthen an indissoluble bond among those who are predestined to form the true Israel, the "corporate Son," the prophetic "remnant." [1] The fundamental mystery of Christianity, namely, the Incarnation of the Son of God who becomes the Head of His Mystical Body which is the Church, embodies within itself the very epitome of the biblical notion of "corporate personality." Jesus Christ is at one and the same time "a life-giving spirit" (1 Cor. 15:45) and the corporate representative of the new humanity, of "many sons" (Heb. 2:10), before the Father. The entire life of the Church—its sacramental life, its prayer life, its life of active charity—all must be viewed in the light of this fundamental conception of

---

1 W. K. Lowther Clarke, *Divine Humanity*, London, 1936, 161.

the Person of Christ, the Messianic King, the new Adam, and the
Servant *par execellence* of Yahweh.[2]

In our first section we wish to show how the notion of "corporate personality," as we have described it, is found throughout the
New Testament.[3] In the second section we will consider it in the
doctrine of the Mystical Body.

A. EXAMPLES OF "CORPORATE PERSONALITY" IN THE NEW TESTAMENT

The idea of "corporate personality" is made up of two facets:
between a group and a determined individual there exists a relationship whereby either the individual is actualized in the group or the
group is encompassed in the individual. These two aspects, as
we have seen, are present in the nine great themes we have studied
in the Old Testament. These same themes have also left their mark
in the New Testament.

1. *Theme of the Father of the Family and His Household*

The unity of the family in the New Testament is such that a
man is hardly ever thought of without his family. That is why it
was necessary on the occasion of the multiplication of the loaves
to specify: "Now the number of these who had eaten was five
thousand men, *without counting women and children*." (Mt. 14:
21, cf. 15:38) The Christians of Tyre who accompany St. Paul

2   Concerning the martyrs cf. H. Von Campenhausen, *Die Idee des
    Martyriums in der alten Kirche*, Göttingen, 1936, 57: "In the per-
    secution of the martyrs it is not a matter of an isolated event in which
    the fate and behavior of individual Christians would be *similar* or
    'comparable' to the fate of Jesus, but an *original unity of the event*
    here as well as there."

3   For examples of "corporate personality" in rabbinic or Jewish apoc-
    alyptic literature at the beginning of the Christian era, see de Fraine's
    article: *Tracce della 'personalità corporativa' nel Giudaismo*, in *BeO*
    3 (1961) 175-179.

are described as follows: "And all of them with their wives and children escorted us." (Acts 21:5) When the people take upon themselves the responsibility for the death of Jesus, they cry out: "His blood be on us *and on our children*" (Mt. 27:25), and Jesus advises the women of Jerusalem who weep for him: "Daughters of Jerusalem, do not weep for me, but weep for yourselves *and for your children.*" (Lk. 23:28)

The royal official whose son Jesus cured "believed, *and his whole household.*" (Jn. 4:53) Lydia, the seller of purple from the city of Thyatira, is baptized together with "her household." (Acts 16:15) Paul and Silas tell their jailor: "Believe in the Lord Jesus, and thou shalt be saved, *and thy household.*" (Acts 16:31) "And he *and his family* were baptized immediately." (Acts 16:33) At Corinth "Crispus, the president of the synagogue, believed in the Lord *and so did all his household.*" (Acts 18:8)

There are certain texts which on the basis of this relationship between the "father" and "his household" speak of Christ as the "father of the family" of his disciples. He calls them "my little children,"[4] (Jn. 13:33: *teknia;* cf. Mk. 10:24: *tekna*) When Jesus is accused of being in the service of the devil, He replies: "If they have called the master of the house Beelzebub, how much more those of his household!" (Mt. 10:25; cf. Jn. 15:20)

2. *Theme of the Beneficial Influence of the Representing Individual*

The extension of the term "son" to include the members of a group who identify themselves with a "father" is no different from the use of the word *bén* in the Old Testament. The subjects of a king are called his "sons" (Mt. 17:24) because together with him they make up a close unity. "All Jerusalem" was troubled with Herod. (Mt. 2:3) [In the French translation of Mt. 9:15 (cf.

---

4 In his *Second Epistle*, St. John speaks of the "children of thy sister Elect." (2 Jn. 13) An analogous terminology is found in the *First Epistle of St. John;* cf. *teknia* (1 Jn. 2:1,2,28; 3:7,18; 4:4; 5:21) or *paidia* (1 Jn. 2:28). Christians are "the children of God" (Jn. 1:12; 1 Jn. 3:2; Lk. 6:35; Jas. 1:18). St. Paul also calls his disciples "my little children." (Gal. 4:19; 1 Cor. 4:15)

Mk. 2:19) the friends of the bridegroom are referred to as the "sons of the bridegroom."][5]

Concerning the "mystery of Jesus," of which we will speak more in the next section, we must note the insistence with which the new Christians join themselves to the beneficent influence of the risen Lord. To become a Christian is to join oneself to the Lord (Acts 5:14) or to become "partakers of Christ." (Heb. 3:14) For God "chose us in him (Christ) before the foundation of the world" (Eph. 1:4) "and raised us up together, and seated us together in heaven in Christ Jesus" (Eph. 2:6); through whom "we have *now* received reconciliation." (Rom. 5:11) All these expressions emphasize the union of the faithful with Christ, who has obtained for them the privileges of the Christian life *once* and for all. The faithful will have no other mission than to continue Christ in their lives, to be the "extension" of His personality. That is why to persecute the faithful is to persecute Christ Himself (Acts 9:5; 26:15); to sin against one's brother is to sin against the Lord Himself. (1 Cor. 8:12)

According to the formula of St. Bernard, the role of Christ is to be *"in nostros usus expensus."* We are all aware of St. John's sublime word play on Caiphas's words: "You know nothing at all; nor do you reflect that it is expedient for us that one man die for

---

5   The metaphorical use of the term *huios* is evident in the following expressions: "the children of the kingdom" (Mt. 8:12; 13:38), the "children of the Most High" (Lk. 6:35; cf. Mt. 5:9: "sons of God" or Rom. 9:4: "sons of the living God"), the "sons of thunder" (Mk. 3:17), "the children of wisdom" (Lk. 7:35), "a son of peace" (Lk. 10:6), "the children of this world" (Lk. 16:8; 20:34), "the children of light" (Lk. 16:8; Jn. 12:36; Eph. 5:8; 1 Thes. 5:5), "the children of the resurrection" (Lk. 20:36), the "sons of perdition" (Jn. 17:12), a "son of consolation" (Ac. 4:36), a "son of the devil" (Ac. 13:10; Mt. 5:45; 12:27; 1 Jn. 3:10; cf. Jn. 8:44), "children of wrath" (Eph. 2:3), the "children of the promise" (Gal. 4:28), children of unbelief, "unbelievers" (Col. 3:6), the "children of the day" (1 Thes. 5:5), children of obedience, "obedient children" (1 Pt. 1:14), "children of a curse" (2 Pt. 2:14), the children of Jezebel "her children" (Ap. 2:23), "sons of Abraham" (Gal. 3:7,29; Jas. 2:21). The meaning of "heir" is apparent in Ac. 3:25: "the children of the prophets" or in Heb. 12:8: "illegitimate children and not sons."

(*huper*—'instead of' or 'in place of') the people, instead of the whole nation perishing." (Jn. 11:50) The high priest thought it necessary to sacrifice Jesus to preserve the nation from the supposed political danger he was causing. But St. John explains: "This, however, he said not of himself; but being high priest that year, he prophesied that Jesus was to die for the nation; and not only for the nation, but that he might gather into one the children of God who were scattered abroad."[6] (Jn. 11:51-52)

The name of the Savior is Jesus, for "he shall save his people from their sins." (Mt. 1:21; Ap. 1:5) Christ is the "good shepherd" who guarantees the unity and well-being of the sheep "who hear his voice." (Jn. 10:16) He is also the vine which unites and vivifies the various branches. (Jn. 15:5) At the end of time he will be "the Lamb" who will overcome *"and they who are with him,* called, and chosen, and faithful." (Ap. 17:14)

The figure of the "grain of wheat" which dies in order to produce its crop (Jn. 12:14) also emphasizes Christ's role in obtaining the well-being of "all the sanctified." (Acts. 20:32; 26:18) Christ and His faithful form a compact group: "the Lord Jesus Christ, *with all his saints"* (1 Thes. 3:13); or in the words of 1 Cor.: "For as in Adam all die, so in Christ all will be made to live. But each in his own turn, Christ as first-fruits, then they who are Christ's, who have believed, at his coming." (1 Cor. 15:23)

In imitation of the example of Jesus, the apostles are from the very beginning a source of joy and universal blessing. They are the "salt of the earth" (Mt. 5:13) because they "prolong" Christ; "He who receives you, receives me; and he who receives me, receives him who sent me."[7] (Mt. 10:40: Lk. 10:16) Timothy

---

6 Compare with Heb. 2:9: "Jesus, crowned with glory and honor because of his having suffered death, that by the grace of God he might taste death for (better: in the place of) all" or with 1 Jn. 2:2: "He is a propitiation for our sins, not for ours only but also for those of the whole world" or with 2 Cor. 5:14: "Since one died for (*huper*) all, therefore all died."

7 It is the principle of the *shâliakh* (Cf. Mk. 9:37; Lk. 9:48; Jn. 12:45; 13:20; 17:18; 20:21). Similary, the "little ones" whom one receives represent Christ. (Mt. 18:5)

is to save "both thyself and those who hear thee" (1 Tim. 4:16);
every high priest "taken from among men is appointed for men."
(Heb. 5:1) When St. Paul is threatened by the storm on the sea,
God promises to save him and all his companions: "Do not be
afraid, Paul . . . God has granted thee all who are sailing *with
thee.*" (Acts 27:24) The power of Peter: "Whatever thou shalt
bind on earth shall be bound in heaven" (Mt. 16:19) is the
power of the Church: "Whatever you (plural) bind on earth shall
be bound also in heaven." (Mt. 18:18) The actions of Peter
are of benefit to the Church as a whole.

The intercessory power of a small group in favor of all the
members is evident in Mt. 24:22: "But *for the sake of the elect*
those days will be shortened (days of the eschatological tribula-
tions)."

3. *Theme of the Harmful Influence of the Representing Individual*

The idea of a collective culpability that begets a collective
responsibility clearly underlies the imperative advice of Ap. 18:4:
"Go out from her (Babylon), my people, that you may not share
in her sins, and that you may not receive of her plagues."

Most often it is a question of a passive responsibility which
the individual brings upon a group. "I will smite the shepherd,
and the sheep of the flock will be scattered." (Mt. 26:30; cf.
Mk. 14:27) Harm or sorrow brought upon one Christian redounds to the entire group: "Now if anyone has caused grief, he
has not grieved me, but in a measure (not to be too severe) all
of you." (2 Cor. 2:5)

The sin of the parents can be the cause of misfortune for
the children. This explains the shifting back and forth in the story
of the man born blind between his personal culpability and that
of his parents: "Rabbi, who has sinned, this man or his parents,
that he should be born blind?" (Jn. 9:2)

4. *Theme of the Ancestor*

In the first place, the Christians obviously look upon themselves as the spiritual "descendants" of their ancestor Abraham.
They are called "sons of Abraham." (Rom. 4:13, 16, 9:7; Lk.

1:73; Heb. 2:16) Besides, Christ is the "seed of Abraham" (Gal. 3:16, 19, 29), and to be a Christian is to be "all one in Christ Jesus."[8] (Gal. 3:28)

Similarly, Jesus appears in the eyes of the New Testament writers to be "the root and offspring of David" (Ap. 22:16), for He fulfills within His person all the Messianic promises: "He shall be great, and shall be called the Son of the Most High. The Lord God will give him the throne of David his father and he shall be king over the house of Jacob forever; and of his kingdom there shall be no end." (Lk. 1:32; cf. Ps. 2:7; 2 K. 7) "From his (David's) offspring, God according to promise brought to Israel a Savior, Jesus." (Acts 13:23) The position of Jesus is analogous to that of the theocratic king, in this sense that in him is summed up all that has made Israel the people of God.[9] (Gal. 3:6; Rom. 9:6-8)

Elsewhere the New Testament presents Christ as "the Son over his own house. We are that house." (Heb. 3:5) In a certain sense Jesus is the spiritual ancestor who is perpetuated in Christians: "the grace which was granted to us in Christ Jesus before this world existed." (2 Tim. 1:9) In his sacerdotal prayer Jesus

---

8 S. Hanson, *The Unity of the Church*, l.c., p. 70. The unity of Christians with Christ is evident in the Western text of Lk. 9:26: "Whoever is ashamed of me and *mine....*"

9 N. Dahl, *Das Volk Gottes*, l.c., p. 155 refers to Mt. 2:2; Lk. 19:38; Jn. 1:49 (Nathanael: "Thou art king of Israel"); Ap. 17:14; 19:16; Mk. 15:2 (Pilate); Lk. 22:30 ("in my kingdom"). This same author finds still other "motifs" which, according to him, demonstrate the royal dignity of Christ; for example, mention of the vine in Jn. 15:1-5 (the king as "tree of life"), and even "the green wood" in Lk. 23:31. The title of "shepherd" which recurs frequently (Mk. 6:34; 14:27; Mt. 25:31-34; Jn. 10:11-16; Heb. 13:20; 1 Pt. 2:25; Mt. 2:6; Mi. 5:1) would also designate the quality of king. The "suffering king" would be represented in Mk. 15:16 (the crowning with thorns) or in Jn. 19:1-3, or in Lk. 24:26 ("Did not the Christ have to suffer these things?"). Dahl also wants to admit the "royal scenes" in Mk. 10:37 (the sons of Zebedee asking to "sit, one at thy right hand and the other at thy left hand, in thy glory") or in Mk. 14:3-7 (the anointing in Bethany). It goes without saying that these comparisons are rather artificial and studied.

is conscious of being glorified in His future members. That is
why he prays to the Father: "I pray for them . . . for those whom
thou hast given to me, because they are thine; and all things that
are mine are thine, and thine are mine; and I am glorified in
them . . . Holy Father, keep in thy name those whom thou hast
given me, that they may be one even as we are." (Jn. 17:9-11, 21)

If Abraham is "the father of all" (Rom. 4:16), it is because
Christians participate in "the promise made to Abraham and to
his posterity." (Rom. 4:13) In the same way Christian women
are the "daughters of Sara," the obedient wife. (1 Pt. 3:6)

5. *Theme of the Beneficial Influence of "Fathers" on Their "Children"*

The *Magnificat* sings the praises of the "fathers" as the guaran-
tors of the welfare of future generations. Redemption comes about
"even as he spoke to our fathers—to Abraham and to his posterity
forever." (Lk. 1:55) The *Benedictus* echoes the same idea: "To
show mercy to our forefathers and to be mindful of his holy
covenant, of the oath that he swore to Abraham our father."
(Lk. 1:72-73)

The promise of Mt. 28:21 expresses the idea of a continuing
divine assistance throughout all Christian generations: "I *am*
with you all days, even unto the consummation of the world."
The "you" of this passage indicates the apostles, but also their
spiritual "sons," the Christians of all times. (cf. Mk. 16:15: "Go
into *the whole world* and preach the gospel *to every creature.*"

Christians are "the children of the prophets and of the covenant that God made with *your fathers*" (Acts 3:25; cf. 26:6),
for "the promise made *to our fathers,* God has fulfilled *to our
children.*" (Acts 13:32; cf. 13:17)

We can add to this same theme the idea of a kind of survival
of an outstanding person: Elias, for example, survives in John
the Baptist. (Mt. 11:14; 17:11-13; Mk. 9:13; Jn. 1:21) Their
influence on their contemporaries is similar.

6. *Theme of the Harmful Influence of "Fathers" on Their "Children"*

In the discourse of St. Stephen (Acts 7) the theme of the

"fathers" recurs constantly: "He dealt craftily with our race and oppressed our fathers" (Acts 7:19); "This is he (Moses) who was in the assembly in the wilderness with the angel who spoke to him on Mount Sinai, and with our fathers" (Acts 7:38); "Our fathers had in the desert the tent of the testimony" (Acts 7:44); "This tent also our fathers inherited." (Acts 7:45) The possessive "our" indicates the living presence of past generations in the mind of the God-fearing deacon. The presence, however, is baneful. It perdures in the continuing resistance to the Holy Spirit: "As *your* fathers did, so *you do also.*" (Acts 7:51)

The Pharisees "fill up the measure of your fathers." Our Lord flails them with the stinging rebuke: "You are witnesses against yourselves that you are the sons of those who killed the prophets." (Mt. 23:31-32) The sarcastic remark of the third Gospel: "You are witnesses and approve the deeds of your fathers; for they indeed killed them, and you build their tombs" (Lk. 11:48) reveals the hypocrisy of the scribes, who thought they were making up for the sins of their fathers, but actually were seconding them. "Some of them (prophets) they will put to death and persecute, that the blood of all the prophets that has been shed from the foundation of the world may be required *of this generation,* from the blood of Abel unto the blood of Zacharias." (Lk. 11:50-51)

7. *Theme of the Identity of the Name of a Person and of a Clan*

The identity of the personal name Jacob-Israel with the over-all group of Israel appears in the speech of St. Stephen: "Jacob went down to Egypt, and he and our fathers died." (Acts. 7:15)

8. *Theme of the Personification of the People*

One or the other time in the New Testament the entire nation is treated as though it were a single person. The picture of Jerusalem as the "mother" of a number of "children" (Mt. 23:37) recalls the texts of the Old Testament which mention the "daughter of Sion" (Jn. 12:15; citation of Za. 9:9) and Sion "the mother of Israel and its peoples." The lament of Jesus reported by Luke suggests the intimate identity between the holy city and the "children of Israel": "Days will come upon thee when thy enemies will throw up a rampart about thee, and surround thee and shut thee in on every side, and will dash *thee* to the ground *and thy children within thee.*" (Lk. 19:43-44) The inhabitants of Jerusalem are looked upon as an individual who has many children. We might compare the quotation with the text of St. Paul which speaks of "that Jerusalem which is above . . . which is our mother." (Gal. 4:26; citation of Is. 54:1)

The Christian collectivity, a people acceptable to God (Tim. 2:14), is also represented by the "sister Elect" (2 Jn. 13) and by the "woman (with) a crown of twelve stars" of *Apocalypse* 12:1. "The male child" of this woman is attacked by the Serpent (Ap. 12:13), but the latter "was angered at the woman, and went away to wage war with the rest of her offspring, who keep the commandments of God, and hold fast the testimony of Jesus." (Ap. 12:17) We readily recognize here the Old Testament picture of the community-mother of several "children," who are, so to speak, brothers of the male child *par excellence,* the Messias.

Together with Jerusalem other cities are spoken of as though they were individual human persons: "And thou, Capharnaum, shalt thou be exalted to heaven? Thou shalt be thrust down to hell." (Mt. 11:23; citation of Is. 14:13)

In the mind of St. Paul the "wild olive" (Rom. 11:17), the Gentile Christians, is thought of as an individual "you" for he says: "But if some of the branches have been broken off, and if thou (singular), being a wild olive, art grafted in their place, and hast become a partaker of the stem and fatness of the olive trees, do not boast against the branches. But if thou dost boast, still it is not thou that supportest the stem, but the stem thee." (Rom. 11:16-18)

9. *Theme of the Legal "Thou"*

In the Sermon on the Mount, the Christian legislation corresponding to the Israelite Torah, we observe a curious phenomenon. Very often a precept of the "New Law" is repeated twice, once in the plural and immediately afterwards in the singular: "When you (plural) pray, you shall not be like the hypocrites . . . But when thou (singular) prayest" (Mt. 6:5-6); "When you

(plural) fast ... But thou, when thou (singular) dost fast"
(Mt. 6:16-17); "Do not judge (plural)... But why dost thou
(singular) see the speck in thy brother's eye?" (Mt. 7:1-3) In
all these precepts (as also in those regarding alms: Mt.
6:2-4), there is question of individual duties, and consequently the "thou"
may well be distributive. But the wording in the prohibitions suggests the abrupt changes of the pronouns "you" and "thou" in
the Old Testament laws. Moreover, prescriptions such as "Thou
shalt love thy neighbor, and shalt hate thy enemy" (Mt. 5:43) are
to be interpreted in a general sense, for Jesus adds: "But I say to
you, love *your* (plural) enemies ... so that you may be children
of your Father in heaven." (Mt. 5:44-45) We have here a fundamental charter of Christianity.[10]

The examples we have given demonstrate quite well that the
nine themes we spoke of previously are found also in New
Testament literature. There is indeed a general substratum of
ideas borrowed from the Old Testament which underlie the
relationships between individuals and society. In this light we
wish to examine the special case of the "Mystical Body of Christ."

B. *THE MYSTICAL BODY*

In his *Epistle to the Smyrnians,* St. Ignatius of Antioch does
not hesitate to say: "Wherever Christ is, there is the Catholic
Church." [11] According to the teaching of St. Paul: "We are ...
always bearing about in our body the dying of Jesus, so that the
life also of Jesus may be made manifest in our bodily frame"
(2 Cor. 4:10), for "since one died for all, therefore all died." [12]

10 E. Von Dobschütz, *Wir und Ich bei Paulus,* in ZST 10 (1933)
    251-77, p. 255 believes that the "thou" of Rom. 2:1; 8:2; 11:17
    designates the nation, as in the philosophical discussion the "I" is
    individual in Gal. 2:19; Rom. 4:23; 1 Cor. 9:19. The link with the
    legal "thou" of *Deuteronomy* seems more plausible to us.
11 C. C. Richardson, *The Church in Ignatius of Antioch,* in *Jer.* 7
    (1937) 428-443.
12 E. Lohmeyer, *Sun Christôi,* in *Festgabe fur Adolf Deissmann,* Tübin-

The unity of Christ with Christians is one of the keystones of the entire New Testament. The statement of Mt. 25:40 is absolute: "And answering the king will say to them, 'Amen I say to you, as long as you did it for one of these, the least of my brethren, you did it for me.'"[13] In order to stress this intimate union between Christ and His followers, the New Testament makes use of a number of figures: All Christians "have put on Christ" (Gal. 3:27); "There is neither Jew nor Greek; there is neither slave nor freeman; there is neither male nor female. For you are all one in Christ Jesus" (Gal. 3:28); All Christians live in Christ: "As the branch cannot bear fruit of itself unless it remain on the vine, so neither can you unless you abide in me. I am the vine, you are the branches." (Jn. 15:4-5) But the most important of all the figures of speech is that of the human body: All Christians form one "body" with Christ. (cf. 1 Cor. 12:12; 27; Rom. 12:4; Eph. 5:30 etc.)

An important discussion regarding this last image[14] has arisen whose solution may perhaps depend on the realization that we are here face to face with the idea of "corporate personality" (themes 1, 2, 4). According to a certain number of exegetes, the imagery of the Mystical Body implies the setting up of a single organism which would be identical with Christ; namely, the "collective person" of the faithful. Other interpreters emphasize especially the salvific action of God in Christ, in virtue of which the individual members of the Church, by undergoing the same spiritual influence,

gen, 1927, 218-257, p. 249: "The dying of the believers (Rom. 6:4,8; Col. 2:13,20) ... follows from the historical dying of Christ which occurred at one time in historical actuality for perpetual significance. With it, in this historical reality, is placed all the 'dying' of the individual believers; every act of 'dying' of the individual, no matter how often it repeats itself in the community, is at the same time a unique and eternal fact of the history of Christ." Cf. also W. Bousset, *Kyrios Christos*, 1926[3], 206.

13   R. Otto, *Reich Gottes und Menschensohn*, Munich, 1934, 187.

14   L. Brun, *Der Kirchliche Einheitsgedanke im Urchristentum*, in ZST 14 (1937) 86-127, p. 109: "More important ... is the recognition that the picture of the body which in St. Paul's authoritative thought is only for visualization and detailing, is used by the Church as the people of God and of Christ."

are united among themselves as to Christ. The two viewpoints—
which we will discuss later on—are not at all incompatible. In
fact they bring out precisely the two inseparable aspects of the
idea of "corporate personality." We know that the idea of "corporate personality" expresses on the one hand the extension of one
person in a group, and on the other hand, the important influence
of this same person on the group and on each member of the
group.

1. *The Mystical Body as an Extension of Christ*

When St. Paul says that "you are all one in Christ Jesus" [15]
(Gal. 3:28), we get the impression that the Apostle is presenting
Christ as a personality who embraces in some way all Christians
and makes of them a unity. Incorporation in Christ seems to
imply a kind of aggregation to a group, which we might designate
(keeping in mind all the while the personal influence of Christ)
as the "collective personality of the Lord into which the baptized
is plunged." [16] The Apostle does not say: "You are Christ," but
together with Christ you form a single being, for you are no
longer a group of isolated beings but a collective personality." [17]
The Lord who is "Spirit" embraces all His followers and incorporates them into His body, but each member retains his
personal individuality in this body: "Now you are the body of
Christ, member for member." [18] (1 Cor. 12:28)

There is no reason to shy away from the term "collective
personality" as though it were a static organism, set up once and
for all, "a *catholica,* gigantic establishment of God into which

15 Compare the identity already pointed out between Christians and
    Christ, who are both "the offspring of Abraham." (Gal. 3:16,29)
16 A. Wikenhauser, *Die Christusmystik des Hl. Paulus,* in BZ XII, 8-10,
    Munster, 1928, 68. Cf. also A. Schweitzer, *Die Mystik des Apostels
    Paulus,* Tübingen, 1930, 119: "A total personality in which the
    peculiarities of the individual personalities as they occur from in-
    heritance, sex, and social position are no longer valid."
17 Fr. Mussner, *Christus das All und die Kirche, Trierer, theol. St.,*
    Trèves, 1955, 127 minimizes Gal. 3:28 when he says, "*Heis* is under-
    stood not 'numerically' but 'qualitatively.'"
18 A. Wikenhauser, *Die Christusmystik,* l.c., p. 105.

individuals are absorbed."[19] St. Paul must be understood in the light of the Old Testament in which the individual and the people are inseparable, and where the idea of the representative role of the individual is current.[20] This role is especially noticeable in the Messias: "As the shepherd is nothing without his sheep, so the Messias is inconceivable without those for whom he is the Messias."[21] Already in the seventh chapter of *Daniel* we meet the idea of "the real identity of one and all: all already one, all belongs to one, and yet all is realized in a collectivity, and all belongs to one people."[22]

Have we a right to reduce these Old Testament ideas to "a very *general* outline which could, to some *indefinable* degree, have provided *some kind of framework* for St. Paul's theological developments," by stating that "traces of them (Old Testament concepts) in Paul's epistles are *very faint?*"[23] For even if "there is no visible link made with the idea of the Church,"[24] we cannot

19   H. Koehnlein, *La notion de l'Eglise,* l.c., p. 377 speaks moreover of a *"civitas platonica,* a total organism, immutable and sealed in its essence." W. Mundle, *Das Kirchenbewusstsein der ältesten Christenheit,* in ZNW 22 (1923) 20-42, p. 39 considers St. Paul as "the founder of the Catholic idea of the Church," because he extols "an ascent of the individual personality in the super-worldly greatness of the body of Christ."

20   H. Koehnlein, *La notion de l'Eglise,* l.c., p. 368. The author recalls that "the king represents the people of God," that "the servant of Yahweh is as much a people as an individual," that "Adam is at one and the same time the first man and all mankind in sin," that "Israel is the name of Jacob and that of the people descended from him," that "the Son of Man is not such without the people whom he represents."

21   H. Koehnlein, *La notion de l'Eglise,* l.c., p. 369. Cf. R. Newton Flew, *Jesus and His Church,* London, 1945[4], 88: "The conception of Messiahship essentially involves the gathering of a community."

22   M. J. Congar, *The Mystery of the Church.* 1960, 60.

23   L. Cerfaux, *The Church in the Theology of St. Paul,* New York, 1959, 284. Italics added.

24   *Ibid.,* p. 285, speaking of the "doctrine of the new Adam," which tends to an interdependence of Christ and mankind."

deny that the fundamental ideas of the Apostle differ little from those of the Old Testament. This is readily observable. Like Adam, Christ is simultaneously leader and representative of all humanity.[25] "As Adam cannot be thought of without those who are subject to sin, so Christ and those whom He came to save, Christ and the Church, are inseparable."[26] Christ—according to the thought of St. Paul—encompasses the People of God. According to Eph. 1:10 it is in Christ that the Father intends to re-establish in unity all those whom Christ represents. The new Israel is "in Christ" as the Jews were in Abraham, as all mankind was in Adam: "The Messiah, the Christ, is at once an individual person—Jesus of Nazareth—and he is more; he is, as the representative and (as it were) the constitutive Person of the New Israel, *potentially inclusive.*"[27] Finally, according to St. Paul, Christ is the vicarious representative of sinful mankind. He has given His life "as a ransom" and "for all" (that is to say "in behalf of" because "in the place of all"). (Mk. 10:45; Gal. 2:20; Rom. 4:25; 5:8)[28] In this way He has reconciled men with God (Rom. 5:10-11; 2 Cor. 5:19-20): "For our sakes he made him to be sin who knew nothing of sin, so that *in him* we might become the justice of God." (2 Cor. 5:21; cf. Gal. 3:13)

25 With good reason T. Schmidt, *Der Leib Christi,* l.c., p. 225 thinks that "this thought of Christ as the second Adam ... determines the entire Christology of the Apostle in a decisive way."

26 H. Koehnlein, *La notion de l'Eglise,* l.c., p. 369. The author refers to 1 Cor. 15:22-23: "For as in Adam all die, so in Christ all will be made to live. But each in his own turn, Christ as first-fruits, then they who are Christ's who have believed in his coming." Cf. J. Weiss, *Das Urchristentum,* Göttingen, 1917, 330: "What happened in Adam is not only his personal experience. He is a representative personality, and his fate (death) is, according to the plan of God, at the same time that of all his posterity. For Adam is in a sense the embodiment of humanity. ... It is now the same way with Christ; He also is an embodiment; what He experiences is not only His fate, but it continues and takes effect in all those who belong to Him."

27 A. E. Rawlinson, *Corpus Christi,* in G. K. A. Bell et Ad. Deissman, *Mysterium Christi,* London, 1930, 225-249, p. 235.

28 S. Hanson, *The Unity of the Church,* l.c., p. 70: "On behalf of men and as their representative."

This vicarious satisfaction (itself based on a vicarious representation) is "the center of Pauline theology"[29] and "the guiding principle in going from the One to the multitude, since humanity is summed up in Christ in so far as it is one body." (Gal. 4:19)[30]

All these doctrines, which are without a doubt Pauline, tend in the same direction. The "Body of Christ" is the Church, which fulfills for humanity the same role as the "remnant," "the people of the saints." But this role was first of all Christ's; who in some way manifests himself in His members, in order to make them capable of "continuing" Him.

It has been said that the Greek expression *sôma Christou,* "body of Christ" cannot have the sense of "society," of a "body made up of members"; that the pre-Christian use of the Greek word does not in any way suggest an organization or a corporate life, but only the concrete, physical and tangible reality, having a unity such as a single material body would have.[31] Perhaps *sôma* does not have in profane Greek the meaning of a "social body." However, we must investigate further. In 1936 T. W. Manson drew attention to the text of an edict of Augustus in 6-7 B. C. in which is found the expression *Hellênôn Sômati,* the community of the Hellenes.[32] In the light of this edict, W. D. Davies writes: "It is no longer possible to say that *sôma* is never used

---

29 E. Percy, *Der Leib Christi (SOMA CHRISTOU) in den paulin-ischen Homologoumena und Antilegomena, Lunds Universitets Ars-skrift,* 38 (1942), 43.

30 O. Cullmann, *Königsherrschaft Christi und Kirche im NT,* in *Theolog. Studien* (K. Barth), Hft. 10, 1940, 38. On page 35 Cullmann sketches the history of salvation as a progressive reduction to the One Messias (Israel—the "remnant" or the community of Yahweh—one single man, the "Servant" or the "Son of Man.") This single person is Christ the King, who spreads out into the many who bear his characteristics.

31 A. E. J. Rawlinson, l.c., p. 226 and 232.—Cf. L. Cerfaux, *The Church in the Theology of St. Paul,* l.c., p. 274. W. Gutbrod, *Die paulinische Anthropologie,* Stuttgart, 1934, 32, paraphrases *sôma* with "the concreteness and actuality of human existence and life." Sometimes the meaning of *sôma* is simply: "external appearance." (Cf. 1. Cor. 13:3; Ph. 1:20; 2 Cor. 5:10)

32 Cf. *JTS* 37 (1936) 385. Quoted by Davies, *Paul and Rabbinic Judaism,* London, 1948, 57.

in pre-Christian Greek for a 'body' of people or society."[33] Another critic, however, says: "It is the very meaning of 'collectivity' which all the authors up to now have given to the word *sôma* that is the essential obstacle to all these interpretations. In spite of all our research, it has proved impossible to discover a single example in which this word designates a collectivity. *Sôma* indicates a unity, a whole, but never a collectivity. And I think that I can assert that this meaning is not a Greek one."[34]

Everything considered, it seems difficult to disassociate a "whole" from a "collectivity"; a whole, even if the emphasis is on the unity, necessarily implies parts that are associated and united in a collectivity.[35] When Plato in his *Timaeus* speaks of *sôma tuo kosmou* (Tim. 31b), he certainly insists on unity, but his formula necessarily implies the existence of diversity in unity (cf. *Tim.* 32c, *sôma tou pantos*, the organized universe). The Latin equivalent, *corpus,* designates professional groups, and that "before the first century."[36] Livy speaks of a *multitudo* which must "*coalescere in populi unius corpus.*" (Livy I, 8:1) The same author speaks of members of the *ordo senatorius* as of "*sui corporis homines.*" (Livy VI, 34:5) Speaking of Capua, he says: "*Corpus nullum civitatis nec senatum nec plebis consilium nec magistratus esse Capuae.*" (Livy XXVI, 16:9) A single town is called "*unum corpus*": "*Nunc in unum corpus confusi omnes, Hispanis prius, postremo et Graecis . . . ascitis.*" (Livy XXXIV, 9:3) A single organization is called "*unum corpus et unum concilium totius Pelopon-*

---

33 A. D. Davies, *Paul and Rabbinic Judaism*, l.c., p. 57—E. Best, *One Body in Christ*, l.c., 223, mentions the application of *sôma* to the state in Plut. *Solon* 18.

34 F. De Visscher, *Les Edits d'Auguste découverts à Cyrène*, Louvain, 1940, 91. Quoted by L. Cerfaux, *The Church in the Theology of St. Paul*, l.c., p. 273.

35 Cf. Flavius Josephus (a contemporary of St. Paul), *Bell. Jud.* 6,4 (#279): the inhabitants of a town, who had been fighting with one another, are reconciled and became "one body"; or *Antiq.* VII, 3,2 (#66): David unites the upper town to Acra and makes them one "body" (a single whole).

36 According to L. Cerfaux, *The Church in the Theology of St. Paul*, l.c., p. 275 this meaning would not have been introduced until the end of the first century after Christ.

nesi." (Livy XXXIX, 37:7) Cicero in turn speaks of certain things *"quae ad corpus civitatis pertinent."* (Inv. II, 168) He also speaks of those who *"totum corpus rei publicae curent."* (De Off. I, 95) Tacitus mentions the *"late fusum corpus libertinorum."* (Ann. XIII, 27)[37] [38]

We might also mention certain parallels to the New Testament usage of the word *sôma*.[39] Philo, for example, asserts that the high priest offers sacrifice "so that all ages and all members of the people, as a single body, may find harmony in a single communion."[40] The Alexandrian writer is evidently thinking of a diversity of members unified in the *hen sôma*. The same meaning of an organized collectivity appears in the Stoic religious writing. Seneca writes to Nero in these words: *"Tu animus rei publicae es, illa corpus tuum."*[41]

Even if we had to concede that the *profane* meaning of *sôma* is never a "social body," we must always keep in mind that the idea of a corporate body was certainly current in Judaism.[42] In

37   Cf. *Thesaurus linguae latinae*, Lipsiae, 1906, vol. IV, col. 1021-22. The numerous inscriptions mentioned by the thesaurus are of uncertain date. They attest irrefutably the meaning of an "organized body."

38   For more examples of the "head" and "body" in classical literature see M. Adinolfi, O.F.M., *Le metafore Greco-Romane della testa e del corpo e il corpo mistico di Cristo*, in *Analecta Biblica* 17-18 (Studiorum Paulinorum Congressus Internationalis Catholicus 1961) Romae, P.I.B., 1963, vol. 2, p. 333-342.

39   W. L. Knox, *Parallels to the N.T. Use of sôma*, in *JTS* 39 (1938) 243-46.

40   Philo, *De spec. Leg.* III, 23 (vol. IV, 187). The term *sôma* seems to translate the rabbinic word *gûf* (cf. A. Ström, *Vetekornet*, l.c., p. 103). On page 112, Ström recalls that Adam contains in his *gûf* all future men.

41   Sen., *De Clem.* I, 5,1. On Stoic *sumpatheia*, the feeling of unity of those who form a single organism, cf. Sext. Empir., *Math.*, IX, 78; Epict., I, 14,2; or Philo, *De migr. Abr.* 180.

42   For four explanations of the origin of Paul's expression, "the body of Christ," see L. Ouellette, C.S.V., *L'Eglise, Corps Du Christ: Origine De L'Expression Chez Saint Paul*, in *L'Eglise Dans La Bible* (Communications Présentées à la XVIIᵉ Réunion Annuelle de l'ACEBAC) Montréal, Declée, 1962, 85-93.

the presence of Yahweh the Israelite people are always a single person—a servant, a wife, a son; the new Israel continues as a single entity: "for you are all one in Christ Jesus." (Gal. 3:28) By the very fact that all Christians are in the one Christ, they constitute one great collective personality, for Christ encompasses them all.[43]

It is appropriate that we read the classical texts regarding the Mystical Body in this perspective. Verse 4 of chapter 12 of the *Epistle to the Romans* treats of the unity of Christians and compares it to the unity in a human body: "For *just as* in one body we have many members, yet all the members have not the same function, so we, the many, are one body in Christ, but severally members one of another." The unity of Christians among themselves *resembles* that among the members of a single human body. The addition of the phrase "in Christ" indicates not only that the individual members are actively influenced by the risen Christ, but also that the totality of the members (all believers) are one with Christ, they are one among themselves.[44] The meaning of the expression *hen sôma* seems to be "a single personality," "a collective personality influenced by the Spirit of Christ."[45] But the comparison (*kathaper*) with the human body, which seems to have been borrowed from popular Hellenistic philosophy,[46] implies very clearly a plurality organized in unity.

We find the same kind of thought in 1 Cor. 12:12: "For as the body is one and has many members, and all the members of

43 T. Schmidt *Der Leib Christi, Eine Untersuchung zum urchristlichen Gemeindegedanken*, Leipzig-Erlangen, 1919, 147. G. Gloege, *Reich Gottes und Kirche im NT*, 1929, 305 n., recalls the etymology of *sôma* from *saos-sôizô*, and translates "die gerettete Restgemeinde."

44 E. Percy, *Der Leib Christi*, l.c., p. 6.

45 T. Schmidt, *Der Leib Christi*, l.c., p. 161. Cf. A. Wikenhauser, *Die Kirche als der mystische Leib Christi nach dem Apostel Paulus*, Munster, 1940², 127.

46 A. Wikenhauser, *Der Kirche als der mystische Leib Christi*, l.c., pp. 84 and 95. Cf. T. Schmidt, *Der Leib Christi*, l.c., p. 129. E. Percy, *Der Leib Christi*, l.c., p. 4 recalls Liv. II, 32, the fable of Menenius Agrippa; cf. also H. Schlier, *Christus und die Kirche im Epheserbrief*, in *Beitr. z. hist. Theol.* 9, 1930, 40.

the body, many as they are, form one body, so also is it with
Christ." The classical apologue comparing society with the human
body here ends with an abrupt and radical twist. To the idea of
the organic unity of the Church is added the idea of dependence
on Christ. "Now you are the body of Christ, member for member."
(1 Cor. 12:27) There is no question of two different conceptions
of *sôma*. On the one hand, we must remember that the Christian
community form "one body" (cf. 1 Cor. 12:13: "For in one
Spirit we were all baptized into one body, whether Jews or Gentiles, whether slaves or free"); on the other hand, we must never
forget that this "body" is "the body of Christ." [47]

The elliptical construction of 1 Cor. 12:12 is very obvious;
the parallelism between the protasis and the apodosis (*houtôs
kai ho Christos*) is defective. Consequently the translation of the
apodosis is extremely difficult. Probably the subordinate part
(*kathaper*) should be understood as though St. Paul had written:
"Just as a man has many members in his one body, so Christ has
many members." [48] Christ—the spiritualized person—and the
community animated by the spirit of Christ—can sometimes be
considered according to the context as relatively autonomous, at
other times as forming a closely-knit unity. [49] Isn't there a difficulty

47   T. Schmidt, *Der Leib Christi*, l.c., p. 141. Cf. E. Percy, *Der Leib
Christi*, l.c., p. 5: "By the sound of the words (1 Cor. 12:12), they
can mean nothing else but that Christ Himself is that body whose
members are the individual believers." According to H. Schlier, *Christus und die Kirche*, l.c., p. 41 the passage of 1 Cor. 12:12-27 would
prove only the attachment to Christ of the "body" formed by Christians, unless St. Paul says explicitly that they are true members of
Christ. This would be taught only in the Epistle to the Ephesians.
But this statement is contradicted by 1 Cor. 6:15 which says that the
bodies of the Christians are the "members of Christ"; Ephesians 5:30 is
even more explicit: "We are members of his body."

48   T. Schmidt, *Der Leib Christi*, l.c., p. 146—Cf. P. Benoit. *Corps, tête
et plérôme dans les Epîtres de la captivité*, in *RB* 63 (1956) 5-44,
p. 15: "So also Christ . . . is a single body whose different members
(Christians) make up the unity."

49   *Ibid.*, p. 147. Schmidt refers to Gal. 3:28: *pantes gar humeis heis este
en Christôi Iêsou*. S. Hanson, *The Unity of the Church*, l.c., 75 uses
1 Cor. 1:13: "Has Christ been divided up?" to deduce that "the unity

with the very term "Christ" ("so also is it *with Christ*)? No, not if we keep in mind that this expression refers at one time to the individual person of Christ and at other times (although this latter usage is quite rare in St. Paul)[50] to the faithful united in Christ.[51] This double reference illustrates precisely what we have been at pains to point out in our study of "corporate personality." "Corporate personality" designates at one and the same time an individual person and the group joined to that individual.[52] In order to distinguish the strictly individual Christ from the "extension" of Christ in the Church,[53] we can call the latter the Mystical Christ.[54] We must not, however, look upon this "mystic person"

of the Church is based on the unity of Christ, with whom it is identical."

50 J. Havet, *Christ collectif ou Christ individuel en 1 Cor.* 12:12? in *ETL* 23 (1947) 499-520, pp. 506 and 508 calls the collective sense of *Christos* a "new" sense; but this sense agrees perfectly with the biblical notion about the corporate personality of the Messias. It is this background which determines the "corporate" exegesis, and not the Greek word *Christos*. We cannot agree with J. Havet, when on page 509 he says that "the Christ of Gal. 3:16 is purely individual"; that is hardly compatible with the word *sperma* which can have a collective meaning.

51 Cf. the interpretation of St. Augustine: "*Loquens de membris Christi, hoc est de fidelibus (Paulus in 1 Cor.* 12:12b) *non sit: Sic et membra Christi, sed tantum hoc quod dixit, Christum appellavit*" (PL 36/232). Immediately before (Enarr. in Ps. 30, II, 3) the same holy doctor, recalling Ac. 9:4; 22:7; 26:14, teaches: "*Non ait: quid sanctos meos, quid servos meos, sed: quid me persequeris? Hoc est: membra mea? Caput pro membris clamabat, et membra in se caput transfigurabat*" (PL 36/231); cf. also *Sermo* 361, 141 (PL 39/1606) or in *Joh.* 28,1 (PL 35/1622).

52 H. Wheeler Robinson, *The Cross of the Servant*, l.c., p. 75: "To be capable of contraction and expansion is precisely the property of 'corporate personality.'" (Translation from the French.)

53 L. Cerfaux, *L'Eglise et le règne de Dieu*, in *ETL* 2 (1925) 181-98, p. 196 n. 91.

54 A. Wikenhauser, *Die Kirche als der mystische Leib Christi*, l.c., pp. 91-92. Cf. F. Prat, *Théologie de St. Paul*, 1[27], 359: "The Mystical Christ is the Church completing its head and completed by Him"; E.

as a "collective I" or an "impersonal Christ" having an existence apart, and being made up of individual Christians as quasi material parts.[55] The only "I" is that of Christ, in whom all the others are present. Ultimately, in order to understand the unity of the Church, we must never lose sight of the Adam-Christ contrast.

Just as Adam is not simply the first sinner in "splendid isolation" but encompasses in himself the entire human race, all of whom share in his fate of sin and death (Rom. 5:19; 1 Cor. 15: 22), so Christ encompasses in Himself in advance all who live or will live the new life of the Spirit of Christ. St. Paul conceives of Adam and Christ in analogous terms: "Adam encompasses and represents the old humanity; Christ, the new. Each is the exponent of a different order of creation ... We have fundamentally the same idea as that expressed by the imagery of the body of Christ."[56] Humanity is a unity, a single body, made up of Adam and all individual men; whenever Adam as the representative, the first sinner, fell, all humanity in so far as it is a body, fell with him. Christ represents redeemed humanity, which forms with Him one single body. In so far as He has given Himself for us (Heb. 2:14), He secured redemption for all those who would become His members, those who would be incorporated into His body.[57]

Mersch, Le Corps mystique du Christ, Brussels, 1936[2], I, 188-189: "The assembly of Christians ... is the one Christ, the mystic Christ."

55 E. Käsemann, Leib und Leib Christi, in Beitr, z. hist. Theol. 9, Tübingen, 1933, 185: "Just as the Church is the concretion of the Christ identical with her, so also for the same reason she cannot be separated from Him; ... only in Christ and his pneuma do the Christians remain the Church."

56 A. Wikenhauser, Die Kirche als Leib Christi, l.c., p. 127. The author refers to G. Kittel, Theologisches Wörterbuch zum NT, Stuttgart, 1935, II, 538, in which Albrecht Oepke thinks that the phrase en Christôi implies that Christ is conceived of as a "universal personality" (Universalpersönlichkeit). Wikenhauser refers also to the Jewish idea of Adam "universal soul (âme), in which all other souls are contained."

57 S. Hanson, The Unity of the Church, l.c., p. 77. On p. 81 the same author compares 1 Cor. 10:2: "And all were baptized in Moses, in the cloud and in the sea." Moses was the representative of the people of

When we go from the two texts just treated (Rom. 12:4 and 1 Cor. 12:12) to the captivity Epistles, we observe a rather notable change of climate. In order to explain this change, the following plan has been suggested.[58] In *Romans* and *Corinthians* there is a simple comparison (Christians form one body among themselves, which belongs to Christ); in *Ephesians* and *Colossians,* however, there is a real identification (Christians belong to Christ as His body). Is it so evident that the text of 1 Cor. 12:27: *"Humeis de este sôma Christou"* should be translated: "You are *a* body which belongs to Christ?"[59] Would it not be simpler and more normal to translate it: "You are *the* body of Christ?" The absence of the article (in Greek) might be readily explained by the basic Semitic thought pattern, even though very frequently the expression "the body of Christ" does contain the article. (Eph. 1: 23: *to sôma autou;* Eph. 4:12: *to sôma tou Christou;* Eph. 5:30; Col. 1:24) Moreover, the captivity Epistles sometimes mention the body of Christians without speaking explicitly of the body of Christ. According to Eph. 2:16: Christ unites Jews and pagans "that of the two he might create in himself one new man, and make peace and reconcile both in one body (*en heni sômati*) to God by the cross, having slain the enmity in himself."[60] The

the Law; to be baptized in him signifies to be associated or incorporated in the Israel that he represents. Cf. T. Schmidt, *Der Leib Christi,* l.c., p. 232: "Thus the entire thought of a total personality in Christ is determined by the idea of the second Adam." P. Benoit, *Corps, tête et plérôme,* l.c., p. 12: "Whereas it never ceases to be the individual body which suffered on the Cross and which rose gloriously from the tomb, this 'body of Christ' does not remain limited to this historical individual; it aggregates to itself all those who are joined to it ... and become its members."

58 H. Schlier, *Zum Begriffe der Kirche im Epheserbrief,* in *TB* 1927, 12; cf. by the same author, *Christus und die Kirche im Epheserbrief,* 1930, p. 40.

59 This is the translation of H. Schlier, in *Christus und die Kirche,* p. 41, according to A. Wikenhauser, *Die Kirche als der mystische Leib,* l.c., p. 100.

60 Cf. Eph. 4:4: "one body and one Spirit." For L. Cerfaux, *The Church in the Theology of St. Paul,* l.c., p. 330, it is question of "the body of Christ with which we are identified, and which is the

"new man" seems to be a new collectivity, the union of all believers with Christ and among themselves. This new collectivity
forms a body which is influenced by Christ. The same idea of an
organism or of an "organized body" appears in Eph. 3:6, where
the pagans are called "fellow-members of the same body" (sus-
sôma) in Christ Jesus, or in Eph. 5:23 where it is said that Christ
is "savior of the body," or in Col. 3:15: "May the peace of Christ
reign in your hearts; unto that peace, indeed, you were called
in one body (en heni sômati)." The last part of the quotation is
explained by a previous verse: "Here there is not 'Gentile and
Jew,' 'circumcised and uncircumcised,' 'Barbarian and Scythian,'
'slave and freeman'; but Christ is all things and in all." (Col. 3:11)
The expression ta panta suggests a limitless extension, and almost identifies Christians with Christ,[61] so great is the union it
establishes between all the elect and Christ the giver of life.[62]

Most often the captivity Epistles explicitly identify the assembly of Christians with the body of Christ. St. Paul wishes to share
in the "sufferings of Christ ... for his body (huper), which is
the Church." (Col. 1:24) The "work of the ministry" must be
considered "for building up the body of Christ." (Eph. 4:12)
Christ is the founder of the Church, for those who were "once afar
off, have been brought near through the blood of Christ." (Eph.
2:13) He is especially the "Leader" of the Church, for He is
the "Savior of the body." (Eph. 5:23) This role as "head over
all the Church, which indeed is his body, the completion of him
who fills all with all" (Eph. 1:23) emphasizes the individual as-

principle of unity." As for the phrase of Eph. 2:16 "in one body," the
same author claims it is meant to mean the crucified body.

61   T. Schmidt, Der Leib Christi, 1.c., p. 150: "(Christ is) the total
personality which embraces all individuals in itself." J. Bonsirven,
Théologie du NT, Paris, 1951, 331 translates: "Christ absolutely."
According to H. Schlier, Christus und die Kirche, 1.c., p. 46, ta panta
would be a gnostic term (Valent. 1:18; 2:9).

62   A. Wikenhauser, Die Kirche, 1.c., p. 163, appeals to a text of Corpus
hermeticum (ed. Scott), XII, 22: "God is all (to pân) and there is
nothing which is not included in this all"; or to the well known text
about Isis "una quae est omnia" (CILX, 3800); or finally to Sir.
43:28: "he (God) is all in all!" It seems to us that the tenor of these
three texts is far from being identical.

pect of the corporate personality, for it implies a personal influence of Christ on the assembly of the Christians. Through the "fullness" of divine life which he receives from Christ (who possesses it; cf. Col. 2:9), the Christian comes to the fullness of the total Christ: the Church and the new Universe.[63] It is necessary in every way to "grow up in all things in him who is the head, Christ. For from him the whole body... derives its increase to the building up of itself in love." (Eph. 4:15; cf. Col. 2:19) But the whole complex of Christ—the "head" of the "body" (Col. 1:18), and Christians together—make up "perfect manhood, to the mature measure of the fullness of Christ" (Eph. 4:13), or the "new man, which has been created according to God in justice and holiness of truth." (Eph. 4:24)[64]

Kaseman[65] and Schlier[66] thought they discerned Gnostic

63 S. Hanson, *The Unity of the Church*, l.c., p. 129 thinks that the *plêrôma* of Eph. 1:23 is a collective designation for all those who are incorporated in Christ, filled by Him with His power and gifts, and who completely represent Him.

64 Cf. Eph. 2:15, which is to be translated according to T. Schmidt, *Der Leib Christi*, l.c., p. 151: "In him Christians become a collective personality (Gesamtpersönlichkeit)." For Fr. Mussner, *Christus das All und die Kirche*, l.c., p. 62, the expression *teleios anêr* (Eph. 4:13) is only a "representation" of the belief of the Church, which is contrasted with *nêpios* of the following verse (Eph. 4:14). P. Benoit, l.c., 42n 1 sees in it "rather the collective meaning, of Christ joining together a single new Man."

65 E. Käsemann, *Leib und Leib Christi*, l.c., p. 149: "Christ is the original man, the total *aion*, as the ikon before all that which is made, and still the original man and redeemer who contains all beings"; p. 155: "The necessity of a gnostic interpretation... might in general be established for the Deutero-Pauline epistles (Eph. Col.)": p. 163: "Phil. 2:6... has its meaning in the gnostic myth according to which the *Anthropos* spans the all in its totality, so that everything is obligated to obey it." On page 68, Käsemann quotes the *Actes de Jean*, 108 (ed. Bousset I, 206), according to which "Christ is the only savior and the only just one; who always sees everything, who is in all, who is present everywhere, and who contains the whole and fills it."

66 H. Schlier, *Christus und die Kirche im Epheserbrief*, in *Beitr. z. hist. Theol.* 6, 1930, 28: "The *teleios anêr* is no one else but the Christ, the anthropos himself, who is thought of as the highest sum-

influences in St. Paul's thought, particularly in *teleios anêr* of the preceding text. In ancient India and ancient Iran there are traces of a divinity which encloses the entire universe as though in a giant body; this being is called *Anthropos*, "the primitive man" or "the great soul" (the totality of souls). Conceived of as a single cosmic person, this *Anthropos* contains all the individual souls as though they were members of its body. Although according to some authors this hypothesis merits serious attention,[67] it is generally agreed that St. Paul's theological conceptions do not rise therefrom. The most we can admit is that the Apostle expressed the beliefs of faith in the terms of current gnosticism.[68] What is noticeably missing in the Gnostic notion of the celestial *Anthropos* and which, in turn, is much in evidence in *Ephesians* and *Colossians* is the value, as a representative, of the one individual who encompasses in his person all the individuals whom he represents.[69]

2. *The Body of the Individual Christ*

We must recognize that the idea of "the body of Christ" is not univocal. As a matter of fact, it alternates between two poles. It passes from the idea that Christ is identical with the entire body to the idea that Christ is the Head, who is distinguished from

> mit of his own pleroma; or, as we might anticipate by saying, as the *kephalê* of his *Sôma*"; p. 42: "That the *ekklesia* is the *sôma* of the redeemer is nowhere presented so completely as in the Valentian gnosis and the gnosis related to it." (Schlier quotes *Exc. ex Theod.* 58:1: "Jesus, the great contender, lifts up the entire Church.")

67 A. Wikenhauser, *Die Kirche*, l.c., p. 239.

68 Fr. Mussner, *Christus das All*, l.c., p. 175. P. Benoit, l.c., 17 notes "that this gnostic conception appears to us only in texts later than Paul."

69 E. Percy, *Der Leib Christi*, l.c., p. 39. On page 41 Percy states with good reason that the notion of "representative" does not flow from syncretism but from an Old Testament background. It is the idea of the identity of the people with their ancestor which has supplied this notion rather than the idea of collecting all individual souls in one single body, which is the body of the heavenly Man.

the body,[70] and *vice versa*. But it is precisely this fluctuation that sets the groundwork for the idea of a "corporate personality."[71] On the one hand, Christ identifies Himself with His members (this is the "collective" aspect of the idea); on the other hand, He is the intimate life of the body (this is the more "personal" aspect of the idea).

Recently some authors[72] have insisted strongly on the individual aspect of the "body of Christ" in St. Paul. Without a doubt this aspect is very real, as we have just seen, and it is fully consonant with the "corporate" interpretation of the union between Christ and the faithful.

From among the Epistles which are universally recognized as being St. Paul's (*Romans, Galatians, Corinthians*), they stress the following passage: "The bread that we break, is it not the partaking of the body of the Lord? Because the bread is one, we though many, are one body, all of us who partake of the one bread." (1 Cor. 10:16-17) They say that the meaning of *sôma* is the same in both verses. In verse 16 *sôma* designates the individual body of Christ ("this is my body"), "His real body becomes present in the Eucharist; therefore, the *hen sôma* of verse 17 also indicates the individual body of Christ present in the

---

70 E. Percy, *Der Leib Christi*, l.c., p. 53. H. Schlier, *Christus und die Kirche*, l.c., p. 38 notes that Christ is sometimes the *kephalê* only, and other times the *sôma* and the *kephalê*.

71 In support of de Fraine's contention here, see J. Luzzi, S.J., *Solidaridad del Soma tou Jristou*, in *CiFe* 16 (1960) 3-45.

72 Besides L. Cerfaux, *The Church in the Theology of St. Paul*, l.c., p. 286 ff., we can point to: H. Koehnlein, *La notion de l'Eglise chez l'Apôtre Paul*, l.c., (1935), p. 365: "The Church is always the result of an action of God in time"; p. 366: the result of the work of Jesus Christ" (Eph. 2:13,15,20: 3:11) and of "the action of the Spirit" (Eph. 2:15,22; 4:4); p. 367: "The people of God actually exist thanks to Christ and the action of his *pneûma*"; p. 371: "The Church is the work of the Lord who lives through the *pneûma*." Among more recent authors we can point to: G. Johnston, *The Doctrine of the Church in the N.T.*, Cambridge, 1943, 89; J. Havet, *Christ collectif ou Christ individuel dans 1 Cor. 12:12? ETL* 23 (1947) 499-520; Fr. Mussner, *Christus das All und die Kirche*, l.c., pp. 119 and 128; P. Benoit, *Corps, tête, Plérôme*, l.c., 12-18.

Eucharist."[73] To the objection which immediately comes to mind: "How can the individual Christian *be* the Eucharistic body of Christ?" (which implies more than an intimate participation in Christ, the one bread) they give the unconvincing answer of a "mystical identification"[74] of all communicants with the Eucharistic body of Christ. Such is not the thought of St. Paul. He is not interested in stressing the union of *each* individual of the faithful with Christ but in emphasizing the unity of the faithful as a group through the action of the one Eucharistic Christ.

In all such unilaterally "personalist" exegesis, there is perhaps too much dependence on the "Greek" point of view,[75] without sufficient awareness of the Semitic ideas we spoke of previously. The Greek point of view would translate the word *sôma* and the expression *hen sôma* in a strictly individual sense. In this perspective there would be room only for Christ's life which flows into all of us who are "in Him,"[76] or for the individual Christians in so far as they have "a mystical identity with the personal Christ."[77] In order to safeguard this personal influence of Christ texts are sometimes forced. The words of 1 Cor. 12:12: "so also is it with Christ" are paraphrased as follows: "So Christ has many mem-

---

73 L. Cerfaux, *The Church in the Theology of St. Paul,* l.c., p. 265.

74 *Ibid.,* p. 279, ft. 33: "We admit that ... there is a mystical identification with the body of Christ which is a mystical identification *sui generis* when it is concerned with the Eucharist." P. Benoit, l.c., 14: "By receiving into their bodies ... the body of Christ, they 'are' all together one single body, that is to say, this body, at first individual, and then assuming to itself all the bodies of those which it unites to itself."

75 *Ibid.,* p. 266: "We have just seen that *Hellenism* (emphasis added) saw the notion of unity in the expression *hen sôma.*" On a later page the same author thinks that the idea of the "body of Christ as the collectivity of the Christians" is "too little Greek." P. Benoit, l.c., 18 thinks: "We must look for the principal source of these categories of Pauline thought in the Old Testament and in Judaism."

76 *Ibid.,* p. 267 concerning Rom. 12:3-6. Would this be the only effect? Christ influences not only *each* of His members, but also the ensemble of His members, since it is the ensemble which is "in Christ."

77 *Ibid.,* p. 268. This phrase is considered to be the opposite of "Christians are the mystic Christ."

bers and *leads* all Christians *to the unity* of His body."[78] If this paraphrase is exact, it is difficult to see how the protasis explains the apodosis, for in the former it is not question of an active force "leading to unity" but rather of the end result of unity.[79] Similarly Gal. 3:28: "For you are all one in Christ Jesus" is interpreted in an individualistic sense: "We are all one new man in Christ; each one becomes an individual (although mystically the same individual) in the new race which God is in the process of forming."[80] Such exegesis, it seems to us, goes counter to the context. In the mind of St. Paul there is not a question of a distributive *pantes* (you all, that is to say, each of you for himself, is a single individual, mystically the same individual), but it is rather the group as a whole which forms a *heis* (a single individual).[81] In fact, St. Paul does not write *hekastos de humôn* or *hosoi* (as in verse 27). Rather he insists on the abolition of every distinction between Christians, and finally he speaks of the totality of Christians as the *Abraam sperma,* an eminently collective term. (Gal. 3:29) There is evidently always the danger of understanding the expression "collective personality" in a static sense, which would exclude the continual activity of Christ

78 Ibid. p. 269. Fr. Mussner, *Christus das All,* l.c., p. 126 sees in the *houtôs* an allusion to the *genesis* of the "single body" rather than to its *existence.*

79 According to L. Malevez, in *RSR* (1944) 27-94, pp. 30-31 the collective meaning is "a necessary interpretation if one does not wish to nullify the comparison introduced by 'sicut.'"

80 L. Cerfaux, *The Church in the Theology of St. Paul,* l.c., p. 246. Cf. J. Havet, *Christ collectif ou Christ individuel,* l.c., p. 515: "Each Christian is united to Christ, is Christ; consequently all are Christ, for several quantities which are each equal to another quantity are equal among themselves." It seems to us that this spiritual arithmetic forgets an important element: not only all Christians individually, but also all Christians as a group, receive the sanctifying influence of Christ, and it is the totality of Christians which is united to Christ (and therefore: "is" Christ).

81 E. Mersch, *Le Corps mystique du Christ,* l.c., p. 175: "A single *heis,* not neuter but masculine because we are dealing with a mystical person." The same author comments regarding 1 Cor. 1:13: "Christ Himself is the Church; we are dealing with the mystic Christ."

as a vivifying principle.[82] But is it not, perhaps, because one thinks that "the Church is a body only by way of allusion to the principle of unity which is the body of Christ,"[83] or that *"sôma,* and even more so *hen sôma,* means a human body or the body of Christ, but always a physical person,"[84] that one is obliged to translate 1 Cor. 12:27 as follows: "Now you are a body, a body which is that of Christ (dependent on Him and in which His life flows)?"[85] The objection that the idea of a total or mystic Christ, "distinct from the personal Christ," destroys the Hellenistic comparison[86] does not take account of the fact that the "mystic" Christ (the ensemble of Christians mystically united to Christ) is not at all distinct from the personal Christ, at least not if we look at the mystery of Christ and His Church in the light of the Semitic and biblical category of "corporate personality." If it is true that the "personal" Christ exerts His salvific activity, "by that very fact He prolongs Himself in the assembly of believers, in such a way that they as a group are identified with Him."[87]

Isn't the idea of "corporate personality" given too short shrift when the "so-called identifications" between the Messias and the

----

82 L. Cerfaux, *The Church in the Theology of St. Paul,* l.c., p. 246 and 269. On the latter page he quotes J. Huby, *Première aux Corinthiens,* Paris, 1946, 286.

83 L. Cerfaux, *The Church in the Theology of St. Paul,* l.c., p. 274.

84 *Ibid.,* p. 274.

85 *Ibid.,* p. 277.

86 *Ibid.,* p. 277.

87 T. Schmidt, *Der Leib Christi,* l.c., p. 153: "Being in Christ does not only lay the basis for the moral-religious life of the individual, but, because it is common to all, it effects also the unity of the community; in Christ all the believers enter into community with each other"; p. 154: "And so it is understandable that the new man who is spoken of here continually is Christ *on the one hand,* but also the community *on the other,* because it is *entirely* united with Christ" (emphasis added). Cf. L. Brun, *Der kirchliche Einheitsgedanke im Urchristentum,* l.c., p. 110: "To be in the Church and to be in Christ is one and the same thing." With good reason, P. Benoit, l.c., recalls that "the (individual) body of Christ gathers together in its risen nature all those who die and rise with him"; and he very clearly appeals to the idea of "corporate personality."

community, the king and his subjects, the Son of Man and the "holy ones of the Most High," the servant of Yahweh and Israel are considered as being of the "juridical or the literary order?"[88] What is evidently undeniable is that for St. Paul the "corporate personality" of Christ is enhanced by the fact that the influence personally exerted by Christ is much more significant than that of any other bearer of a "corporate personality," regardless of whether he is leader or ancestor.[89] The reality of the life of Christ shared in by the faithful is due to the sanctifying action of Christ's resurrected body which is filled with the divinity.[90] But this is no way prevents "all Christians as a group, in so far as they are a spiritual organism" from being "mystically identified with the body of Christ."[91] Do we really go beyond this assertion "when we identify the organism with the *person* of Christ, or when we speak of a mystical body of Christ as a collective person which forms the Church?"[92] We reply in the affirmative if we understand the term "identification" in too Greek a sense; we reply "not necessarily" if we keep in mind the fluidity of a "corporate personality" which at one time is considered as an active individual and at another time as the extension of this individual.

The individual aspect of the "corporate personality" of Christ and of His Church is particularly manifest in the Captivity Epistles.[93] Because "the peace of Christ" reigns in their hearts,

88 L. Cerfaux, *The Church in the Theology of St. Paul*, l.c., p. 284. On page 344 the same author speaking of the expression "body of Christ" says: "the expression is always metaphorical: it is rooted in the real body of Christ, his risen body, which pours out its life on Christians."

89 A. Wikenhauser, *Die Kirche*, l.c., pp. 127-28: "Christ is ... the sustaining foundation, the bond which merges the Christians together, the power which replaces them into the pneumatic sphere, the source which nourishes them with new life."

90 In reality it is the glorified Body of the Risen Lord which exercises its activity of the "vivifying Spirit"; cf. L. Cerfaux, *The Church in the Theology of St. Paul*, l.c., p. 331.

91 L. Cerfaux, *The Church in the Theology of St. Paul*, l.c., p. 282.

92 *Ibid.*, p. 282.

93 *Ibid.*, p. 334. The author believes that "for an exact understanding of Paul's expressions, it is useful to maintain the distinction between

Christians are "called in one body." (Col. 3:15) The central idea in this sphere is that of the "head"; Christ has been set up by God the Father as "head over all the Church, which indeed is his body." (Eph. 1:22; 4:15; Col. 2:19) He is "head of the Church, being himself savior of the body." (Eph. 5:23) The meaning of *kephalê* is rather "master" or "leader" than "head" properly speaking. The term brings out the universal influence of Christ over His Church.[94]

Doesn't St. Paul go further and use the term *sôma* in the Captivity Epistles in the sense of the "real (risen) body of Christ?"[95] It seems very doubtful. In Col. 1:18 and 24 he speaks of *sôma tês ekklêsias and sôma ho estin ekklêsia*. In these expressions the term *sôma* can hardly refer to the real body of Christ,[96] for Christ is not the head of His own body, and it is difficult to see how the sufferings of the Apostle could serve the real body of Christ. Furthermore, in Eph. 5:23 Christ is called *sôter tou sômatos,* a term which can scarcely be applied to His own "real (risen)" body.[97] Logically then we must admit that the term "body of Christ" in the Epistles of the Captivity (and perhaps also in the other Epistles) expresses together with the spiritual activity of Christ in glory, both the constitution of the Church as a body which is "an expansion of Christ, His fulness and His flowering"[98] and the identity of the body of Christ as the

the two theories on the 'body of Christ'; namely, that held in the major epistles (Christians are united to the Eucharistic body) and the one found in the epistles of the captivity (in which the 'body which is the Church' is identified with the glorious body of the Risen Lord)." Parentheses added.

94 *Ibid.*, p. 334.
95 *Ibid.*, p. 337. The meaning of "the real body of Christ" is found elsewhere, e.g., in Rom. 7:4; Ph. 3:21; Col. 1:22; 2:17; Heb. 10:10; 1 Pt. 2:24.
96 *Ibid.*, p. 337. Cerfaux explains it by a vague "disconnection."
97 P. Benoit, l.c., p. 19 says without flinching: "Christ is the savior of the body," "this body which is his (??) and of which we are the members (?)."
98 L. Cerfaux, *The Church in the Theology of St. Paul,* l.c., p. 342. On

Church with His physical and personal body. Precisely these three aspects of the mystery of Christ and of the Church constitute a striking example of "corporate personality." The risen Christ and the Church are a) one "body," one identical reality, b) they are so because of the mystical identity between the Church and Christ, and c) because of the infusion of the divine life of Christ into the believers.

In this perspective it is difficult to maintain that "the idea of 'body' is never connected with the Church as a social body" or that "the word refers to the Church only by means of an always perceptible reference to the real body of Christ." [99] It seems to us more exact to say that the term "body of Christ" includes *at one and the same time* a reference both to the personal Christ, to His real and physical body, and to the organized plurality of the faithful. It is exact to speak of the identity of the Church as a social body and as the "body of Christ," that is to say in so far as it is unified through the activity of Christ. Certainly we can maintain a distinction between the personal body of Christ—the cause of the holiness of the Church—and the social body of the Church—the effect of Christ's activity; but they are two inseparable aspects of the one single reality. [100] It is proper to the idea of "corporate

page 393 the author says very well: "The Church goes to heaven with the risen Christ, and so the 'body of Christ,' the Church, is his glorified body, made spiritual. It is the fulness of God's sanctifying power in Christ."

99   *Ibid.*, p. 344.

100   *Ibid.*, p. 344: "However, in these epistles (of the captivity) we see a tendency to disconnect (?) the effect from the cause, and thus the Church is as a rule called 'the body of Christ' because of its own life ... And so the Church-body of Christ, although a manifestation of that body, can be considered as a reality distinct from the physical body." The expression "disconnect" which occurs also in another place seems too strong to us. Rather, we think, it is a question of another dialectical aspect of the same reality. P. Benoit, l.c., p. 20 insists on the fact that "the Body is first of all Christ Himself, but *also* all those whom He bears in Himself as the New Adam," who dies and rises for the whole human race.

personality" to emphasize at one time the cause (the person of Christ) and at another time the effect (the Church unified in Christ) while firmly maintaining at the same time the simultaneity of the two. Neither the idea of the Church as a collective personality in some way disassociated from Christ,[101] nor the idea of the Church as an assembly of individuals separately influenced by Christ (without forming a body in Christ) does justice to the Pauline texts. We must maintain at one and the same time that the Church is a unified assembly (because it is the one body of Christ) and that Christ exerts over all an undeniable supremacy (which, ultimately, assures its unity). There is no incompatibility in these two notions, if we keep in mind the biblical notion of "corporate personality."[102] St. Paul goes as far as a Hebrew suitably can when he personifies the society of believers and emphasizes the unity of this society in Christ.[103] We do not fall into pan-Christism (the identification of the Church and Christ in the ontological order)[104] when we interpret St. Paul as teaching that the entire Church is really and mystically in Christ.[105] The person of Christ is always present in the whole Church, which He makes, as it were, a body for Himself and in which He manifests Himself tangibly and corporally.[106] The

101   A kind of "impersonal being"; cf. *Coll. Dioec. Torn.* 28 (1933) 85.
102   Cf. E. Best, *One Body in Christ*, l.c., 111: "The conception of c.p. cannot be reduced to logical terms."
106   T. Schmidt, *Der Leib Christi*, l.c., p. 144.
104   G. Gloege, *Reich Gottes und Kirche im NT*, l.c., p. 311: "All the mystic rules are lacking which somewhat in the sense of an ontological metaphysics wipe away the line between Christ and His community." The argumentation of Gloege strenuously attacks any static doctrine (which would deny, or rather seem to deny the direct action of God the sanctifier).
105   L. Malevez, *L'Eglise dans le Christ*, in RSR 25 (1935) 257-291 and 418-440 has even tried to express this incorporation of all mankind in Christ "in terms of Thomistic Aristotileanism" (p. 418); cf. p. 430: "Each man includes *virtually* in himself all the others"; p. 436: "Christ, as man, contains all of us virtually (potentially)."
106   T. Schmidt, *Der Leib Christi*, l.c., p.144.

Church is the "body of Christ" only in so far as Christ is the "head."[107] The disjunction "collective Christ *or* individual Christ" is artificial.[108] The existence of a mystical Christ is nothing "else"[109] than the idea of the union of the faithful with Christ, since it is this union of the First Born with His brothers (Col. 1: 18) which is the basis of the mystical Christ. The community is inseparable from its leader, the Messias, the Son of man, "who is *at the same time* the head and the embodiment."[110] To speak of the Christian community as "the body of Christ" is to assert that it is a living, unified organism "in accordance with the principle of 'corporate personality' so common in the Semitic world; Christ is the community, and the community is 'in Christ.' "[111]

The basic idea of St. Paul on this subject; namely, that the One unifies the multitude whereas the multitude is only the extension of the One,[112] fulfills precisely the two complementary aspects of "corporate personality." It is, therefore, legitimate to explain the idea of the body of Christ by means of this idea. "The new Israel, according to the New Testament thought, is 'in Christ' as the Jews were in Abraham, or as mankind was in Adam. The Messias, the Christ, is *at once* an individual person— Jesus of Nazareth—and he is more: he is the representative and

107 G. Gloege, *Reich Gottes und Kirche im NT*, l.c., p. 299.
108 J. Havet, *Christ collectif ou Christ individuel*, l.c.
109 *Ibid.*, p. 513, regarding Rom. 6:3-5.
110 F. J. Leenhardt, *Etudes sur l'Eglise dans le NT*, 1940, 14: emphasis added. E. C. Hoskyns and N. Davey, *The Riddle of the NT*, London, 1931, 34-35, n. 1 note a bit exaggeratedly: *'ekklêsia* is equivalent to the word *kuriakon*, "that which belongs to the Lord."
111 G. E. Wright, *The Biblical Doctrine of Man in Society*, l.c., p. 81. Cf. A. E. J. Rawlinson, *Corpus Christi*, l.c., p. 235: "To be 'in Christ' and to belong to the New Israel are from henceforth the same thing."
112 J. A. T. Robinson, *The Body. A Study in Pauline Theology*, London, 1952, 61, is of the opinion that "It is not the One who represents the many.... Rather, it is the many who represent the One." The "rather" seems inexact to us. It is necessary to maintain both affirmations at the same time.

(as it were) the constitutive Person of the New Israel, potentially inclusive."[113]

113   A. E. J. Rawlinson, *Corpus Christi*, l.c., p. 235. P. Benoit, l.c., 21: "It would be vain, and even false, to recognize under these expressions ('a single Body and a single Spirit') *only* the individual body of Christ and His Spirit, or *only* His Mystical Body and the Spirit communicated to Christians. *They are both* indissolubly bound *together*: the individual body of Christ enlarged by the addition of all Christians who join themselves to Him by faith and baptism; the Spirit penetrating the individual body of Christ, and through it all members of His Mystical Body."

Conclusion [114]

The idea of "corporate personality" seems strange to us. We live in an age of individualism, and our thought patterns do not ordinarily embrace the "corporate." Contrariwise, the inspired writings of the Old and New Testaments are animated by a deep faith in the solidarity of the group.

The long analysis of the biblical texts, which at times may have seemed tedious, has shown the great variety of expression in the Scriptures based on this solidarity. The two patterns, that of the *pater familias* (the horizontal pattern) and that of the ancestor (the vertical pattern) are frequently in evidence in the four great subdivisions of the Old Testament and in the New Testament. What is noteworthy is not so much the coexistence of a given individual and a given group, with the group (the tribe, the nation, the family) being thought of as a single individual, but rather the fact that the two points of view are dominant in turn. At one time it is the group which is summed up in a single individual; at another time the exact same group becomes the "extension" of the single individual member.

There is no reason to disassociate the two points of view or to oppose the one to the other (either the individual *or* the col-

114 For a summary of the CONCLUSION see *Adam and Christ as Corporate Personalities*, in *TD* 10 (1962) 99-102; for a summary of the highlights of the entire book see J. de Cock, S.J., *La personalità corporativa*, in *BeO* 3 (1961) 1-5.

lective). The biblical idea of "corporate personality" is characterized by the great fluidity and the extreme ease with which the
two aspects of the total phenomenon succeed each another, are intertwined, and complete each another in consciousness. Because
many authors have failed to keep in mind this quality proper to
all living dialectic, they have poorly understood the idea of "corporate personality." They imagine that one must choose between two incompatible conceptions: either a personality definitely individual, or a group which does not possess any characteristics of the individual.

Along side this "logical" error, which holds that the dialectical
simultaneity of the one and the many is contrary to the principle
of contradiction, is another, observed in the preceding pages, which
is also based fundamentally on a latent individualism. Its proponents are willing to admit that a definite individual—the father of
the family, the king, or the prophet—can occupy such an important
place in the midst of his group that his action has repercussions on
the other members of the group for weal or for woe. But they hold
that this repercussion and this contact is explained by a "causality"
which comes from outside and which this outstanding member
exercises on the group. But in the biblical category of "corporate
personality," on the contrary, this causality is based on a prior and
fundamental metaphysical unity. Because the group is one with
the individual, the latter can express himself through this "extension of his personality," even after a considerable length of
time. Unity (profoundly intrinsic) precedes causality (and always somewhat external). In a very concrete sense, the individual
and the group together form one single reality, whose structure
can further expand in a relationship of causality. Basically the
individual does not fulfill his role by representing the group, or
even by influencing it for the good or for the bad; in the framework of "corporate personality" we can say very objectively that he
is the group and that group *is* he. When we come right down
to it, we are here face to face with one of the most profound in-
tuitions of biblical metaphysics; namely, the dynamic (not at all
static) character of the idea of "being": the individual tends to become the group, and the group tends to be identified with the representing individual.

One last remark is necessary. Several times in the preceding pages, we have had occasion to show that the biblical idea of "corporate personality"—the dynamic and hence fluid union which exists between a group and an individual—always presupposes a special regard for the individual. In fact, the group is conceived very realistically as a single individual. If the emphasis put on unity does not exclude the reality of the many, the latter in turn is always envisaged under its aspect of belonging to the one rather than under its aspect of multiplicity. The French sociological school was perhaps wrong in underestimating the individual and in believing that "in the beginning there was the community." Because the notion of "corporate personality" smacks somewhat of this overly "collective" interpretation, many authors have indicated their disapproval when there is question of finding the idea of "corporate personality" in the Bible. Thanks, however, to the correction (specifically biblical?) which resolutely accentuates the role of the individual, we are hardly treading on dangerous ground when we advance the thesis that the scriptural idea of "corporate personality" is one of the most important categories of thought for the understanding of the inspired books. Even if we experience a certain difficulty in accepting as our own this Semitic or Oriental mode of thought, rather than reject it we should adapt ourselves to this scriptural category in which the divine Word has been clothed.

More than once in the course of our exploration of the biblical texts, we have observed that the category of "corporate personality" furnishes a means of resolving one or the other *"crux interpretum."* Great light is thrown on the figure of the Savior King if we give proper value to the great unity which binds the representing sovereign to the people whom he represents (or is). This figure of the king served as a prototype of that of the Messias who will obtain for Himself an acceptable people, with whom He will enter into a profound unity by associating them to His most intimate life.

The two other Messianic titles—besides that of King, there are those of the Servant of Yahweh and the Son of Man—take on a striking lustre when interpreted in the light of the idea of "corporate personality." The Servant *par excellence* is the Chosen People in its most sublime sense, or the single individual who is the true "remnant" and therefore the authentic nucleus of the

people. The Son of Man is also an individual figure who sums up
in himself the 'holy ones of the Most High." The vexing problem
of the "I of the psalms" (with the frequent shift from the singular
to the plural and *vice versa*) loses some of its knottiness if instead
of presenting two diametrically opposed solutions (the individual
and the collective) we remember that these two views, far from
being mutually exclusive, can very well be reconciled in the idea
of "corporate personality." The "I of the psalms" can well be
an individual figure (king, priest, or outstanding layman) who
sums up within himself the aspirations of the community: aspirations to prayer, to repentance, to the liturgical glorification of
"the God of the heart."

In the New Testament we have met two antithetical figures:
Adam and Christ. We have shown that the very etymology of
the expression *bèn-'âdâm* forces us to see in the term *'âdâm* not
a single individual but all humanity. To be *bèn-'âdâm* therefore
means: to belong to the human race (rather than "to descend
physically from the first Adam.") However, since the unity of a
group ultimately presupposes an outstanding individual, and since
the term *Adam* seems to have sometimes in the Old Testament,
and a fortiori in the New Testament, the meaning of a proper
name, it seemed to us that in Rom. 5:12-21 St. Paul is thinking
of a single individual. But we must add immediately that if the
Apostle thinks of Adam as a single individual, *at the same time*
(in virtue of a normal and immediate turn of thought) he sees
him under his corporate aspect, in so far as the "many" form one
with him. The fact that Adam can affect the *massa damnata* follows from his deep-seated identity with it. Because Adam constitutes a "corporate personality" in union with all mankind, his
sin has its effects *ipso facto* on all men of all times.

In the same way Christ exercises a causality of grace among
Christians. As the transcending Messias He is intimately one with
His people, the *ekklesia,* that is to say, the community of the
chosen ones. Here again it is not the activity of the individual
Christ in favor of individual Christians which begets the unity
of the Body of Christ; rather it is this prior fundamental unity
which serves as the basis for the sanctifying influence of the
Word Incarnate.

We see now that the idea of "corporate personality" is of

unquestionable help in expressing the dogmatic truths of original sin and of Redemption. It is precisely in these doctrines that the idea of "corporate personality" is of ultimate interest for Catholic theology. Since our times are marked by an interest in getting back to the original biblical categories in which our dogmas were first expressed, and since Sacred Scripture is the privileged expression (because inspired) of the truths preached by the Apostles, we must make every effort to get to the basic and exact meaning of the biblical category of "corporate personality."

If we conceive of Adam as a "corporate personality" we can understand a bit more readily how all humanity was "placed in the state of sin" because the first sinner revolted against God. Adam is not simply an isolated individual of primordial times (whose sin has mysterious effects on all his descendants, even the most distant), but he *is* also the entire human race, which he encompasses within himself in a very real and true sense. Whenever the first man sinned (Rom 5:12), all those who belong to the human race, (in so far as they are "sons," that is to say, descendants) become in very truth sinners. Every man who is born into the world is, by the very fact that he is part of the human community, in some way an "extension" of the original sinner. This is the teaching of a very happy formula of one of the Fathers of the Council of Trent, Cornelius Mussus, O.F.M. Conv., bishop of Bitonto: "Before our births, we were all in Adam when he sinned; when we are born, Adam is in us." (S. Ehses, *Concilii Tridentini Actorum Pars altera,* Fribourg, 1911, 175)

The same Father of the Council of Trent immediately adds: "In the same way, when Christ suffered for us, we were all in Him; in this way our sins were taken away." The dogma of the Redemption in turn can be advantageously phrased on the basis of the biblical category of the "corporate personality" of Christ. The Savior suffering for us (that is to say in our place and therefore for our benefit) merited for us objective redemption which was obtained once and for all; but its grace is distributed to each individual in the subjective redemption.

All Christology takes on a new light and greater depth if Christ no longer appears only as an individual man but rather as a real "corporate personality." Because He encompasses (dynamically speaking *is*) all Christians, Christ is so intimately united to His followers that everything He does has its effect on them: "Much more has the grace of God, and the gift in the grace of the one man Jesus Christ, abounded unto the many ... Much more will they who receive the abundance of the grace and of the gift of justice reign in life through the one Jesus Christ ... So also by the obedience of the one the many will be constituted just." (Rom. 5:15, 17, 19)

All the titles of Christ—the second Adam, king, prophet, suffering servant, son of man, priest *par excellence*—lead us inevitably to this conclusion: in order to get back to their original and profound meaning, that is to say, to regain the fundamental theological expression, we must make use of the biblical idea of "corporate personality."

This same idea will also initiate us into a number of insights of contemporary theology. Will it not help to illustrate in a more striking manner the *'filii in Filio"* of the theology of grace? Will it not help us to realize more forcefully that the Church is the "extension of Christ," the "first sacrament?" What new light will it not throw on the theology of the priesthood according to which all human priests are summed up in the single personality of the High priest (which will, for example, assure unity of intention in the rite of concelebration)? Will it not be a great help in the Marian theology which describes the Blessed Virgin as the "image of the Church," that is to say, she who "represents," in fact, in a certain sense, *is* the entire Church (at the moment of the objective Redemption, for example)?

Considering these many theological applications of the idea of "corporate personality," we are convinced that we have done a useful work in going to the very heart of Old Testament revelation. In this idea of "corporate personality," we may legitimately conclude, we have found one of the richest of categories for use in working out a truly Catholic and biblical theology, something our contemporaries so ardently desire and clamor for.[115]

---

115   As examples of favorable and unfavorable reviews of de Fraine's book
      see respectively: J. P. Audet, O.P., *RB* 67 (1960) 297-298; J.
      Coppens, *ETL* 35 (1960) 488-490.

Principal Works Consulted

Abbreviations

JTS   The Journal of Theological Studies

KVSW   Kölner Vierteljahrschrift für Socialwissenschaften

NTT   Norsk Teologisk Tidsskrift

RB   Revue Biblique

RHPR   Revue d'Histoire et de philosophie religeuse

RHR   Revue de l'Histoire des Religions

RPh   Revue Philosophique

RSR   Recherches de Science religeuse

SBU   Symbolae biblicae Uppsalienses

SEA   Svensk exegestisk Arsbok

TB   Theologische Blätter

TD   Theology Digest

TLZ   Theologische Literaturzeitung

VD   Verbum Domini

VT   Vetus Testamentum

WZKM   Wiener Zeitschrift für die Kunde des Morgenlandes

ZAW   Zeitschrift für die alttestamentliche Wissenschaft

ZNW   Zeitschrift für die neutestamentaliche Wissenschaft

ZST   Zeitschrift für die systematsiche Theologie

Albright, W. F., *From the Stone Age to Christianity*, 1946[2].

Aubrey, E. F., *The Holy Spirit in Relation to the Religious Community*, in *JTS* 41 (1940) 1-13.

Balla, E., *Das Ich der Psalmen*, in *BRLANT* 16, Göttingen, 1912.

Baron, S. W., *Histoire d'Israël. Vie sociale et religeuse*, 1956.

Baumgärtel, Fr., *Die Eigenart der alttestamentlichen Frömmigkeit*, Schwerin in Mecklenburg, 1932.

Benoit, P., *Corps, Tête, Plérôme dans les épîtres de la captivité*, in *RB* 63 (1956) 5-44.

Berdiaeff, N., *Die menschliche Persönlichkeit und die überpersönlichen Werte*, Vienna, 1937.

Bertholet, A., *Histoire de la civilisation d'Israël,* French translation of J. Marty, Paris, 1929.

―――― *Dynamismus und Personalismus* (Sammlung gemeinverständlicher Vorträge 142). Tübingen, 1930.

Best, E., *One Body in Christ,* London, 1955.

Birkeland, H., *Die Feinde des Individuums in der israelitischer Psalmenliteratur,* Oslo, 1933.

Black, M., *The Son of Man in the Old Biblical Literature,* in ET 60 (1948/9) 11-15.

Boehmer, J. *Wieviel Menschen sind am letzten Tage des Hexaëmerons geschaffen worden?* in ZAW 34 (1914) 31-35.

Bogardus, Emory S., *Fundamentals of Social Psychology,* 1931[2].

Boman, T., *Das hebräische Denken im Vergleich mit dem griechischen,* Göttingen, 1954[2].

Bonhoeffer, D., *Sanctorum Communio,* Berlin, 1930.

Bonsirven, J., *Théologie du Nouveau Testament,* Paris, 1951.

Borch, H. von, *Das Gottesgnadentum. Historisch-soziologischer Versuch über die religiöse Herrschaftslegitimation,* Berlin, 1934.

Bousset, W., *Die Religion des Judentums im neutestamentlichen Zeitalter,* 1913[2].

―――― *Kyrios Christos,* 1926[2].

Brockington, L. H., *The Hebrew Conception of Personality in Relation to the Knowledge of God,* in JTS 47 (1946) 1-11.

Brun, L., *Der kirchliche Einheitsgedanke im Urchristentum,* in ZST 14 (1937) 86-127.

Campenhausen, H. von, *Die Idee des Martyriums in der alten Kirche,* Göttingen, 1936.

Causse, Ant., *Du groupe ethnique à la communauté religeuse. Le problème sociologique de la religion d'Israël,* Paris, 1937.

Cazelles, H., *Loi israélite,* in DBS V, 497-530.

―――― *Etudes sur le Code de l'Alliance,* Paris, 1946.

―――― *Les poèmes du Serviteur,* in RSR 43 (1955) 2-51.

Cerfaux, L., *L'Eglise et le Règne de Dieu,* in ETL 2 (1925) 181-198.

―――― *La Théologie de l'Eglise suivant St. Paul,* Paris, 1948[2].

Clarke W. K. Lowther, *Divine Humanity*, London, 1936.

Congar, Y., *Esquisses du Mystère de l'Eglise*, Paris, 1941.

Cook, Stanley A., *Cambridge Ancient History III*, Cambridge, 1925.

―――― *The Old Testament. A Reinterpretation*, Cambridge, 1936.

Cooley, C. H., *Social Organisation*, New York, 1909 (1914[2]).

Cullmann, O., *Königsherrschaft Christi und Kirche im NT* (Theologische Studien, Karl Barth, 10), Zurich, 1940 (1950[3]).

Dahl, N. A., *Das Volk Gottes, Eine Untersuchung zum Kirchenbewusstsein des Urchristentums*, Oslo, 1941.

Dalman, G., *Die Worte Jesu* 1, Leipzig, 1930[2].

Davies, W. D., *Paul and Rabbinical Judaism*, London, 1948.

De Fraine, J., *Individu et societé dans la religion de l'Ancient Testament*, in *Bb* 33 (1925) 324-355 and 445-475.

―――― *L'aspect religieux de la royauté israélite. L'institution monarchique dans l'AT et dans les textes mésopotamiens*, Rome, 1954.

Dobbschütz, E. von, *Wir und Ich bei Paulus*, in *ZST* 10 (1933) 251-77.

Dodd, C. H., *The Apostolic Preaching and its Developments*, London, 1936 (1944[2]).

―――― *The Epistle of Paul to the Romans* (*The Moffatt NT Commentary*), London, 1946[11].

―――― *According to the Scriptures*, Oxford, 1952.

Dupont-Sommer, A., *Adam, "Père du Monde" dans la Sagesse de Salomon*, in *RHR* 119 (1939) 182-203.

Durkheim, E., *Les formes élémentaires de la vie religieuse*, Paris, 1925[2].

Eissfeldt, O., *The Ebed-Jahve in Isaiah in the Light of the Israelitic Conception of the Community and the Individual, the Real and the Ideal*, in *ET* 44 (1932/33) 261-268.

―――― *Der Gottesknecht bei Deuterojesaja*, Halle, 1933.

Engnell, I., *Studies in Divine Kingship in the Ancient Near East*, Uppsala, 1943.

―――― *The 'Ebed-Yahweh Songs and the Suffering Messiah in "Deutero-Isaiah"*, in *BJRL* 31 (1948) 54-93.

Euler, F. K., *Die Verkündigung vom leidenden Gottesknecht aus Jes. 53 in der griechischen Bibel*, in *BWANT* IV, 14, Stuttgart, 1934.

Faris, E., *The Nature of Human Nature*, New York, 1937[2].

Feuillet, A., *Le Fils de l'homme de Daniel et la tradition biblique*, in *RB* 60 (1953) 197 ff.

Flew, R. N., *Jesus and His Church*, London, 1954[4].

Frazer, J. G., *Les origines magiques de la royauté*, Paris, 1920.

Galling, K., *Die Erwählugstraditionen Israels*, in ZAW Beiheft 48, Giessen, 1928.

———— *Vom Richteramt Gottes*, in *DT* 6 (1939) 86-97.

Gillischewski, E., *Der Ausdruck 'am hā'ârèc im AT*, in ZAW 40 (1922) 37-42.

Gloege, G., *Reich Gottes und Kirche im NT*, Gütersloh, 1929.

Graham, W. C. and May, H. C., *Culture and Conscience*, Chicago, 1936.

Gressmann, H. *Der Messias*, Göttingen, 1929.

Gutbrod, W., *Die paulinische Anthropologie*, Stuttgart, 1934.

Hanson, S., *The Unity of the Church in the NT*, Uppsala, 1946.

Havet, J., *Christ collectif ou Christ individuel en 1 Cor. 12.12?* in *ETL* 23 (1947) 499-520.

Heaton, E. W., *The Book of Daniel* (Torch Bible), London, 1956.

Hempel, Joh., *Das Gottesvolk im Alten und Neuen Testament*, in *Auslanddeutschtum und evangelische Kirche* (Jahrbuch), Munich, 1933.

———— *Gott und Mensch im AT*, in *BWANT III*, 2, Stuttgart, 1936[2].

———— *Das Ethos des AT*, in ZAW Beiheft 67, Berlin, 1938.

Hooke, S. H., *The Labyrinth*, London, 1935.

Hoskyns, E. C. and Davey, N., *The Riddle of the NT*, London, 1931.

Hubert, H. and Mauss, M., *Mélanges d'Histoire des Religions*, Paris, 1929[2].

Jepsen, A., *Nabi. Soziologische Studie zur alttestamentlichen Literatur und Religionsgeschichte*, Munich, 1934.

Jeremias, J., *Jesus als Weltvollender*, in *BFCL* 33,4, Gütersloh, 1930.

Jerusalem, F. W., *Über den Begriff der Kollektivität und seine Stellung im Ganzen der Soziologie*, in *KVSW II*, 1 (1922) 47-53.

Johannson, N., *Parakletoi. Vorstellungen von Fürsprechern für die Menschen vor Gott in der alttestamentlichen Religion, im Spätjudentum und Urchristentum*, Lund, 1940.

Johnson, R. Aubrey, *The One and the Many in the Israelite Conception of God*, Cardiff, 1942.

—— *The Vitality of the Individual in the Thought of Ancient Israel*, Cardiff, 1949.

—— *Sacral Kingship in Israel*, Cardiff, 1955.

Johnston, G., *The Doctrine of the Church in the NT*, Cambridge, 1943.

Käsemann, E., *Leib und Leib Christi*, Tübingen, 1933.

Kattenbusch, F., *Der Quellort der Kirchenidee*, in *Festgabe für A. Harnack*, 1921, 153-172.

Kissane, E. J., *The Book of Isaiah II*, Dublin, 1943.

Knox, W, L., *Parallels to the NT Use of sôma*, in *JTS* 39 (1938) 243-246.

Köhler, L., *Theologie des Alten Testaments*, Tübingen, 1953².

Koehnlein, H., *La notion de l'Eglise chez l'apôtre Paul*, in *RHPR* 17 (1937) 357-77.

Kraeling, C. H., *Anthropos and the Son of Man*, New York, 1927.

Kraeling, E. H., *Babylonian and Iranian Mythology in Daniel*, ch. 7 in *Oriental Studies in Honour of C. E. Pawry*, Oxford, 1933.

Kümmel, W. G., *Kirchenbegriff und Geschichtsbewusstsein in der Urgemeinde und bei Jesus*, in *SBU* 1 (1943) 33 ff.

Labat, R., *Le caractère religieux de la royauté assyro-babylonienne*, Paris, 1939.

Lafont, G., *Sur l'interprétation de Romains V, 15-21*, in *RSR* 45 (1957) 481-513.

Lagrange, M. J., *Le judaïsme avant J.C.*, Paris, 1931².

Lattey, C., *Vicarious Solidarity in the OT* in *VT* 1 (1951) 267-74.

Le Bon, G., *Psychologie des foules*, Paris, 1939⁴¹.

Leenhardt, F. J., *Etudes sur l'Eglise dans le NT*, Neuchâtel, 1940.

Leeuw, V. de, *Le serviteur de Yahvé, figure royale ou prophétique?* in *L'attente du Messie*, Paris, 1954.

—— *De Ebed-Jahweh-Profetieën*, Assen, 1956.

Lefrois, B. J., *The Woman Clothed with the Sun (Ap. 12). Individual or Collective? An Exegetical Study*, Rome, 1954.

—— *Semitic Totality Thinking*, in *CBQ* 17 (1955) 315-323.

Leroy, O., *La raison primitive. Essai de réfutation de la théorie du prélogisme*, Paris, 1927.

Lévy-Bruhl, L., *La mentalité primitive*, Paris, 1925[4].

―――― *L'âme primitive*, Paris, 1927.

―――― *Les fonctions mentales dans les sociétés inférieures*, Paris, 1928[9].

Lindblom, J., *The Servant Songs in Deutero-Isaiah*, Lund, 1951.

Lindhagen, C., *The Servant Motif in the OT. A preliminary Study to the 'Ebed Yahweh Problem in Deutero-Isaiah*, Uppsala, 1950.

Litt, Th., *Individuum und Gemeinschaft*, 1924[2].

Lockner, R., *Deskriptive Pädagogik*, Reichenberg, 1927.

Lods, Ad., *Israël des origines au milieu du VIIIe siècle*, Paris, 1930.

―――― *Les prophètes d'Israël et les débuts du judaïsme*, Paris, 1935.

―――― *Les antécédents de la notion d'Eglise en Israël et dans le Judaïsme*, in *Origine et nature de l'Eglise;* lectures given to the Faculty of Protestant Theology, Paris, 1939, 7-50.

Löhr, M., *Sozialismus und Individualismus im AT*, in ZAW Beiheft 10, Giessen, 1906.

Lohmeyer, E., *Sun Chroistôi*, in *Festgabe für Ad. Deissmann*, Tübingen, 1927, 218-57.

Lowie, R., *Traité de sociologie primitive*, Paris, 1935.

Lyonnet, S., *Le péché originel et Rom. 5:12-14*, in *RSR* 44 (1956) 63-84.

Malevez, L., *L'Eglise dans le Christ*, in *RSR* 23 (1935) 257-291 and 418-440.

Manson, T. W., *The Teaching of Jesus*, Cambridge, 1931 (1943[2]).

―――― *The Son of Man*, in *BJRL* 32 (1949/50) 171-193.

Marmorstein, A., *Paul und die Rabbinen*, in ZNW 30 (1931) 271-85.

McDougall, W., *The Group Mind. A Sketch of the Principles of Collective Psychology with the Attempt to Apply to the Interpretation of National Life and Character*, Cambridge, 1920.

McIver, R. M., *Community. A Sociological Study*, London, 1924.

―――― *Society. A Textbook of Sociology*, New York, 1937.

McKenzie, J. L. *Royal Messianism*, in *CBQ* 19 (1957) 25-52.

Mehlis, G., *Lehrbuch des Geschichtsphilosphie*, Berlin, 1915.

Mersch, E., *Le corps mystique du Christ I*, Brussels, 1936[2].

Messel, N., *Der Menschensohn in den Bilderreden des Henoch*, in ZAW Beiheft 36, Giessen, 1922.

Meyer, E., *Geschichte des Altertums V*, Stuttgart, 1913[2].

Michel, O., *Prophet und Märtyrer*, in BFCT 37, 2 Gütersloh, 1932.

Morgan, L. C., *Individual and Person*, in AJS 34 (1928/29) 623-631.

Mowinckel, S., *Der Knecht Jahwäs*, in NTT 22 (1921) Beiheft 43.

―――― *Psalmenstudien I. Awän und die individuelle Klagepsalmen*, Kristiana, 1921.

―――― *Psalmenstudien II. Das Thronbesteigungsfest Jahwäs und der Ursprung der Eschatologie*, Kristiana, 1922.

―――― *V. Segen und Fluch in Israels Kultur und Psalmendichtung*, Kristiana, 1925.

Müller, W. E., *Die Vorstellung vom Rest im A.T.*, Leipzig, 1939.

Mundle, W., *Das Kirchenbewusstsein der ältesten Christenheit*, in ZNW 22 (1923) 20-42.

Murmelstein, B., *Adam. Ein Beitrag zur Messiaslehre*, in WZKM (1928) 242-275 and 36 (1929) 51-86.

Mussner, Fr., *Christus das All und die Kirche*, Trier, 1955.

Neher, A., *L'essence du prophétisme*, Paris, 1955.

―――― *Amos. Contribution à l'étude du prophétisme*, Paris, 1950.

North, C., *The Suffering Servant in Deutero-Isaiah*, Oxford, 1956[2].
Noth, M., *Das System der Zwölf Stämme Israels*, in BWANT IV, 1, Stuttgart, 1930.

―――― *Gesammelte Studien zum Alten Testament*, Munich, 1957, 274-290.

Nyberg, H. S., *Studien zum Hoseabuche*, Uppsala, 1935.

―――― *Smärtornas man. En studie till Jes. 52:13-53:12*, in SEA 7 (1942) 5-82.

Oepke, A., *Leib Christi oder Volk Gottes bei Paulus?* in TLZ 79 (1954) 363-368.

Otto, R. *Reich Gottes und Menschensohn*, Munich, 1934.

Pakody, L. M. von, *Deutero-jesajanische Studien, II: Der Ebed in der Theologie Deutero-jesajas*, 1942.

Peake, A. S., *The People and the Book*, Oxford, 1925.

Peck, R. E. and Burgers, E. W., *Introduction to the Science of Sociology*, Chicago, 1928.

Pedersen, J., *Israel. Its Life and Culture, I-II*, Copenhagen, 1946, *III-IV*, Copenhagen, 1947[2].

Percy, E., *Der Leib Christi (SOMA CHRISTOU) in den paulinischen Homologoumena und Antilegomena*, Lund, 1942.

Quispel, G., *Der gnostische Anthropos und die jüdische Tradition*, in *EJ* 22 (1953) 195-234.

Radin, P., *Primitive Man as Philosopher*, New York and London, 1927.

Rawlinson, A. E. J., *Corpus Christi*, in G.K.A. Bell-A. Deissman, *Mysterium Christi*, London, 1930, 225-249.

Richardson, C. C., *The Church in Ignatius of Antioch*, in *JR* 7 (1937) 428-443.

Robinson, H. Wheeler, *The Christian Doctrine of Man*, Edinburgh, 1913[2].

—— *The Psychology and Metaphysic of "Thus saith Yahweh,"* in *ZAW* 41 (1923) 1-15.

—— *The Cross of the Servant*, London, 1926.

—— *The Hebrew Conception of Corporate Personality*, in *ZAW* Beiheft 66 (1936) 49-61.

—— *The Old Testament. Its Making and Meaning*, London, 1937.

—— *Redemption and Revelation*, London, 1944[3].

—— *Inspiration and Revelation in the Old Testament*, Oxford, 1946.

—— *The Religious Ideas of the Old Testament*, London, 1949[8].

Robinson, J. A. T., *The Body. A Study in Pauline Theology*, London, 1952.

Rost, L., *Die Bezeichnungen für Volk und Land im A.T.*, in *Festschrift O. Procksch*, 1931, 125-148.

—— *Israel bei den Propheten*, in *BWANT* IV, 19, Stuttgart, 1937.

—— *Die Vorstufen von Kirche und Synagoge im AT*, in *BWANT*, Stuttgart, 1938.

Rowley, H. H., *The Rediscovery of the Old Testament*, Philadelphia, 1946.

—— *The Biblical Doctrine of Election*, London, 1950.

—— *The Unity of the Bible*, London, 1953.

—— *The Servant of the Lord*, 1954².

—— *The Faith of Israel*, London, 1956.

Rudolph, W., *Volk und Staat im AT*, in *Volk, Staat, Kirche. Ein Lehrgang der theologischen Fakultät Giessen*, Giessen, 1933, 21-33.

Scharbart, J., *Solidarität in Segen und Fluch im AT und in seiner Umwelt, I. Vaterfluch und Vatersegen*. Bonn, 1958. De Fraine himself reviews and compares this book with his own in *VD* 38 (1960) 45-48.

Schlier, H., *Zum Begriff der Kirche im Epheserbrief*, in *TB* 1927, 12 ff.

—— *Christus und die Kirche im Epheserbrief*, in *BHT* 6, Tübingen, 1930.

Schmidt, T., *Der Leib Christi—sôma Christou—Eine Untersuchung zum urchristlichen Gemeindegedanken*, Leipzig-Erlangen, 1919.

Schweitzer, A., *Die Mystik des Apostels Paulus*, Tübingen, 1930.

Seidelin, P., *Der 'Ebed Jahwe und die Messiasgestalt im Jesajatargum*, in *ZNW* 35 (1936) 194-231.

Simpson, D. C., *The Psalmists*, Oxford, 1926.

Sjöberg, E., *Der Menschensohn im aethiopischen Henochbuch*, Lund, 1946.

Smend, R., *Ueber das Ich der Psalmen*, in *ZAW* 8 (1888) 49-147.

Smith, W. Robertson, *Lectures on the Religion of the Semites*, London, 1927³.

Spann, O., *Kategorienlehre*, Jena, 1939².

—— *Religionsphilosophie auf geschichtlicher Grundlage*, Vienna, 1947.

Staerk, W., *Soter I. Die biblische Erlösererwartung*, Gütersloh, 1933.

—— *Soter II. Die Erlösererwargung in den östlichen Religionen*, Stuttgart, 1938.

Ström, A. V., *Vetekornet. Studier över Individ och Kollektiv i Nya Testamentet*, Stockholm, 1944.

Sutcliffe, E. F., *Providence and Suffering in the Old and New Testaments*, London, 1953.

Tennant, F. R., *The Source of the Doctrines of Fall and Original Sin*, Cambridge, 1903.

Tournay, R. J., *Les chants du Serviteur dans la seconde partie d'Isaïe*, in *RB* 59 (1952) 355-84; 481-512.

Tresmontant, C., *Etudes de métaphysique biblique*, Paris, 1955.

Weber, M., *Aufsätze zur Religionssoziologie III. Das Antike Judentum*, Tübingen, 1921.

Weiss, J., *Das Urchristentum*, Göttingen, 1917.

Widengren, G., *The King and the Tree of Life in Ancient Near Eastern Religion*, Uppsala, 1951.

———— *Religionens Värld*, Stockholm, 1953².

———— *Sakrales Königtum*, Stuttgart, 1955.

Wikenhauser, A., *Die Christusmystik der Hl. Paulus*, in *BZF* XII, 8-10, Munster, 1928.

———— *Die Kirche als der mystische Leib Christi nach dem Apostel Paulus*, Munster, 1940².

Wing, J. van, *Etudes Bakongo*, Louvain, 1920.

Wolf, W., *Individuum und Gemeinschaft in der ägyptischen Kultur*, Glückstadt, 1935.

Wright, G. E., *God Who Acts*, London, 1952.

———— *The Biblical Doctrine of Man in Society*, London, 1954.

Young, Kimball, *Social Psychology*, New York, 1946.

Zimmerli, W., *Das Alte Testament als Anrede*, Zurich, 1956.

ALBA HOUSE is staffed by the Pauline Fathers and Brothers. The operations going into the making of this book were carried out by the Fathers and Brothers as part of their publishing apostolate. The Society of St. Paul was founded to work exclusively in communications. By this is meant that it was instituted to preach and teach the word of Christ via the press, radio, motion pictures and television.

PAULINES reach thousands daily — by each book, pamphlet, production — multiplying the good message and at times carrying it into places almost impossible to reach. It is their mission in the Church to staff editorial offices, publishing plants, film studios, etc., and to develop those fields of communications still comparatively un-touched for Christ. The **Vatican Council's** decree on the media of social communications has been a great source of renewed energy for them.

INTERNATIONAL as the air-waves, the Pauline Fathers and Brothers are located in twenty-three countries, with headquarters in Rome. In the United States they are in New York City, Buffalo, Detroit, Boston and Youngstown.

A BROCHURE on the Society and its aims can be obtained for yourself, or any young man whom you feel might qualify to become a Pauline Priest or Brother, by simply sending a card to: The Pauline Fathers and Brothers, Vocation Office, 2187 Victory Blvd., Staten Island, N. Y.